AN ARK ON THE NILE

An Ark on the Nile: The Beginning of the Book of Exodus

KEITH BODNER

OXFORD
UNIVERSITY PRESS

Great Clarendon Street, Oxford, OX2 6DP,
United Kingdom

Oxford University Press is a department of the University of Oxford.
It furthers the University's objective of excellence in research, scholarship,
and education by publishing worldwide. Oxford is a registered trade mark of
Oxford University Press in the UK and in certain other countries

© Keith Bodner 2016

The moral rights of the author have been asserted

First Edition published in 2016

Impression: 1

All rights reserved. No part of this publication may be reproduced, stored in
a retrieval system, or transmitted, in any form or by any means, without the
prior permission in writing of Oxford University Press, or as expressly permitted
by law, by licence or under terms agreed with the appropriate reprographics
rights organization. Enquiries concerning reproduction outside the scope of the
above should be sent to the Rights Department, Oxford University Press, at the
address above

You must not circulate this work in any other form
and you must impose this same condition on any acquirer

Published in the United States of America by Oxford University Press
198 Madison Avenue, New York, NY 10016, United States of America

British Library Cataloguing in Publication Data
Data available

Library of Congress Control Number: 2016933206

ISBN 978-0-19-878407-4

Printed in Great Britain by
Clays Ltd, St Ives plc

Table of Contents

Abbreviations   vii

Introduction   1

1. Images of Egypt in Genesis   17
2. Old Promise, New King   40
3. Pharaoh's Midwife Crisis   64
4. The Waters of Chaos   89
5. Criminal Charges   117
6. The Stranger in Midian   146
7. Exodus 1–2 and the Sojourn of Israel   174

Bibliography   187
Index   203

Abbreviations

AB	Anchor Bible
ABD	*Anchor Bible Dictionary*
ACEBT	*Amsterdamse Cahiers voor Exegese en bijbelse Theologie*
AnBib	Analecta biblica
BCBC	Believers Church Bible Commentary
BDB	Brown, F., S. R. Driver, and C. A. Briggs. *A Hebrew and English Lexicon of the Old Testament*, Oxford 1907.
BibInt	*Biblical Interpretation*
BIS	Biblical Interpretation Series
BKAT	Biblischer Kommentar, Altes Testament
BZAW	Beihefte zur Zeitschrift für die alttestamentliche Wissenschaft
CBQ	*Catholic Biblical Quarterly*
CBR	*Currents in Biblical Research*
ECC	Eerdmans Critical Commentary
ESHM	European Seminar in Historical Methodology
EQ	*Evangelical Quarterly*
FAT	Forschungen zum Alten Testament
FCB	Feminist Companion to the Bible
FOTL	Forms of the Old Testament Literature
HAR	*Hebrew Annual Review*
HBM	Hebrew Bible Monographs
HCOT	Historical Commentary on the Old Testament
HS	*Hebrew Studies*
ICC	International Critical Commentary
ITC	International Theological Commentary
JAAR	*Journal of the American Academy of Religion*
JAOS	*Journal of the American Oriental Society*
JBL	*Journal of Biblical Literature*
JBQ	*Jewish Bible Quarterly*
JETS	*Journal of the Evangelical Theological Society*
JHS	*Journal of Hebrew Scriptures*
JJS	*Journal of Jewish Studies*
JPS	Jewish Publication Society
JQR	*Jewish Quarterly Review*
JSJSup	Journal for the Study of Judaism Supplement
JSNT	Journal for the Study of the New Testament
JSOT	*Journal for the Study of the Old Testament*

JSOTSup	Journal for the Study of the Old Testament: Supplement Series
JTS	*Journal of Theological Studies*
KJV	King James Version
LHBOTS	Library of Hebrew Bible/Old Testament Studies
LXX	Septuagint (the Greek OT)
MT	Masoretic Text (of the Hebrew Bible)
NCB	New Century Bible
NIBC	New International Biblical Commentary
NICOT	New International Commentary on the Old Testament
NIV	New International Version
NIVAC	New International Version Application Commentary
NRSV	New Revised Standard Version
OBO	Orbis biblicus et orientalis
OTL	Old Testament Library
OTM	Oxford Theological Monographs
OTS	Old Testament Studies
OTT	Old Testament Theology
SBL	Society of Biblical Literature
SBT	Studies in Biblical Theology
SBLDS	Society of Biblical Literature Dissertation Series
SBLMS	Society of Biblical Literature Monograph Series
SBLSymS	Society of Biblical Literature Symposium Series
SNTSMS	Society for New Testament Studies Monograph Series
VT	*Vetus Testamentum*
VTSup	Supplements to Vetus Testamentum
WBC	Word Biblical Commentary
WUNT	Wissenschaftliche Untersuchungen zum Neuen Testament
ZAW	*Zeitschrift für die alttestamentliche Wissenschaft*

Introduction

Early in the book of Exodus the people of Israel are enslaved in the land of Egypt, brutally commandeered as a labor-force tasked with building supply cities for the king. But in the midst of this hopelessness, a story is told about a mother who gives birth to a favored child. Hiding him from the tyrannical king's edict of destruction, the mother boldly prepares a papyrus ark and floats the child on the Nile river—perhaps as a desperate measure, or maybe trusting in the guiding hand of providence for the boy's future. Whether the mother is aware of it or not, there are some poignant parallels with the earlier story of Noah's ark that preserves life in the midst of violence, the only other time the word "ark" (תבה) occurs in the Bible. In due course the diminutive ark is drawn from the Nile, but with an unexpected twist of fate, the child is rescued by none other than the tyrannical king's own daughter, who adopts the boy as her own. As a crowning irony, the boy grows up to become the key figure in the liberation of the oppressed people of Israel, leading them out of slavery to commence a journey where they build a sanctuary and edge closer toward a return to their long-promised inheritance.

The events narrated in the book of Exodus have absorbed the attention of readers across the ages, and its plot of rescue remains among the foundational paradigms of redemption in the Hebrew Bible. Having experienced substantial growth after moving to the land of Egypt, in due course the people of Israel are forced into slavery by a crafty pharaoh of veiled provenance. Outmaneuvered in turn by spirited midwives and a Levite woman, there is one particular survivor—the young Moses—who proves highly influential in the story. Forced to flee the country after an impetuous homicide, Moses subsequently returns with a divine commission to liberate the enslaved

Israelites. Yet the king of Egypt is unyielding, even through a series of climactic plagues and changes of mind. Although he eventually grants permission for the Israelites to depart, he quickly reverses the order and pursues his slave-force. But the panic-stricken Israelites, seemingly trapped by the manic king behind them and the waters of the Red Sea before them, are miraculously able to walk on dry ground, with their improbable victory made complete when the same waters subsequently drown their pursuing enemies. After liberation from Egypt, what appears to be a circuitous wandering in the wilderness is actually a divinely led journey to Mount Sinai where the laws of the covenant are unveiled, and even a massive infidelity in chapter 32 cannot break the divine resolve and commitment to the people of Israel. The latter parts of Exodus feature elaborate instructions for the building of a sanctuary, and the book concludes with the divine presence infused in the newly constructed tabernacle.

Compared to the epic sweep of the book of Genesis, Exodus covers a much more limited time period, and it also begins in a rather different manner than both Genesis before it and the book of Leviticus after it. If Genesis has no equal in terms of time and space in the Pentateuch—the book begins at the dawn of time and covers a vast amount of the earth—then Leviticus is much more restricted, with the only location in the book being the spatial setting of the Tent of Meeting. The opening chapters of Exodus move between Egypt and Midian, but after a genealogical prologue that enumerates the population increase of the Israelites in the land of Egypt, there is a rapid pace and flow of action. Seventy descendants of Jacob migrate to Egypt in order to escape the famine and take refuge with Joseph, and the first segment of the book of Exodus outlines the prolific growth of this family. The downside of such numerical expansion is that the people attract the attention of an enigmatic new king of Egypt, who—in what seems like paranoia—rationalizes that this group could cause a problem in the event of war. The ensuing policy of slavery is relentlessly oppressive, but proves ineffective in stemming the fruitfulness of the Israelites, who simply become more numerous, resulting in a command to the midwives to destroy the male population. Yet the midwives bravely disregard their orders and spare the Israelite males, although after interviewing the midwives the king orders that every male child be thrown into the Nile. As chapter 2 begins, a Levite child escapes death, but not because of the midwives' intervention this time. Rather, the lad survives because his mother places him in an ark (תבה) and floats him on the river. Serendipitously, Pharaoh's own daughter retrieves the boy, adopts him, and preserves the account of this watery rescue by means of her naming-speech. In the wake of this extraordinary account of survival, the rest of Exodus 2 narrates the early career of Moses: his murder of an Egyptian and subsequent flight to Midian, his marriage to the daughter of a Midianite priest, and the birth of his son. Finally, the last notice of the chapter is God's perspective on the Israelite slavery, with a conspicuous hint that a new phase of the plot is poised to unfold.

As well as glancing back in a number of ways to the antecedent material in Genesis, there are grounds for suggesting that Exodus 1–2 foreshadows various plot-movements in the rest of the book. For example, consider Terence Fretheim's summary comment: "The book of Exodus moves from slavery to worship, from Israel's bondage to Pharaoh to its bonding to Yahweh. More particularly, the book moves from the enforced construction of buildings for Pharaoh to the glad and obedient offering of the people for a building for the worship of God. Exodus advances from an oppressive situation in which God's presence is hardly noted in the text to God's filling the scene at the completion of the tabernacle."[1] Each of these aspects of the story—servitude, building, and the divine presence—is enhanced or even reversed from the early portions of the book of Exodus through its later developments and conclusion. Other examples also can be cited, including the large-scale irony in Pharaoh's actions: Pharaoh commands that Israelite males be drowned in the waters of the Nile, only to have Egyptian male warriors drowned in the waters of the Red Sea later in chapter 14.[2] Moreover, in Exod 2:14 Moses intervenes in a dispute between two Israelites, only to be verbally accosted by one in the wrong: "Who made you a prince and judge over us?" Unintentionally, in this accusation the angry Israelite underscores key aspects of Moses' future as both a judge and mediator for the community, in addition to his role as a distributor of the law to the people of Israel. It is striking, overall, how many aspects of the forthcoming storyline are presaged early in the book of Exodus, and even in the opening chapters a sense of anticipation is generated. Due to the richness of

---

[1] Terence E. Fretheim, *Exodus. Interpretation: A Bible Commentary for Teaching and Preaching* (Louisville: John Knox Press, 1991) 1.

[2] Robert Alter, *The Five Books of Moses: A Translation with Commentary* (New York: W. W. Norton, 2008) 395.

the narrative, Exodus 1–2 has garnered a fair amount of critical attention in recent days. As part of the introduction to this present study, some of the notable works will now be canvased briefly.

The monograph of Gordon Davies provides a helpful starting point for a survey of recent research, even if his stated decision to focus on the opening segment of Exodus was driven by other factors: "Practical needs directed the choice of the first two chapters of Exodus as the material for this study. They were not chosen for any special beauty or depth of thought. But once the work of reading is underway, one notices their spread in the tissue of the Bible."[3] Of central interest to Davies is the application of his reading method, one that is comprehensively applied at every juncture. As such, he is able to take advantage of a host of secondary studies, both theoretical (e.g., Meir Sternberg) and more specific to his chosen textual sample (e.g., George Coats, Michael Fishbane, and D. W. Wicke).[4] Although it may be only the most committed reader who will persevere through Davies' detailed theoretical mappings, for the interpreter of Exodus 1–2 there are a number of serviceable observations along the way. Consider his reflection on the genealogical prologue to the book of Exodus where he comments: "The list in Exod. 1.1–7 is original. It follows the broad genealogical framework of Genesis 46, but drops the details of the sons of the sons. It copies Genesis 35 in citing the sons of the wives before those of the concubines, the eldest to the youngest by each mother. But it drops the explicit mention of the women. The result is the creation out of the Genesis tradition of a simplified and implicit hierarchical order, detailed chronologically."[5] Some readers may be tempted to overlook the genealogy, but the idea that the opening inventory of names can have a more programmatic function is a fertile one, and when combined with the work of other

---

[3] Gordon F. Davies, *Israel in Egypt: Reading Exodus 1–2* (JSOTSup 135; Sheffield: Sheffield Academic Press, 1992) 13.

[4] Meir Sternberg, *The Poetics of Biblical Narrative: Ideological Literature and the Drama of Reading* (Indiana Studies in Biblical Literature; Bloomington: Indiana University Press, 1985); George W. Coats, "A Structural Transition in Exodus," *VT* 22 (1972) 129–42; Michael Fishbane, *Text and Texture: Close Readings of Selected Biblical Texts* (New York: Schocken Books, 1979; republished as *Biblical Text and Texture: A Literary Reading of Selected Texts*, Oxford: Oneworld, 1998); D. W. Wicke, "The Literary Structure of Exodus 1.2 –2.10," *JSOT* 24 (1982) 99–107.

[5] Davies, *Israel in Egypt*, 33.

scholars (e.g., William Propp) can provide the materials for some useful analysis.[6] Jopie Siebert-Hommes has also written a monograph that further equips the reader with a solid foundation for interpreting the opening chapters of Exodus. Originally composed as a Dutch dissertation, the author begins with a short overview of literary-orientated scholarship beginning with W. M. L. de Wette, and then provides definitions of central terms in her book, such as repetitions, key words, motif and theme, structural patterns, and polysemy. Among the helpful features of the book is an annotated translation with ample discussion of more elusive words or phrases. Combined with a rigorous attention even to seemingly incidental details, her exegesis cannot be lightly dismissed. Of particular value is Siebert-Hommes' attention to the many female characters in Exodus 1–2, headlined by her discussion of the 12 sons at the beginning of chapter 1: the future of the 12 sons of Israel relies on the involvement of 12 daughters in the story—the number of women she counts in the opening chapters, from the midwives to the daughters of the Midianite priest.[7] Siebert-Hommes is also keen to connect the opening chapters with later events in Exodus, as in her discussion of the king who "sought (בקש) to kill Moses" in Exod 2:15 that is brought to a close with God's announcement to Moses in 4:19 that all those seeking (בקש) his life are dead.[8] At an introductory level, then, there is some good material to work with in this concise book that provides a primer on the basic coherence of Exodus 1–2.

On a larger scale than the monographs of Gordon Davies and Jopie Siebert-Hommes, the sprawling book of James Nohrnberg takes on the complex representation of the multivalent figure of Moses across the Pentateuch and beyond. An impressive and creative literary appraisal with numerous strengths, for the interpreter of Exodus 1–2 Nohrnberg is particularly helpful in his section entitled "The Birth of the Life of Moses."[9] There are a plethora of observations that

---

[6] William H. C. Propp, *Exodus 1–18: A New Translation with Introduction and Commentary* (Anchor Bible 2; New York: Doubleday, 1999) 128: "the major difference from Gen 35:23–6 is that Joseph receives special treatment in Exod 1:5."

[7] Jopie Siebert-Hommes, *Let the Daughters Live! The Literary Architecture of Exodus 1–2 as a Key for Interpretation* (BIS 37; Leiden: Brill, 1998) 112.

[8] Siebert-Hommes, *Let the Daughters Live!*, 87.

[9] James Nohrnberg, *Like Unto Moses: The Constituting of an Interruption* (Indiana Studies in Biblical Literature; Bloomington and Indianapolis: Indiana University Press, 1995) 133–52.

can be appropriated in this section of Nohrnberg's book. For instance, in the above paragraph it is mentioned that Siebert-Hommes identifies a linkage between the confrontation of an unnamed Israelite assailant in Exod 2:14 and the later career of Moses. Nohrnberg likewise draws a similar conclusion, but takes it in a slightly different direction: "The rebellious Hebrew of Exodus 2:14 questions Moses as if he were an illegitimate successor to the presumptuous Joseph: 'Who made thee a prince and a judge over us?' Some time thereafter, in Midian, Moses asks the same kind of question about himself: 'Who am I, that I should go unto Pharaoh, and that I should bring forth the children of Israel out of Egypt?' (Exod. 3:11)."[10] Perhaps reflecting the tutelage of Northrop Frye and Marshall McLuhan, Nohrnberg exhibits great interest in typologies and intertextual linkage; he writes, "Moses is the human hero of the exodus, and the life of the human hero is determined by its singularity or individuation, and this is so even if the hero represents a collective: the collective itself is individuated in the hero's name."[11] To what extent, we may ask by extension, is the story of Israel inscribed in the life of Moses (drawn out of the waters, fleeing to the wilderness, brought to Mount Sinai)? The fecundity of this line of reasoning hardly needs defense, and such is Nohrnberg's strength and why his book—one that is not overly cited among biblical scholars, so it would appear—merits attention. As a further example, consider his argument on the significance of Pharaoh's daughter paying wages for the nursing of her adopted son to the boy's own mother:

> Fated to be thrown into the Nile by Pharaoh's edict in Exodus 1:22, Moses is paradoxically saved by his mother's exposing him on the river. On the one hand, the bondwoman's son is adopted by Pharaoh's maternally-inclined daughter, while his fellow Hebrews have been conscripted for Pharaoh's work; on the other hand, the bondwoman is able to hire herself out as the foundling's nurse, and thus get herself reinstated as the child's mother. The servants are doing their masters' living for them, and the royal house is paying for what ordinarily a child secures for free. For the mother takes wages for nursing her own son. The despoiling of the Egyptians, a motif that turns up three times in

---

[10] Nohrnberg, *Like Unto Moses*, 134–5.
[11] Nohrnberg, *Like Unto Moses*, 133.

Introduction 7

the exodus narrative proper (Exod. 3:21–2, 11:2, 12:35–6), has already begun.[12]

The three books of Davies, Siebert-Hommes, and Nohrnberg represent a selective sample of research in the past two decades and illustrate that there are still areas to mine in the rich vein of Exodus 1–2. In addition to these longer studies, there also is a fund of scholarly articles on the literary qualities of this material, and any short survey would do well to begin with the contributions of James Ackerman and Charles Isbell. To start with Ackerman, it should be noted that his weighty article is a pioneering work in a number of respects, writing as he was at the crest of the wave and the surge in popularity of literary approaches to biblical narrative. Combining a sensitive reading of the text with some engagement with secondary studies has enhanced the value of this article among biblical scholars. During the course of his discussion, to cite one example, Ackerman remarks on the surprising and benevolent role of foreigners in the early career of Moses that forms a contrast to his later experiences with some of the Israelites: "An Egyptian princess spares him; a Midianite priest will welcome him into the clan; his own Hebrew people will turn upon him, challenging his claim to authority."[13] Of course, not every proposal needs to be accepted, and critical fashions have changed since the publication of this piece, but on the whole it is still worth consulting 40 years later. Like Ackerman, Charles Isbell's essay is part of a volume dedicated to newer rhetorical approaches

---

[12] Nohrnberg, *Like Unto Moses*, 136. Note the polite disagreement with Brevard Childs in a discursive endnote (p. 359): "Some commentators have wondered whether this is a form of irony directed toward the Egyptians, but in the light of the favorable portrayal of the Egyptian princess, this is hardly likely" (citing Childs, *The Book of Exodus: A Critical, Theological Commentary* [OTL; Louisville: Westminster, 1974] 18–19). Nohrnberg responds, "I do not agree. The princess belongs to the house of Pharaoh, and Pharaoh's house is to be despoiled. The prediction of the enriching of Israel is made in the vicinity of the story of the wages (Exod. 2:7–9, Exod. 3:21–22), and in the prediction that 'each woman shall ask of her neighbor' clothing to be put on the Hebrew's sons and daughters. The irony lies in the prediction's already being partly fulfilled, i.e., in the appropriation of Pharaoh's house for the nurturing of a despoiler whom God is yet to commission."

[13] James S. Ackerman, "The Literary Context of the Moses Birth Story," pp. 74–119 in *Literary Interpretation of Biblical Narrative*, Volume 1, edited by Kenneth R. R. Gros Louis, James S. Ackerman, and Thayer S. Warshaw (Nashville: Abingdon, 1974) 93.

and a showcase for literary-oriented readings of the biblical text.[14] Taking his opening cue from Martin Buber, Isbell searches for key words and overarching patterns in Exodus 1–2 that later recur, often with an inversion or a reversal of expectation.[15] So, consider the spatial setting of the *water's edge*, first occurring in Exod 2:3 when the mother of Moses hides the child among the reeds "at the edge of the Nile" (על־שׂפת היאר). It may seem immaterial at first glance, but years later the plague sequence begins with a dialogue between Moses and Pharaoh "at the edge of the Nile" (על־שׂפת היאר) in Exod 7:15, reaching a climax when God defeats Pharaoh "at the edge of the sea" in 14:30. For Isbell, "This transformation from a place of hiding to a place of confrontation to a place of victory signaled by 'at the edge of' (על־שׂפת) parallels the development of the story line in general."[16] Again similar to Ackerman, after several decades Isbell's work still retains its currency.

The contribution of feminist criticism to the interpretation of Exodus 1–2 can hardly be overstated here, as attested by the helpful work of Siebert-Hommes. Moreover, a number of important studies by feminist scholars have appeared in print, and three are highlighted here. First, Cheryl Exum's *Semeia* article is replete with insights at every turn, as her piece "seeks to illuminate the role of women in Exod. 1.8–2.10, the story of events surrounding the birth of Moses. It investigates the narrative in its present form on the premise that an understanding of its literary contours will aid us in perceiving its meaning."[17] Exum draws attention to shades of irony throughout the

---

[14] Charles Isbell, "Exodus 1–2 in the Context of Exodus 1–14: Story Lines and Key Words," pp. 37–61 in *Art and Meaning: Rhetoric in Biblical Literature*, edited by David J. A. Clines, David M. Gunn, and Alan J. Hauser (JSOTSup 19; Sheffield: JSOT Press, 1982). As the editors of the collection state in the preface: "The received text is not viewed, that is, as a barrier beyond which one must—in order to do Biblical scholarship—necessarily press, nor an end product that should most properly be analysed for evidences of its origins. True though it is that its literary history may at times encompass many centuries, several strata of tradition, and a variety of editorial influences, it is itself—the final text—susceptible of study as a system of meaningful and artistic wholes."

[15] Martin Buber, *Moses: The Revelation and the Covenant* (New York: Harper Torchbacks, 1958).

[16] Isbell, "Exodus 1–2 in the Context of Exodus 1–14," 48.

[17] J. Cheryl Exum, "'You Shall Let Every Daughter Live': A Study of Exodus 1:8–2:10," *Semeia* 28 (1983) 63–82, reprinted in pp. 37–61 in *A Feminist Companion to Exodus to Deuteronomy*, edited by Athalya Brenner (FCB 6; Sheffield: Sheffield Academic Press, 1994) 37.

narrative, discusses subtle motivations of female characters with their acts of defiance, and occasionally points out textual variations in the Septuagint that are of literary interest to the interpreter. Second, Esther Fuchs' essay in a collection of papers devoted to various forms of interreligious dialogue begins with an outline of her personal journey and a comment that her reading of Exodus 1–2 "is an attempt at deconstructing the immasculating process as it unfolds in the text and as it already has come to construct me as a reader."[18] Her reading contains several valuable observations, such as her discussion of the identity and actions of the (unnamed) daughter of Pharaoh in Exodus 2: "The surrogate mother who saves the infant's life is not a biological relative. She is a foreigner. She shares neither family nor national kinship with the future savior of the Israelites. She is the pharaoh's own daughter. Once again the narrative pokes fun at the Egyptian ruler by aligning his own daughter with the Israelite cause." Fuchs also connects the actions of Pharaoh's daughter with the "trope of the foreign woman who sides with the Israelites appears in Josh 2 in the character of Rahab the Canaanite and later in the character of Jael the Kenite (Judg 4)," and there is ample scope for expanding this kind of insight.[19] Third, Phyllis Trible's essay in the recent Tamara Eskenazi *festschrift* also presents a critical reading of Exodus 1–2 that focuses on female characters, and notable is her evaluation of the role of the sister (presumably Miriam) in Exodus 2 who crucially intervenes at a pivotal moment in the story: "The sister neither identifies herself nor indicates that 'a woman' is the baby's own mother. By a shrewd choice of vocabulary—what she says and what she says not—the sister protects all the characters. She avoids arousing suspicion, reservation, or resistance on the part of Pharaoh's daughter. Using the interrogative form, she offers assistance to royalty while respecting its power to decide."[20] The timely intervention of the sister—who is clever with language, like the midwives in

---

[18] Esther Fuchs, "A Jewish–Feminist Reading of Exodus 1–2," pp. 307–26 in *Jews, Christians, and the Theology of the Hebrew Scriptures*, edited by Joel S. Kaminsky and Alice Ogden Bellis (SBL Symposium Series 8; Atlanta: Society of Biblical Literature, 2000) 309.
[19] Fuchs, "A Jewish–Feminist Reading of Exodus 1–2," 314.
[20] Phyllis Trible, "Difference Among the Distaff: A Reading of Exodus 1.1–2.10," pp. 292–306 in *Making a Difference: Essays on the Bible and Judaism in Honor of Tamara Cohn Eskenazi*, edited by David J. A. Clines, Kent Harold Richards, and Jacob L. Wright (HBM 49; Sheffield: Sheffield Phoenix Press, 2012) 303.

Exodus 1—is an important facet of the story that deserves more scrutiny.[21]

From this admittedly brief survey of scholarship—and one could add numerous other studies and commentaries by Cornelis Houtman, Brevard Childs, John Durham, Thomas Dozeman, Moshe Greenberg, Nahum Sarna, Walter Brueggemann, and Carol Meyers, among others—it is apparent that some thoughtful research has been done, and in light of this strong groundwork, other angles of the text can be explored. In this book I will undertake a close reading of Exodus 1–2 with an interest in the literary devices and aesthetic elements such as intertextuality, irony, characterization, spatial settings, point of view, repetition and contrast, plot reversals, and motif and theme. I also build on previous arguments suggesting that the larger contours of the book of Exodus are foreshadowed in these opening chapters that operate as both a transition from Genesis and an overture to the rescue of Israel, the journey to Mount Sinai replete with grumbling as well as divine provision, and construction of the tabernacle in the wilderness. Although the subject can only be pursued in passing during the course of this study, I am also interested in the theoretical notions of *beginnings* in a work of literature: to what extent do the opening chapters of Exodus represent an ideological or a rhetorical beginning to the book? Utilizing the work of scholars like Edward Said, Brian Richardson, and J. Hillis Miller, I will tentatively probe this idea of beginnings as we proceed, and suggest that this is a fertile area for further research.[22] In terms of broader methodology, this book adopts a narrative-critical approach that I have discussed at

---

[21] Other contributions could be included, such as Drorah O'Donnell Setel, "Exodus," pp. 26–35 in *The Women's Bible Commentary*, edited by Carol A. Newsom and Sharon H. Ringe (Louisville: Westminster/John Knox Press, 1992); Alice Ogden Bellis, *Helpmates, Harlots, and Heroes: Women's Stories in the Hebrew Bible* (Louisville, KY: Westminster/John Knox Press, 1984); Adele Berlin, "Giving Birth to a Nation," in *The Torah: A Women's Commentary*, edited by Tamara Cohn Eskenazi and Andrea L. Weiss (New York: URJ Press and Women of Reform Judaism, 2008) 305–23.

[22] For instance, Edward Said (*Beginnings: Intention and Method* [New York: Basic Books, 1975] 41) writes, "Very frequently, especially when the search for a beginning is pursued within a moral and imaginative framework, the beginning implies the end—or, rather, implicates it; this is the observation around which Aristotle builds the *Poetics*." Such an observation squares with Brevard Childs' comment about the "dual function" of Exod 1:1–7, as it looks back to the ancestral age and looks forward to the exodus events (*The Book of Exodus*, 2; cf. Exum, "'You Shall Let Every Daughter Live,'" 38).

length elsewhere.[23] By way of succinct overview, Helmet Utzschneider and Wolfgang Oswald provide a summary of the kind of reading strategy of the received text that will be used in this study. In their detailed commentary on Exodus 1–15, the authors provide a magisterial synthesis of diachronic and synchronic approaches, aligning the latter with an appreciation of the text as a "literary–aesthetic subject," that is, "an independent literary work that *can* be meaningfully read without reference to the intentions of its authors and without knowledge of the history of its development." Utzschneider and Oswald conclude:

> Synchronic interpretation in this sense is directed towards the literary form, the poetic formation of the traditional Hebrew text, as well as its aesthetic response. Its most defining poetic form is narrative. This form is realized by means of the specific features of ancient Hebrew narrative style (e.g., syntax, textual incipits), as well as more general narrative techniques that are also typical of modern narrative texts. At its heart, therefore, synchronic interpretation is representation of the narrative profile of the exodus narrative.... Literary–aesthetic interpretation also focuses its attention on the historical textual forms, i.e. genres, motifs, motif-constellations and traditions, that have formed the text and which have each undergone their own specific individual formation within it. Synchronic interpretation, therefore... is not a-historical. Literary-aesthetic interpretation is conscious of its indebtedness to the tradition of Old Testament genre and genre-historical criticism.[24]

In the remaining portion of this introduction there is a preview of the forthcoming chapters of this book. Since the major strands of plot and the characters of Genesis are assumed at the outset of Exodus, some preliminary matters need to be considered. Therefore, Chapter 1

---

[23] E.g., Keith Bodner, *Elisha's Profile in the Book of Kings: The Double Agent* (Oxford: Oxford University Press, 2013) 11–14; *The Artistic Dimension: Literary Explorations of the Hebrew Bible* (LHBOTS 590; London: T & T Clark, 2013) 1–6; *After the Invasion: A Reading of Jeremiah 40–44* (Oxford: Oxford University Press, 2015) 150–60.

[24] Helmet Utzschneider and Wolfgang Oswald, *Exodus 1–15* (trans. Philip Sumpter; International Exegetical Commentary on the Old Testament; Stuttgart: Kohlhammer, 2015) 19–20; cf. Walter Brueggemann, "The Book of Exodus: Introduction, Commentary and Reflections," pp. 675–981 in *The New Interpreter's Bible*, Volume 6, edited by Leander E. Keck (Nashville: Abingdon, 1994) 681; note also Dennis T. Olson, "Literary and Rhetorical Criticism," pp. 13–54 in *Methods For Exodus*, edited by Thomas B. Dozeman (Methods in Biblical Interpretation; Cambridge: Cambridge University Press, 2010).

("Images of Egypt in Genesis") evaluates several narratives in Genesis where Egypt is the central locale and where Egyptian characters are featured. We begin with the Abraham cycle where Egypt is a prominent spatial setting early in the ancestor's career: travelling to the land of Canaan after being given an astonishing divine promise, upon arrival Abram is faced with a famine in the land. Consequently, he makes the decision in Gen 12:10 to travel to Egypt, the first formal mention of the country in the Hebrew Bible (cf. the proper name in Gen 10:6, 13). Our analysis focuses on what happens there, including the appropriation of Sarai into Pharaoh's house and the subsequent enriching of Abram, and the great plagues (נגעים גדלים) that befall Pharaoh culminating in Abram's abrupt expulsion from the country when Pharaoh discovers that Sarai is not—as advertised—the sister of Abram. As a spatial setting Egypt essentially fades from the story after these memorable events in Genesis 12 and is only mentioned in passing in the rest of the Abraham narrative, although when it is referenced there is usually some larger significance. For example, in Gen 13:10 Abram's nephew Lot lifts up his eyes to survey the Jordan Valley, and makes a mental comparison to the land of Egypt. The most well-known Egyptian character in this stage of Genesis is Hagar, Sarah's Egyptian maid-servant, and her characterization also is probed in this chapter. There is only one reference to Egypt in the career of Isaac—the divine admonition *not* to go down to Egypt in Gen 26:2—and none during the major account of Jacob's life, focused as it is with the land of the Arameans to the east. By far the highest concentration of references to Egypt in the book of Genesis is found in the Joseph narrative near the end of the book (Genesis 37–50), and so the rest of Chapter 1 surveys the images of Egypt in this section. Certainly the decisive moment in the story is when Joseph's brothers sell him as a slave to a caravan of merchants heading down to Egypt in Gen 37:25–8, but despite some vicissitudes of fortune, Joseph prospers in Egypt. Remarkably, being sold as a slave eventually results in Joseph's elevation as Pharaoh's senior advisor and allows his own brothers to survive the ravages of a widespread famine. In this chapter we also explore the characterization of Pharaoh, and reflect on the concluding moments of Genesis 50 as a transition to the book of Exodus.

Having discussed the necessary background in Genesis, the next stage of our study proceeds with a reading of Exodus 1–2 in its sequential unfolding. Terence Fretheim remarks on the expansiveness of the opening of Exodus: "The wide-ranging scope of these chapters is breathtaking. They move back and forth from the familial to the national, from the personal to the cosmic, from courageous women to arrogant kings, from endangered babies to a concerned God."[25] To commence our analysis, Chapter 2 of this book ("Old Promise, New King") focuses on Exod 1:1–14, a stretch of text that can be divided into two parts. First, Exod 1:1–7 starts with an enumeration of the sons of Jacob and their proliferation in Egypt, to the point that they "swarmed" (שׁרץ) and the land was filled with them. Recalling God's promise in Genesis, Abraham is told that his descendants would be as numerous as the sand on the seashore, and they would be given the land of Canaan. So, part of the promise certainly appears to moving along, but the many offspring of Abraham are not residing in their own land. The second section consists of Exod 1:8–14, and introduces a new king who arises over Egypt. The identity of this unnamed king is discussed in this chapter, as is his evident anxiety about the teeming Israelites: in a short speech laced with hypothetical exigencies, the king's concern with the Israelites eventually results in a coercive policy of enslaving them. Yet the slavery does not impede the growth of the Israelite nation—counter to Pharaoh's obvious expectation—but it does prove to harden his resolve.

Chapter 3 ("Pharaoh's Midwife Crisis") turns to Exod 1:15–22 where a heroic element is introduced into the storyline. The king of Egypt orders the Hebrew midwives to destroy every male child born to the Hebrews, but in a treasonous act of defiance, the midwives allow the boys to live. Although this is a compact textual sequence, a

---

[25] Fretheim, *Exodus*, 23. As my study is interested in the aesthetics of the final form of the canonical text, I will not pursue the legion of source-critical questions that are often posed; for a critique ("Those scholars who argue for compositional unity in these chapters also tend, not surprisingly, to ignore these narrative difficulties in favor of structural or thematic considerations"), see Joel S. Baden, "From Joseph to Moses: The Narratives of Exodus 1–2," *VT* 62 (2012) 133–58. Such a caution is duly noted, but as the intended audiences for this book are students and general readers rather than specialists, my own reading follows the lead of Exum, "'You Shall Let Every Daughter Live,'" 37–8: "Analyses that divide the material between the pentateuchal sources, J, E and P, and discussions of the growth of the tradition are available in the commentaries, and it is not my intention to delve into these matters here. There are, to be sure, logical inconsistencies and tensions in the narrative which bear witness to a long and complicated process of development. As they meet us in the narrative now, however, they contribute to its richness, its irony and its humor, and, as in the case of Moses' sister, who appears suddenly out of nowhere, they surprise us by giving the story a new direction."

number of questions surface and occupy our attention in this chapter. Why are only two midwives presented, and are they intended as typological characters or is this an example of a folktale motif at work? Similarly, there is some debate about their ethnicity: are the midwives Hebrew or Egyptian women, and what difference does it make to the interpretation of this scene? We also find an intriguing translation issue in Exod 1:16, where Pharaoh's order to the midwives is rendered by the NRSV as follows: "When you act as midwives to the Hebrew women, and see them on the birthstool," but Gordon Davies opts for, "When midwifing the Hebrew women, look at the stones." This is a quite different understanding of the verse, and the various options are weighed in the chapter. For their part, the midwives adopt a creative strategy of deception, and this strategy is also explored as our chapter proceeds, both in terms of how it works in the context of Exodus 1–2 and in relation to comparable deceptions practiced by other laudable female characters in the Hebrew Bible. If there is a striking absence of God until this point in the book of Exodus, an abrupt intrusion occurs when God is formally mentioned in this sequence. Unlike Pharaoh, God neither speaks nor commands, and only gives the midwives "houses" (בתים). Furthermore, we will inquire as to how the king of Egypt discovers the deception of the midwives, and in his final moments of direct speech in Exodus 1 (the last words in the rest of his career, for that matter) he addresses a larger audience and commands that male babies be thrown into the Nile. Indeed, the Nile river is the central spatial setting for the next scenes of the story. The backbone of Egypt's religious and commercial economies, the Nile is the stream of life that ensures the prosperity of the nation, but now it chaotically becomes a mechanism for destroying the future of Israel.

One of the more memorable episodes of the Pentateuch takes place in Exod 2:1–10, and is the subject of Chapter 4 ("The Waters of Chaos") of this book. Bearing in mind the bleakness of the previous scenes, Exodus 2 begins on an ominous note with the birth of a male child to Levite parents, but the actions of the mother reveal a courage and tenacity that give the boy a chance to survive. The father is absent for the most part—perhaps the reader is to infer that he is forced to return to the building projects—leaving the mother as the principal actor. The allusion to the ark of Noah in Exodus 2 has already been mentioned, but the contrasts should also be adumbrated: Noah is provided with specific divine instructions for the schematics of the ark, whereas the mother in this story acts apparently of her own initiative alone. Cut from the same cloth, in this chapter we also explore the role of the unnamed sister who watches at a distance until it is time to take action; when the sister acts, new possibilities emerge in the storyline. The unnamed sister forthrightly converses with Pharaoh's daughter, another dauntless character who will be analyzed at length in this chapter: is her father aware of her conduct? Is she presented as a "righteous Gentile" in the narrative as some scholars have suggested? Moreover, it is Pharaoh's daughter who finally names the child "Moses," and this chapter concludes with a discussion of the etymology of this name and its significance for the larger dramatic sequencing at work in the book of Exodus.

Filmmakers and other interested parties have long been interested in the dual citizenship of Moses: a rescued Hebrew who grows up in the exotic Egyptian court, perhaps even with a disguised identity. But the book of Exodus is teasingly laconic about the youth and intellectual development of Moses in this locale, and instead fast-forwards to a momentous event of confrontation. It is the first actions of a grown-up Moses in Exod 2:11–15 that form the subject matter of Chapter 5 ("Criminal Charges"), as Moses' intervention when he sees an Egyptian beating a Hebrew results in a murder. The details of this crime are mysteriously discovered both by other Hebrews and the king of Egypt himself, precipitating the flight of Moses from the land of Egypt. Among the various issues that are considered in this chapter, it should be noted that when Moses sees a fellow Hebrew striking his brother in Exod 2:13, he pointedly addresses the one *in the wrong* (רשע). Not only does this term recur later in the book during a dialogue with Pharaoh (Exod 9:27), but it also anticipates the legal role of Moses among the Israelites. Moreover, the theoretical accusation leveled against Moses ("Are you thinking of killing me just like the Egyptian?") by the hostile Israelite foreshadows the contentious nature of his leadership and the fractiousness he faces at nearly every turn, both before and after the Israelites depart from Egypt. Moses' reaction to the king's knowledge of his crime, we observe, is "fear," and this is the first but certainly not the last time that fear is part of his experience, and we will assess various implications as he opts to exit the country and seek refuge in the land of Midian.

Fleeing from Egypt as a fugitive with scant prospects for a comfortable future, a turning-point in the career of Moses occurs as he sits down near a well of water in the liminal territory of Midian. It may seem inconsequential to the casual reader, but Moses' proximity to a well of water fits with an established pattern already seen several times in the book of Genesis, and labeled by scholars as the *type-scene* of the maiden at the well. Jacob and Isaac before him (albeit by proxy) also had such an encounter where they meet their bride at a well of water, and so now Moses joins this group. In Chapter 6 ("The Stranger in Midian") we turn to Exod 2:16–25, where the type-scene serves to connect Moses with the great ancestral promise in the book of Genesis, and strongly suggests that his career is far from over despite his flight from Egypt and fugitive status. Besides the type-scene, we will discuss the role of the Midianite priest in this episode, Moses' marriage to Zipporah, as well as the birth and naming of Moses' son in order to determine how such matters fit in the larger scheme of the chapter. The last verses in Exodus 2 present some important developments in Egypt even as Moses now seems reasonably ensconced in the land of Midian. The Israelites groan under their yoke of servitude, but God hears their cry for help and "remembers" the covenant made with Israel's ancestors. Since the verb *remember* (זכר) is a call to action based on a prior commitment (cf. Gen 8:1), there is every indication that the divine response will officially set in motion the liberation from Egyptian slavery.

Chapter 7 ("Exodus 1–2 and the Sojourn of Israel") provides a short conclusion to this book, and begins by summarizing several of the key literary features of the story such as allusion, foreshadowing, irony, and characterization. Not only does Exodus 1–2 serve to anticipate significant aspects of Israel's experience in the book of Exodus itself, but some of the themes in the opening section of the story also resonate with other portions of the Hebrew Bible and the New Testament. Is it possible, for instance, that distinct allusions to Exodus can be found in the book of Esther, with its secret identity of the main character in the royal court and a deadly threat aimed against the entire people? Or is it possible that Matthew 1–2 draws on images of Exodus and the career of Moses in order to establish a sophisticated typology in its opening pages? Delving into these questions as well as the reception history of this text is too ambitious a task for the end of this study, but I will submit that narratives such as Esther or the opening chapters of Matthew's gospel would be fruitful avenues that other scholars can explore as this memorable beginning to the book of Exodus—with its arresting plot, ensemble of characters, and poignant themes—is further studied and appreciated in the days to come.

1

Images of Egypt in Genesis

*Lot lifted up his eyes, and he saw the entire plane of the Jordan, that all of it was watered—before the L*ORD *destroyed Sodom and Gomorrah—like the garden of the L*ORD, *like the land of Egypt, all the way to Zoar.*

Genesis 13:10

Not only is the book of Genesis foundational for the story of Israel as a nation, but also its major themes and characters are presupposed in Exodus. For the study of Exodus 1–2, therefore, a number of events and figures from Genesis need to be surveyed in order for the reader to fully appreciate the background and context. Both in the book of Genesis and elsewhere in the Hebrew Bible, Egypt undoubtedly is portrayed as a daunting superpower whose economic security is assured by the rhythmic undulations of the Nile river that annually distributes its alluvial bounty. "In the famous phrase of the ancient Greek historian Herodotus, Egypt is the 'gift of the Nile.'"[1] Occasionally in Israelite history the nation of Egypt appears to be an ally, as when Solomon secures the daughter of Pharaoh as a wife in 1 Kings

---

[1] Michael D. Coogan, "In the Beginning: The Earliest History," pp. 3–24 in *The Oxford History of the Biblical World*, edited by Michael D. Coogan (New York: Oxford University Press, 1998) 7. Coogan further notes, "The Nile was thus the lifeline of Egypt, providing water year-round and guaranteeing food production. More than any other factor it explains the extraordinary longevity, stability, and conservatism of Egyptian culture" (p. 7). "The most remarkable of the ancient world's river systems," writes Bruce B. Williams, "the Nile formed an indispensable resource for Egypt and a series of cultures in Nubia and Sudan in ancient times" ("Nile [PLACE], Geography," in *Anchor Bible Dictionary*, edited by David Noel Freedman, 6 vols [New York: Doubleday, 1992] 4:1112–16). See also Diana Edelman, "The Nile in Biblical Memory," pp. 77–102 in *Thinking of Water in the Early Second Temple Period*, edited by Ehud Ben Zvi and Christoph Levin (BZAW 461; Berlin: Walter de Gruyter, 2014).

3:1. More often, however, seeking alliance with Egypt is portrayed as a perilous undertaking, not just during the reign of Solomon—where, incidentally, the fugitive Jeroboam is granted asylum in 1 Kings 11:40, and not long after Pharaoh Shishak directs an incursion against Judah and Jerusalem in 1 Kings 14:45—but at numerous points afterward. An oracle of Isaiah summarizes the imprudence of such dependency: "Oh, rebellious children, says the LORD, who carry out a plan, but not mine; who make an alliance, but against my will, adding sin to sin; who set out to go down to Egypt without asking for my counsel, to take refuge in the protection of Pharaoh, and to seek shelter in the shadow of Egypt; therefore the protection of Pharaoh shall become your shame, and the shelter in the shadow of Egypt your humiliation" (30:3, NRSV). Although I can only offer a limited number of examples here, the point remains that Egypt is portrayed as an attractive but unreliable partner during Israel's turbulent monarchic history.[2]

In this opening chapter, I would like to undertake a literary appraisal of those sectors of Genesis where Egypt is prominent, and investigate how Egypt is delineated in the text. As noted by Walter Brueggemann and Tod Linafelt, "The narrative materials of Genesis 12–50 present the tradition of the earliest ancestors of Israel wherein the most elemental themes of faith are rooted and paradigmatically articulated."[3] There are five parts in this chapter, starting with the experience of Abram in Egypt during his south-western trek in Gen 12:10-20. This first section assesses, among other things, the perceived tension between God's promise to give him and his descendants the land of Canaan and the subsequent decision to enter Egypt

---

[2] Such an argument could certainly be expanded; note the summary of John Goldingay, "Jeremiah and the Superpower," pp. 59–77 in *Uprooting and Planting: Essays on Jeremiah for Leslie Allen*, edited by John Goldingay (LHBOTS 459; New York: T & T Clark, 2007) 59: "Through most of Old Testament Israel's history, one superpower or another dominated the political, economic, cultural, and religious life of the world as Israel knew it—Assyria, then Babylon, then Persia, then Greece." For the portrayal of Assyria as an analogy, see Peter Machinist, "Assyria and Its Image in the First Isaiah," *JAOS* 103 (1983) 719-37; Marvin A. Sweeney, "The Portrayal of Assyria in the Book of Kings," pp. 274-84 in *The Bible as a Human Witness to Divine Revelation: Hearing the Word of God through Historically Dissimilar Traditions*, edited by Randall Heskett and Brian Irwin (LHBOTS 469; London: T & T Clark, 2010). For a diachronic study, see Stephen C. Russell, *Images of Egypt in Early Biblical Literature: Cisjordan-Israelite, Transjordan-Israelite, and Judahite Portrayals* (BZAW 403; Berlin: Walter de Gruyter, 2009).

[3] Walter Brueggemann and Tod Linafelt, *An Introduction to the Old Testament: The Canon and Christian Imagination*, Second Edition (Louisville: WJKP, 2012) 65.

because of the famine. Second, we review several other mentions of Egypt in the Abraham cycle, including the perspective of Abraham's nephew Lot in Gen 13:10—as quoted at the commencement of this chapter—and the character of Hagar who occurs at several junctures in the story. Third, we move to the narrative of Joseph and consider his experiences after being sold as a slave, and how Egypt is represented in his early career. Fourth, the characterization of Pharaoh in the Joseph narrative is discussed, and this includes a comparison with the Pharaoh of Genesis 12 during the peregrination of Abram. The fifth section of this chapter turns to the final parts of the story, especially the instructions of Jacob to carry his bones from Egypt in Gen 47:29–30, and the portentous words of Joseph about God "visiting" the family of Israel in Gen 50:24 and taking them up from the land of Egypt, before turning to the opening chapters of the book of Exodus.

FAMINE IN CANAAN

An oft-quoted statement by David Clines outlines the following thesis: "The theme of the Pentateuch is the partial fulfilment—which implies also the partial non-fulfilment—of the promise to or blessing of the patriarchs. The promise or blessing is both the divine initiative in a world where human initiatives always lead to disaster, and are an affirmation of the primal divine intentions for humanity."[4] Clines is referring to God's promise to Abraham first articulated in Gen 12:1–3 and reiterated on several occasions. This divine promise includes several elements: the gift of land, an abundance of progeny, and the assurance that through Abraham's offspring every family on earth will be blessed. It would be difficult to overstate the importance of this promise for the rest of the biblical text. For a related thread of interpretation, consider Gerhard von Rad's classic summary: "From the multitude of nations God chooses a man, looses him from tribal ties, and makes him the beginner of a new nation and the recipient of great promises of salvation. What is promised to Abraham reaches far

---

[4] David J. A. Clines, *The Theme of the Pentateuch*, Second Edition (JSOTSup 10; Sheffield: Sheffield Academic Press, 1997 [originally published 1978]) 30.

beyond Israel; indeed, it has universal meaning for all generations on earth."[5]

From a literary vantage point there is a certain drama that emerges after reflecting on these words: Abraham is bequeathed a great promise, and thus as a character and a bearer of this promise, many readers will have a vested interest in the fortunes of this figure. Furthermore, for the book of Exodus this promise is of tremendous import and is certainly under threat, although in the Genesis narrative there are some formidable obstacles as well: Abraham and his wife Sarah are both advanced in years, and Sarah is barren. Nonetheless, Abraham's willingness to make the journey to Canaan given such impediments is almost universally appreciated as a laudable act of faith.

A clear timeline is not given, but it can be assumed that a reasonably short time after entering the land of Canaan there is a famine in the land (Gen 12:10), and this crisis leads to Abraham's decision to find a safe harbor in Egypt. Whether this move springs from a momentary lack of faith has troubled commentators. Later in Abraham's life (Gen 22:1) there is a chilling "test," yet no such language is used here, so it could be suggested that an ambiguity is presented. But for Terence Fretheim there is a particular rationale in the move toward Egypt: "Abraham must move out of the land of promise in order to survive. It would have been no demonstration of faith in God to not take appropriate action and wait for God to perform a miracle. This trek is but the first of a number of such journeys away from the land of promise, often into alien and dangerous territory."[6] Apart from the faith question that interpreters debate, Fretheim's point about dangerous territory is worth pursuing on two levels.[7] First, Egypt has not

---

[5] Gerhard von Rad, *Genesis: A Commentary* (OTL; Philadelphia: Westminster, 1972) 152, cited in R. W. L. Moberly, *The Theology of the Book of Genesis* (OTT; Cambridge: Cambridge University Press, 2009) 144.

[6] Terence E. Fretheim, *Abraham: Trials of Family and Faith* (Columbia, SC: University of South Carolina Press, 2007) 48.

[7] On the faith question, Jon Levenson is more equivocal (*Inheriting Abraham: The Legacy of the Patriarch in Judaism, Christianity and Islam* [Princeton: Princeton University Press, 2012] 142), as is Dennis T. Olson, "Abram had just received God's promise that God would bless Abram and make him a 'great nation' (12:2–3), but Abram seems not to trust fully in God's blessing and protection in this instance" ("Genesis," pp. 1–32 in *The New Interpreter's Bible One-Volume Commentary*, edited by Beverly Roberts Gaventa and David L. Petersen [Nashville: Abingdon, 2010] 12). For a slightly different view, see J. Gerald Janzen, *Abraham and All the Families of the Earth: A Commentary on the Book of Genesis 12–50* (ITC; Grand Rapids: Eerdmans, 1993) 24.

been mentioned as a place prior to this particular point in the story, only as a proper name in the table of nations in Genesis 10 as part of the Hamite branch. In the context of Abraham's story, then, Egypt is immediately configured as a place of shelter or survival from the exigencies of famine. Scrutinizing the language of 12:10 more closely—"Then there was a famine in the land, and Abram went down to Egypt to sojourn (גור) there, because the famine was heavy in the land"—one of the controversial terms is *sojourn*, and the reader is unsure whether a temporary or long-term stay is intended. Gordon Wenham opts for the latter, inferring that Abraham deems it advantageous to remain in Egypt instead of risking the anxiety of Canaan.[8] It may be preferable to reserve judgment on how long Abraham intends to sojourn, but the point remains that there is a danger of staying too long in Egypt. Second, it is at the boundary of Egypt that Abraham speaks for the first time in the narrative. He makes the journey to Canaan with no recorded speech, only wordless obedience, as it were. But on the threshold of Egypt, Abraham's opening dialogue in vv. 11–13 is fraught with apprehension and the potential for death as he speaks to his wife Sarai: "Behold, I know that you are a beautiful woman, and when the Egyptians see you, they will say 'This is his wife,' and they will kill me, but let you live. Please say that you are my sister in order that it might go well for me for your sake, and that I will live on account of you."

Based on Abraham's actions and first words in the story, Egypt is initially pictured as a place to escape the crisis in Canaan, but also a spatial setting where danger lurks. As he predicted, the beauty of Sarah attracts Egyptian attention and she is taken into Pharaoh's house. Given Sarah's advanced age, her appropriation could contain shades of satire on Egyptian standards or Pharaoh's personal preferences, but the immediate beneficiary is "her brother" Abraham, on whom gifts are lavished because of her: sheep, oxen, male and female servants, male and female donkeys and camels. Walter Brueggemann argues that this episode has elements of humor that involve "the shrewdness of father Abraham, the irresistible beauty of mother

---

[8] E.g., Gordon J. Wenham, *Genesis 1–15* (WBC; Waco: Word, 1987) 287: "It is striking that Abram is said to have gone to 'settle in' Egypt, to be an immigrant there. To live as an immigrant (גור) suggests the intention of long-term settlement, which is somewhat alien to Abram's wandering lifestyle. It also comes as quite a surprise to hear that Abram is ready to settle in Egypt so soon after he has been promised 'this land' (12:7)."

Sarah (in the present form, an aged beauty), and the crippling lust of Egypt and its Pharaoh. Of all the women available in the empire, they want mother Sarah! So the story," Brueggemann concludes, "has a sociological function. It moves in the arena of liberation, of dramatic and linguistic delegitimization of imperial authority."[9] Regardless of any satire, it could be supposed that the divine promise is jeopardized by Abraham's machination, as there is a plausible link between taking Sarah and the arrival of "great plagues" sent by God. Numerous commentators aver that the plagues of Exodus are anticipated at this point in Abraham's career, even if slightly different language is used.[10] Of course, in Exodus Pharaoh is a guilty party, whereas here Abraham is prevaricating. How Pharaoh finds out that he has been hoodwinked is not revealed in the story, but his anger is palpable—perhaps the plague renders him impotent—and results in the expulsion of Abraham. The final combination of plagues, confrontation, and dismissal from Egypt serves to foreshadow the events of Exodus, and notwithstanding the serious differences and reversals, the episode hints that Abraham's descendants will too depart Egypt with riches (more explicitly raised in Gen 15:14). For now, however, the initial images of Egypt are ambivalent, as F. V. Greifenhagen observes: "The first instances of Egypt in the Abraham cycle thus portray Egypt as a dangerous place that one enters and leaves quickly, but which promises riches at the cost of deception. As a proto-exodus narrative, the story presents Egypt as a detour."[11] It could also be suggested that in this episode God intervenes and initiates a rescue because of the promise, despite Abraham's less-than-admirable conduct.

---

[9] Walter Brueggemann, *Genesis* (Interpretation; Atlanta: John Knox Press, 1982) 128.

[10] E.g., R. R. Reno, *Genesis* (Brazos Theological Commentary on the Bible; Grand Rapids: Brazos Press, 2010) 148. Robert Alter, *Genesis: Translation and Commentary* [New York: W. W. Norton, 1996] 52) notes that the phrase "you they will let live" is "a pointed echo of Exodus 1:22, 'Every boy that is born you shall cast into the Nile and every girl you shall let live.'" See also Fretheim, "The Book of Genesis: Introduction, Commentary, and Reflections," pp. 321–674 in *The New Interpreter's Bible*, Vol. 6, edited by L. E. Keck (Nashville: Abingdon, 1994) 428: "God's action constitutes the turning point in the story, in spite of Abram's duplicity. A comparison with the plague stories (Exod 11:1) brings out a notable contrast. While plagues are visited upon the Egyptians in both cases, the reasons differ. In Exodus, the conduct of the Egyptians elicits them. Here the behavior of God's own chosen one leads to Pharaoh's action, which engenders the plagues."

[11] F. V. Greifenhagen, *Egypt on the Pentateuch's Ideological Map: Constructing Biblical Israel's Identity* (JSOTSup 361; Sheffield: Sheffield Academic Press, 2002) 31.

OTHER REFRACTIONS

There are several other texts where Egypt is mentioned or alluded to in the Abraham narrative, and in this section three are discussed: the perception of Lot in Gen 13:10; God's words to Abraham about his descendants in Gen 15:13-14; and several scenes that involve the character of Hagar, Sarah's Egyptian maidservant. Starting with Lot, it should be said from the outset that Lot is not a simple character to interpret. As the nephew of Abraham, the reader could be under the impression that Lot is the heir of his childless uncle—which explains why Abraham takes him to Egypt—though later developments in the story reveal otherwise. Indeed, the later episodes of Lot in the city of Sodom and the subsequent impregnation of his own daughters hang like a cloud over this character.[12] But in Genesis 13 matters are still open, as all Lot has done is venture with his uncle Abraham to Egypt and departed with him when Pharaoh ejects them from his country. The context for Lot's next appearance in Gen 13:5-12 is a quarrel among the herdsman, leading to Abraham's offer for him to choose his portion of land.[13] In the passage cited at the beginning of this chapter, Lot lifts up his eyes and his inner perception is refracted in the narrative, as he compares the Jordan Valley to both the garden of the LORD and the land of Egypt. Lot's focalization reinforces the notion that Egypt is an enticing spatial setting: with the famine in Canaan occurring not so long ago in the narrative, the well-irrigated landscape akin to Egypt represents a lucrative prospect for Lot. Bringing both Egypt and the garden into the same orbit may appear positive, but both places have been recent sites of temptation, judgment, and banishment.[14]

A question arises as to why this picture of Egypt—and the comparison with Eden—is filtered through the perspective of Lot, a relation of Abraham's who has a somewhat idealized view of Egypt. Lot's perception of Egypt will by no means remain unique to him, but

---

[12] For a study of Lot's characterization, see Robert I. Letellier, *Day in Mamre, Night in Sodom: Abraham and Lot in Genesis 18 and 19* (BIS 10; Leiden: Brill, 1995).

[13] Daniel Rickett, "Rethinking the Place and Purpose of Genesis 13," *JSOT* 36.1 (2011) 31-53.

[14] Laurence A. Turner, *Genesis* (Readings; Sheffield: Sheffield Academic Press, 2000) 68; Greifenhagen *Egypt on the Pentateuch's Ideological Map*, 29: "the implicit comparison of Egypt with the garden of YHWH, in the light of Gen. 3, suggests that Egypt is a place of temptation."

resurfaces in the later story with Israel's longing for Egypt (e.g., Num 11:5, "We remember the fish that we would eat for free in Egypt, the cucumbers, the melons, the leeks, the onions, and the garlic"). A comparatively minor character, Lot prefigures the perspective of later descendants of Abraham who do not learn from the past, and yearn for well-watered Egypt and tend to complain about the deficiencies of Canaan. Hence Gordon Wenham understands Lot as a character endowed with typological qualities here, and "it may be that Lot is seen as typical of the wrong attitudes within the nation. His choosing of territory like the land of Egypt foreshadows the oft-repeated desire of the wilderness rebels to return to Egypt (Exod 16:3, Num 11:5; 14:2–3). Both ended in destruction."[15] The differences between Canaan and Egypt in Lot's perception are stressed by Robert Kawashima in a slightly different framework, as the comparison between the plain (prior to its ecological ruination through divine judgment) and Eden/Egypt "implies that to live in a state of paradisiacal ease, where one can simply 'irrigate by foot' (Deut 11:10–12), inevitably leads human societies into moral decline."[16] Like later Israel, Lot has recently lived in Egypt but fails to learn that the country of the Nile—with all of its well-watered attraction—ultimately does not provide the kind of security that is so desperately coveted.

Egypt next features in the Abraham narrative during the encounter with God in chapter 15, where God reveals that his descendants will suffer enslavement in a foreign nation, certainly the most specific and foreboding anticipation of the Exodus experience in the book of Genesis. The context of this encounter is when Abraham falls into a deep sleep and darkness descends upon him, setting the tone for the divine words about the forthcoming dark night of the soul for Abraham's descendants. Earlier in the scene God declares "I am the LORD who brought you from Ur of the Chaldeans" (Gen 15:7) in language that will be reappropriated in Exodus, and the scene concludes with God's reiteration of the covenant with Abraham and the gift of the land to his seed (15:18–21), assurances that are threatened in the early

---

[15] Wenham, *Genesis 1–15*, 300.
[16] Robert S. Kawashima, "Sources and Redaction," pp. 47–70 in *Reading Genesis: Ten Methods*, edited by Ronald Hendel (New York: Cambridge University Press, 2010) 60.

plot movements of Exodus 1-2. The pivotal moment of the scene is Gen 15:13-14 and God's ominous disclosure about the future:

> Know for certain that your seed will be a stranger in a land that is not theirs, and they will serve them, and be afflicted (ענה) by them for four hundred years. But also, on the nation that they serve I will act as judge, and afterward they will march out with great property.

The period of 400 years has been variously interpreted by scholars, but for the purposes of this book the point need not be a literal one; instead, it is established that Abraham's offspring will experience times of terrifying darkness where the great promises of land and covenant appear to have been erased, and oppression by an empire dominates their worldview. Undoubtedly the exodus events are in view, but why is Egypt not explicitly mentioned? With the long-term horizon in view, perhaps this is not the only trial that Abraham's descendants will endure, as Fretheim suggests: "Since 'Egypt' does not appear in v. 13, the author does not appear concerned to speak about the future with precision. Hence, readers might apply the word to more than one life situation (fourth-generation language would work well for the exiles)."[17] But if Exodus is squarely in view, then the image of Egypt that emerges in this scene is rather different than Abraham's recent experience, with mass enslavement and affliction. Moreover, the absence of any direct mention of Egypt here keeps the reader's mind open about the character of Hagar, the next figure to consider in our survey of the images of Egypt in Genesis.

Abraham is enriched by Pharaoh on account of his "sister" in Gen 12:16, and included in the inventory of gifts are maidservants. Hagar the Egyptian is presumably one of these maidservants, and when Abraham is dismissed by an angry Pharaoh and exits with all of his possessions in Gen 12:20, it can be surmised that Hagar is part of the group that departs with Abraham, Sarah, and Lot. Hagar is a main character in chapter 16, a unit that, in the judgment of Ernst Axel Knauf, is "a short story of high literary standing: human attempts to implement the divine promise (Gen 15:4) prove counterproductive; they lead to the anarchy of the desert (Gen 16:12)."[18] Sarah's attempt at surrogate motherhood backfires when Hagar becomes pregnant

---

[17] Fretheim, "The Book of Genesis," 446-7.
[18] Ernst Axel Knauf, "Hagar," in *The Anchor Bible Dictionary*, 6 volumes, edited by David Noel Freedman (New York: Doubleday, 1992) 3:18-19.

through Abraham but then she treats Sarah "lightly," and Hagar herself is subsequently afflicted (ענה) by Sarah. Fleeing from the house, Hagar hears the voice of an angel of God near a spring of water in the desert, providing reassurance for the present and hope for the future with respect to her offspring. Our interest here is how this Egyptian character is portrayed, and in the first instance there is an analogy with Lot. When Lot lifted his eyes he perceived a well-watered valley, like the land of Egypt. Now, Hagar from Egypt is fertile while Sarah is barren in Canaan: "just as Egypt has food during famine, so it harbors fertility during barrenness."[19] In Genesis 16 it should also be noted that Sarah is the one who afflicts Hagar, even if the roles are reversed in Exodus 1 and the Egyptians afflict the Israelites. Consequently, Hagar generates more sympathy from the reader, and despite the fact that she treats Sarah with contempt (Gen 16:5), she does not appear in a wholly negative light. Because of the harsh treatment of the Israelites in Exod 1:11–12—note the verb "afflict" (ענה) occurring twice—the reader might expect the Egyptian (s) to be vilified in Genesis, but this is not exactly the case.[20] In fact, God's care for Hagar in the wilderness setting might best be appreciated in light of Israel's own experience after leaving Egypt, where water is miraculously provided and the divine presence accompanies them during their sojourn. Hagar's encounters in the wilderness lead to another significant feature within her portrayal in this section of Genesis. As Thomas Dozeman outlines at length, there are a series of intriguing similarities between the experiences of Hagar and the career of Moses.[21] Both, for instance, are dislocated characters: Hagar is an Egyptian in Abraham's house, and Moses is an Israelite in an Egyptian house. Both figures experience God in the wilderness, have

---

[19] Greifenhagen, *Egypt on the Pentateuch's Ideological Map*, 32. He further notes the echoes of Eden in this episode: "But, just like Abram's move to Egypt, Sarai's decision, while seeming on the surface to have the desired result, conceals a hidden danger. A verbal allusion to Gen. 3 underlines the potential problem. There, the deity berated Adam for listening to Eve (3:17), who took of the fruit and gave of it to her husband (3:6); so also here the same language is used to describe how Abram listens to Sarai, who takes Hagar and gives her to her husband (16:2-3). In both cases, the desired result leads to unforeseen consequences" (citing Wenham, *Genesis 16-50* [WBC; Dallas: Word, 1994] 7–8).

[20] Fretheim, "The Book of Genesis," 429.

[21] Thomas B. Dozeman, "The Wilderness and Salvation History in the Hagar Story," *JBL* 117 (1998) 23–43; cf. Athalya Brenner, "Female Social Behavior: Two Descriptive Patterns within the 'Birth of the Hero' Paradigm," *VT* 36 (1986) 257–73.

an encounter at a well or spring of water, and endure a deadly crisis with their offspring. Altogether, these similarities create a favorable role for Hagar the Egyptian, perhaps anticipating other positive Egyptian characters in the story of Exodus and inviting reflection on further parallels:

> The prominent role of the wilderness outside of Genesis raises the question of whether Hagar's repeated journey there is intended to embed her story in a larger history in which parallels are created between the lives of Hagar and Moses, and also between the Ishmaelites and Israelites.... Hagar becomes the first person in the Pentateuch to undergo transformation in the wilderness leading to the founding of a wilderness nation, while Moses is the second. In both instances, the history now accentuates how God transforms family conflict into an instance of liberation, which results in the separation of people—Ishmaelites from Israelites and Israelites from Egyptians.[22]

FROM ADVERSITY TO ELEVATION

The character of Hagar—finally driven out (גרש) from Sarah's house with a verb that is important in the book of Exodus (e.g., 2:17, 6:1; cf. Gen 3:24)—is worthy of more sustained treatment, but our attention now turns instead to the images of Egypt in the Joseph narrative of Genesis 37–50. Prior to the descent of Joseph, Egypt is not a major spatial setting: Abraham's visit does not seem overly long, Lot's perspective is wistful, and Hagar only secures a wife for her son in a fleeting mention of Egypt (Gen 21:21). In fact, Egypt does not feature in the story for prolonged stretches. During another famine in the land, Isaac is explicitly told by God in Gen 26:3, "Do not go down to Egypt," perhaps a censorious reference to Abraham's earlier conduct since it takes place during another *sister act* controversy. Egypt as a site of potential danger and temptation is held in abeyance until a turning point occurs in the Joseph narrative, as Egypt becomes the principal location and dwelling-place of the Israelites by the end of the story. By way of background, we recall that the favoritism Jacob bestows on his young son Joseph does not have a salutatory effect in the narrative. On the contrary, combined with Joseph's immature

---

[22] Dozeman, "The Wilderness and Salvation History in the Hagar Story," 33.

temperament, the simmering rivalries are barely contained in the early part of Genesis 37. Comparable jealousy and resentment seem to reappear in Exod 2:14 with the accusation against Moses. When Joseph has dreams of grandeur—poignantly imparted in the form of grain and harvest, in light of Joseph's future leadership in Egypt—the wrath of the brothers is kindled.[23] The brothers' resentment reaches its culmination with a plot to destroy Joseph, as he is seized and thrown into an empty cistern presumably to die of starvation. Indeed, the story could well end here, except for a strange happenstance where the land Egypt is involved, albeit circuitously, in Gen 37:25–8:

> As they sat down to eat their bread, they lifted up their eyes and looked, and behold, a caravan of Ishmaelites were coming from Gilead! Their camels were loaded with spices, balm, and myrrh, going on their way down to Egypt. Then Judah said to his brothers, "What is the profit that we should kill our brother and cover up his blood? Come now, and let's sell him to the Ishmaelites so that our hand won't be upon him—for he is our brother, our flesh is he." His brothers listened. Then, some Midianite traders passed by, and they drew out Joseph and brought him up from the cistern. They sold Joseph to the Ishmaelites for twenty silver pieces, and so they brought Joseph to Egypt.

So far in Genesis, Egypt has generally been pictured as a place of refuge and survival when the land of Canaan poses risks and uncertainty; if Canaan periodically is besieged with famine, Egypt is consistently unaffected. But in Genesis 37 there is a slightly different depiction, as Egypt becomes a place for the brothers to hide their guilt. Though the market for slaves in Egypt may sound an ominous note, it certainly helps to assuage the brothers' collective conscience here. Earlier Abraham acquired maidservants and menservants during his sojourn, but now his grandson is taken down to Egypt and sold as a slave. The Ishmaelites, who mediate the transaction by both

---

[23] Jon D. Levenson, *The Death and Resurrection of the Beloved Son: The Transformation of Child Sacrifice in Judaism and Christianity* (New Haven: Yale University Press, 1993) 166. On the element of binding sheaves in Joseph's first dream (Gen 37:7), Levenson notes an insight of David Qimchi and the significance of grain in Joseph's rapid promotion in Egypt: "it was 'because of grain that he rose to prominence.'" Also, "the image of the brothers' sheaves bowing while Joseph's own remained upright (Gen 37:7) might have suggested that his supply of grain would be full when theirs had already given out. The collapsed sheaves would then have foreshadowed the brothers' empty sacks, and Joseph's upright sheaf would, by the same logic, have suggested that his sack would be abundant when they were in dire need."

transporting and selling Joseph, are an intriguing but perhaps underestimated part of the story. An apparent confusion has taxed scholars, as the Midianites are also mentioned in the paragraph of Gen 37:25-8. A standard solution has been to recognize a merging of traditions here, with the Ishmaelite strand identified with the J source and the Midianite reference ascribed to the E source.[24] Without casting any aspersion on the assured results of source-critical stratigraphy, from a literary perspective the matter has been investigated differently, and it is argued that when Joseph is sold as a slave there are echoes of the earlier Ishmael ordeal. More specifically, the Ishmaelites (descended from Hagar) and the Midianites (descended from Keturah in Gen 25:2) "are both mentioned since their forefathers were both banished by Abraham."[25] Joseph and Ishmael have some common threads in their careers, and when the Ishmaelites arrive en route to Egypt, an intertextual reflex is activated:

> Its purpose is to trigger an association: just as Ishmael was sent into the wilderness as the intended victim of a murderous plan motivated by family enmity, so also Joseph is unknowingly sent out to a desolate place where he falls victim to his brothers' animosity. But in the end both are rescued. It is a strange turn of fate that those who arrive to "save" Joseph are descendants of the same one who had earlier been targeted for such treacheries by the same family—but survived. The irony is vexing: if Ishmael had not survived his betrayal in the wilderness, Joseph may not have survived his.[26]

Ishmael survives his expulsion from Abraham's house and has descendants just as God promised (Gen 16:10). Yet after he is brought down to Egypt by Ishmael's offspring, Joseph too thrives after his expulsion, and God is with him and causes him to prosper in

---

[24] E.g., David W. Cotter, *Genesis* (Berit Olam; Collegeville: Liturgical Press, 2003) 276; E. A. Speiser, *Genesis* (AB 1a; New York: Doubleday, 1964) 291. Cf. Judges 8:24, where it is explained that Midianites have a cache of gold earrings because they are "Ishmaelites."

[25] S. Nikaido, "Hagar and Ishmael as Literary Figures: An Intertextual Study," *VT* 51 (2001) 237-8, citing Joel Rosenberg, *King and Kin: Political Allegory in the Hebrew Bible* (Bloomington: Indiana University Press, 1986) 237.

[26] Nikaido, "Hagar and Ishmael as Literary Figures," 238. It remains to be seen if it is significant that Moses flees to Midian, which Greifenhagen (*Egypt on the Pentateuch's Ideological Map*, 65-6) labels "liminal territory."

Potiphar's house (Gen 39:2–5). The divine words to Abraham about his descendants suffering in another land (Gen 15:13) coupled with the Egyptian market for slaves may have inclined the reader to think the worst for Joseph in Potiphar's house, but his initial experiences are far from negative: he fares better as a slave in Egypt than at the hands of his brothers in Canaan. Despite such a fortuitous start, Joseph's darkest trial in Egypt has to be his imprisonment on false charges after resisting the seductive advances of Potiphar's wife. Earlier in Egypt the beautiful Sarah was taken into Pharaoh's house; in an inverted manner, the handsome Joseph too is the object of attraction, though matters take a more claustrophobic turn when the spurned wife's testimony results in Joseph's incarceration. Yet another comparison with Ishmael can be observed in Gen 39:14 when the wife accuses Joseph of trying to "sport" (צחק) with her, the same verbal root that prompts Sarah's anger against Ishmael and Hagar in Gen 21:9. "Ishmael in like manner can be compared to Joseph's character in that both are unjustly expelled from their advantageous positions because of their masters' wives, yet prosper in exile."[27] Slavery and imprisonment are bleak, but they are not the end of Joseph's story in the land of Egypt. The narrative of Genesis 39 begins with the statement that God is with Joseph, and the chapter ends with the same language, as God is with Joseph in the jail. Through an astounding sequence of events, the imprisoned Hebrew slave ends up gaining an audience with Pharaoh, where his gift of dream interpretation and administrative counsel give him the highest-ranking civilian post in Egypt as the vizier of Pharaoh. One would be hard-pressed to come up with a more radical career trajectory, as practically overnight Joseph is vaulted from prison to the prime minister's office, and thus the images of Egypt in Genesis 40–1 are quite unlike earlier sectors in the book of Genesis as Joseph inaugurates preparations to rescue Egypt from a famine, surely an unimaginable exigency. These themes of Egypt as a place where God's presence abides with Abraham's descendant(s) in spite of the bitterness of slavery and false imprisonment are important for appreciating the opening moments of the book of Exodus when the entire family of Israel suffers enslavement and oppression.

---

[27] Nikaido, "Hagar and Ishmael as Literary Figures," 242.

IN PHARAOH'S HOUSE

Joseph's elevation in Egypt is launched by dreams and interpretation, and through Pharaoh's dreams some of the more notable aspects of his own characterization are distilled. A significant moment of Pharaoh's individuation occurs at the beginning of chapter 41, when Pharaoh's dream is narrated at the spatial setting of the Nile river. Not only is Pharaoh baffled by the cows and the grain in his two dreams, but the magicians of Egypt are also at a loss. This is the only appearance of the magicians in the Joseph narrative, but it might anticipate their significance later in the book of Exodus where they are at first antagonists to Moses and Aaron and replicate some of the signs (e.g., turning the Nile to blood and staffs into sea-monsters [תנין]), but eventually confess their inadequacy when they fail to bring forth gnats by means of their secret arts in Exod 8:18–19 ("This is the finger of God!"). There is no reported objection to Joseph's arrival in Pharaoh's court among the magicians, but given the later storyline in Exodus, the absence of any confrontation or ideological conflict is striking. Instead, the court officials and magicians "are portrayed less as opponents and more as providing exotic color and a foil for the superior abilities of Joseph. Joseph emphasizes that the dream content and the events they forebode, as well as the correct interpretation of the dreams, come from God. Pharaoh does not argue with this position and in fact recommends Joseph to his court because he obviously has the רוח אלהים ('spirit of God,' 41:38)."[28] Based on Pharaoh's agitation and testimony after his dreams ("I have never seen such ugly cows in the land of Egypt"), the reader can assume that such sights are uncommon in his experience, and that the land of the Nile has stood aloof from the catastrophes of famine. Even in Pharaoh's report he stresses the negative sights. When he speaks, the hideous cows are overwhelming and the sleek are eclipsed, suggesting that strength is a matter of course but he can hardly process the image of weakness swallowing strength. Based on the confusion and vulnerability, a larger theme can be glimpsed:

> The dreams about reversal of position, about strength and weakness, about the mystery of human responsiveness to divine tides, though integral to the Joseph story and vital for building its particular potentate,

---

[28] Greifenhagen, *Egypt on the Pentateuch's Ideological Map*, 36.

are challenging beyond it as well. If the story of the exodus from Egypt is arguably the fundamental pattern of the whole biblical narrative, then the Joseph story, its action propelled by the dreams, poses the question of why the going-out was necessary. The dreams in the Joseph story refer obliquely to an untold story, to an unnamed danger that makes escape even in Egypt a necessity. What is the danger lurking that makes Egypt a refuge, even if only for a time? What is the secret of human potency and coherence, whether at the mundane, geopolitical, or spiritual levels that unwinds so easily?[29]

Back in Genesis 12 during Abraham's sojourn to Egypt the Pharaoh is only minimally characterized, but there is a measure of sympathy when he takes Sarah to be his wife on account of the sister ruse. Pharaoh has only one speech in the story, brimming with anger and rhetorical questions because of the great plagues that are inconveniencing both him and the royal house (12:18–19). As mentioned earlier, there is a gap in the episode, and no direct indication as to how Pharaoh uncovers the connection between Abraham's marriage and the arrival of the plagues. But commentators also point out that "Abram and Sarai's experience foreshadows that of their descendants in the first half of the ensuing book," and thus Genesis 12 has a "typological function" within the broader storyline.[30] By comparison, the Pharaoh in the Joseph narrative is much more perplexed with his circumstances, and the descendant of Abraham arrives in his court as the solution, not the problem. The surprising volume of "God" language in Genesis 40–1 creates a different tone than the Abraham episode, culminating with Pharaoh's own pronouncement in Gen 41:39: "Since God has shown you all this, there is no one so discerning and wise as you. You will be over my house, and all my people will comply with your words; only with regard to the throne will I be greater than you." Echoes of the earlier promotion in Potiphar's house can be heard in Pharaoh's words, reminding the reader that adversity in Egypt has perhaps brought out new and more attractive

---

[29] Barbara Green, "The Determination of Pharaoh: His Characterization in the Joseph Story (Genesis 37–50)," pp. 150–71 in *The World of Genesis: Persons, Places, Perspectives*, edited by Philip R. Davies and David J. A. Clines (JSOTSup 257; Sheffield: Sheffield Academic Press, 1998) 170–1.

[30] Jon D. Levenson, "The Conversion of Abraham to Judaism, Christianity, and Islam," pp. 3–40 in *The Idea of Biblical Interpretation: Essays in Honor of James L. Kugel*, edited by Hindy Najman and Judith H. Newman (JSJSup 83; Leiden: Brill, 2004) 6, cited in Moberly, *The Theology of the Book of Genesis*, 210.

qualities in Joseph, of which Pharaoh is a beneficiary.[31] The adversity is inscribed in the text when Joseph is given a new name and a wife by Pharaoh toward the end of chapter 41, but his attempts to erase his memory and modify his identity are not entirely successful even when he names his son Manasseh (מנשה), "for God has made me forget (נשה) all the trouble in my father's house." Joseph is not the last Hebrew who will be a member of Pharaoh's house, nor the last to name his firstborn son in recollection of painful experiences.[32] Under quite different circumstances, Moses also enters Pharaoh's house, although his firstborn son Gershom is born and named far away from the royal court, in the land of Midian.

Meanwhile, as Joseph forecasts in Gen 41:29–30, the seven bountiful years end and the period of famine begins. This dismal situation happens to be the catalyst for Joseph's own family to join the rest of the nations in trudging to Egypt in order to buy grain. From the brothers' perspective, the journey to Egypt is more than simply an opportunity to purchase food, for they also have some defining theological experiences along the way. More than any previous point in Genesis, the land of Egypt becomes a place of theological discernment, and in strange situations the sons of Israel have an experience in Egypt that they never have in the spatial setting of Canaan. Gen 42:7 narrates a moment of dramatic irony, as the brothers face the vizier of Egypt when attempting to acquire grain, unaware that they are facing their long-lost sibling whom they sold as a slave. After a closely worded interview, Joseph put the brothers in prison (משמר), reminiscent of his own recent internment in Gen 40:3 where the same term is used. After two days, dialogue with the vizier resumes in Gen 42:18–23:

> On the third day Joseph said to them, "Do this and live, for I fear God. If you are honest, let one of your brothers remain bound in the prison house, and the rest of you go and bring grain to your famished houses. But your youngest brother you will bring to me, so your words can be

---

[31] Cf. the summary of Brent A. Strawn, "Pharaoh," pp. 631–6 in *Dictionary of the Old Testament: Pentateuch*, edited by T. Desmond Alexander and David W. Baker (Downers Grove: InterVarsity Press, 2003) 635: "Pharaoh is powerful and yet powerless, despotic and yet determined by a will not his own, self-sufficient and yet massively reliant on Yahweh's chosen servant, Joseph, and therefore also on Yahweh."

[32] Note also Thomas Römer, "The Exodus in the Book of Genesis," *Svensk Exegetisk Årsbok* 75 (2010) 10: "In the final context of the Torah, Joseph even seems to be a forerunner of Moses, since like the latter he too is integrated into Pharaoh's family."

confirmed, and you will not die." They did so. Then they said to one another, "Truly, we are guilty for our brother! We saw his soul's distress when he cried for mercy to us, and we didn't listen! Therefore, this distress has come upon us!" Reuben answered them, saying, "Didn't I say to you, 'Don't sin against the boy'? But you wouldn't listen, and now, look, his blood is seeking justice!" But they did not know that Joseph was listening, because an interpreter was between them.

For the purposes of this study, it can be argued that Egypt is configured in this section of Genesis as a place where God is much more active than may have been supposed, or at the very least, where the characters have an awareness of God in relation to their own misdemeanors. It is in Egypt that the reader learns from the brothers' private dialogue that Joseph cried out for mercy in what Robert Alter refers to as "a remarkable instance of withheld narrative exposition," and that here Reuben returns to the storyline as "the chief spokesman for their collective guilt."[33] Far from trivial, this movement in the narrative is relevant for our study of Exodus. In the misery of Israel's enslavement in Egypt as pictured in Exodus 1 it may be thought that God is absent, but on the basis of the Joseph narrative in Genesis, the reader can infer that Egypt is a place where God does not abandon prior commitments. Several other instances confirm this notion. When Joseph dismisses the brothers—with the bound Simeon remaining as a kind of security deposit—he also orders that the men's silver be returned to their sacks. During the march back to Canaan in Gen 42:28, one of them opens his sack to find the silver, causing the others to tremble and ask, "What is this God has done to us?"

A larger sense of providential design also can be discerned in the march back to Egypt to acquire more food. When the brothers prepare to depart, their father tells them to bring double the amount of silver along with other commodities, including spices, balm, and myrrh. As we recall, these are the items that the Ishmaelite merchants were bringing down to Egypt when Joseph was taken as a slave. "The wheel seems to have come full circle," writes Meir Sternberg. "The plot movement that started with a brother leaving home in all innocence to join his brothers, only to find himself the property of a trading caravan bound for Egypt, now presses for closure once the

---

[33] Alter, *Genesis*, 247.

Images of Egypt in Genesis 35

brothers leave home in a caravan to rescue a brother in Egypt."[34] During our survey of Abraham's detour to Egypt, it was suggested that the land of the Nile is a place of refuge and survival, albeit fraught with danger and temptation. At this point in the Joseph narrative, it can be further perceived that Egypt is a place where God's justice is at work, even when it is not immediately obvious. A further illustration can be found in the chief steward of Joseph's house, a minor character in Genesis 43-4 who plays an interesting role as the story moves closer to its denouement. When the brothers arrive with Benjamin, Joseph directs the steward to take the men to his house to dine, and the scene in Gen 43:18-24 is worth quoting at length:

> The men were afraid because they had been brought to Joseph's house, and they said, "This is because of the silver that was returned in our sacks the first time that we are being brought here, in order to roll us over and fall upon us, so we can be taken as slaves! And our donkeys!" So they drew near to the man who was over Joseph's house, and they spoke to him at the door of the house. They said, "My lord, indeed we came down the first time to buy grain. But when we arrived at the lodging-place, we opened our sacks, and behold, each man's full weight of silver was in the mouth of his sack! So we brought it back in our hand. We brought down other silver in our hand to buy grain, but we don't know who put our silver in our sacks!" He said, "Peace to you. Don't be afraid, your God and the God of your father has given you treasure in your sacks. Your silver came to me." Then he brought Simeon out to them. So the man brought them into the house of Joseph. He gave them water and they washed their feet, and he gave fodder to their donkeys.

The steward of Joseph's house—and there is every reason to assume that he is an Egyptian—appears at an important juncture in the story as a mediating figure between the vizier of Egypt and the brothers. But even as he plays a significant role in maintaining the pretense and preparing for the climactic scenes, the steward is also depicted as a character in his own right whose actions and words are integrated into the thematic web of the narrative. The brothers' panic upon being brought to Joseph's house is no doubt compounded because of their residual guilt: the silver is their immediate item of confession,

---

[34] Sternberg, *The Poetics of Biblical Narrative*, 300-1, cited in Wenham, *Genesis 16-50*, 421. Cf. Alter, *Genesis*, 253: "As with the silver sent back and forth, the brothers are thus drawn unwittingly into a process of repetition of and restitution for their fraternal crime."

but the brothers must fear that other sins are finding their day of reckoning. There is a slight discrepancy in the story—after all, only one brother initially finds the silver back in Gen 42:27-8, then all of them find their silver returned in 42:35—but their sincerity is hardly in question here.³⁵ The steward does not interrupt their effusive protestation, but when they conclude the steward utters a word of *shalom* and dispels their fear. This kind of language is often associated with later Israelite prophets as a preface to an oracle of salvation. If the first words of the steward are a preface, they are followed by a most remarkable theological explanation that points to God's activity even in hostile circumstances in Egypt. For Gerhard von Rad, the steward's words contain a "dark ambiguity" that "touches the innermost mystery of the whole Joseph story: God's concealed guidance."³⁶ The reader may also pause and ask about the effect of such words about God's hidden actions spoken by an Egyptian minor character. For Terence Fretheim, the steward's status needs to be taken seriously: "One who stands outside the community announces this word of comfort to the people of God (even if he learned it from Joseph). This may be disconcerting to insiders, but they must be open to God's capability of working on their behalf in and through such persons. Outsiders, too, can be the vehicle for a word of God's peace."³⁷

It will be suggested in a moment that similarly configured minor characters are encountered early in the book of Exodus. Before that, however, it should be noted that Joseph's steward follows up his words with actions confirming that nothing disingenuous can be found in the speech. He begins by bringing Simeon back to them, a token of good faith in the immediate context but for the reader it anticipates a more dramatic fraternal reunion shortly to come. When the steward next gives them water to wash their feet (רגליהם), the gesture of hospitality can also be interpreted as a reversal of Joseph's contrived accusation of spying (מרגלים) back in Gen 42:9, cleverly exploiting the wordplay.³⁸ The steward's welcome extends to caring for the donkeys; it sounds faintly ridiculous that the viceroy of Egypt would want to steal the brothers' donkeys, but even this false fear is

---

³⁵ Turner, *Genesis*, 185.
³⁶ Gerhard von Rad, *Genesis*, 388, cited in Victor P. Hamilton, *The Book of Genesis: Chapters 18-50* (NICOT; Grand Rapids: Eerdmans, 1995) 550.
³⁷ Fretheim, "The Book of Genesis," 636.
³⁸ Cf. Hamilton, *The Book of Genesis*, 551.

assuaged by the steward. To be sure, in Gen 44:1–12 Joseph outlines a machination wherein the steward is the leading actor, but this tableau is only directed toward bringing about the reconciliation after a very long passage of time. Again, there are numerous reasons why the biblical writer could use the steward in these roles—simple plot contrivance could be among them—but one guesses there is a more significant utility. The pattern of anonymous minor characters who act on behalf of the sons of Israel certainly can be seen in Exodus 1–2. The midwives, for instance, fear God in Exod 1:17, and this quality leads to their intrepid and resourceful actions that sustain the people's growth in a time of persecution. So, one might suggest that the words and actions of Joseph's steward set the tone for these subsequent characters, as his surprising discourse about God's involvement with the brothers and their silver is surely an intriguing element of the storyline.

CONCLUDING DATA

More could be said about images of Egypt in the Joseph narrative, but in the last moments of this chapter our discussion is limited to just a few more passages that help to frame the context of Exodus 1–2, beginning with the divine word in Gen 46:3–4 that prompts Jacob's departure from Canaan in accordance with Joseph's wishes and Pharaoh's provisions. During a night vision in the vicinity of Beersheba, God speaks to Jacob: "I am God, the God of your father. Don't be afraid of going down to Egypt, for there I will make you into a great nation. I am going down to Egypt with you, and I will certainly bring you back up, but Joseph will put his hand over your eyes." The declaration that opens the speech creates a link between previous divine words and the present one to Jacob. When God spoke after the sunset to Abraham back in Genesis 15 there was specificity about the length of time of his descendants' oppression and the certainty of their deliverance, but no details about the whereabouts, only that they would be sojourners in a land that was not their own (15:13). The divine word here in Gen 46:3–4 also describes a return from Egypt—in language that almost suggests a personal escort—but not before Jacob's offspring become a "great nation" there. As the euphemism implies, Jacob himself will die in Egypt, but his descendants will one day be brought out, and therefore residence is not a permanent arrangement: "This represents a deep commitment of God to enter into all the dynamics of the Egyptian experience. With the promise that God will bring him back to Canaan, the exodus and related events come into view."[39] Such a commitment needs to be kept in mind by the reader during the initial chapters of Exodus in the midst of Pharaoh's brutal subjugation. Moreover, there is a theological interplay here that certainly extends into the book of Exodus and beyond, as Robert Alter contends:

> The reassurance God offers—which is already the kernel of a theological concept that will play an important role in national consciousness both in the Babylonian exile and after the defeat by the Romans in 70 C.E.— is necessary because in the polytheistic view the theater of activity of a deity was typically imagined to be limited to the territorial borders of the deity's worshippers. By contrast, this God solemnly promises to go down with His people to Egypt and to bring them back up.[40]

In the final chapter of Genesis there are two speeches of Joseph that require our attention, the first concerning a wider theme, and the second regarding a more specific prediction. First, after the funeral of Jacob, the brothers are scared that with their father gone Joseph will seize the opportunity and seek retribution for their crimes against him in an outburst of *schadenfreude*. But Joseph's response to them in Gen 50:20 is a potent articulation of a theme repeatedly seen in the book of Genesis: "You designed evil against me, but God designed it for good, in order to make it happen as it is today, that many people are kept alive." Throughout the vicissitudes of Genesis this theme has been operative: despite myriad hardships and often self-inflicted disasters of human actors in the story, God consistently transforms

---

[39] Fretheim, "The Book of Genesis," 652.
[40] Alter, *Genesis*, 274. Greifenhagen (*Egypt on the Pentateuch's Ideological Map*, 43) argues that after Jacob's death, the journey taken by the funeral entourage is not geographically straightforward: "Jacob insists that he should not be buried in Egypt (49:29-32), and when he dies and is embalmed, a funeral procession winds its way back to Canaan for the burial (50:2-14). This 'exodus' of Jacob from Egypt, with its strange round-about route around the Dead Sea through the Transjordan, seems to be meant proleptically to evoke the route of a very different exodus to come." Greifenhagen further notes, "A much more direct route leads from Egypt to Hebron. However, just as the Israelites leaving Egypt in the exodus are diverted from a direct route to the Promised Land (Exod 13:17-18), so also the funeral procession follows a similar indirect route."

evil designs into something good that results in the saving of many lives. Joseph's slavery and adversity epitomize what the nation will soon experience, and the brothers may have acted as evil as any tyrannical Pharaoh, but God's promise is unwavering. As Norman Whybray puts it, Joseph "attributes all that had happened to the hidden hand of God, whose purpose had been to preserve their lives so that they would become a 'numerous people' (the word *'am*, 'people,' can denote a group or family, but here has also overtones of 'nation')."[41] There may be some variation, but this thematic emphasis will extend into the book of Exodus, as we will see in due course. The second speech of interest is Joseph's utterance in Gen 50:24 as he approaches his death. He gives instructions to his brothers: "I am about to die, but God will surely visit you (פקד יפקד), and bring you up to the land that he swore to Abraham, to Isaac, and to Jacob." Joseph reiterates this certainty in the next sentence, and adjures the Israelites to carry up his bones with them when they leave. The last image in the book of Genesis is a coffin in Egypt, a conclusion that must demand a sequel. To be sure, Joseph's coffin does not remain forever in Egypt, but indeed accompanies the Israelites on the way out in Exod 13:19: "Moses took the bones of Joseph with him, because he had made the Israelites solemnly swear, saying, 'God will surely visit you, and you must take up my bones from here with you!'" Merging the words and speeches of Abraham, Jacob, and now Joseph, the reader has ample expectations for the next phase of the story as the book of Exodus begins: oppression may be inevitable, but God will somehow orchestrate a departure.

---

[41] R. N. Whybray, "Genesis," pp. 38–66 in *The Oxford Bible Commentary*, edited by John Barton and John Muddiman (Oxford: Oxford University Press 2001) 66.

2

Old Promise, New King

> *The paradox of beginning is that one must have something solidly present and preexistent, some generative source or authority, on which the development of a new story may be based.*
>
> J. Hillis Miller[1]

In any sequel to a great literary work there are elements of continuity and discontinuity, and when turning to the opening chapters of the book of Exodus there are immediate points of contact with the preceding Genesis narrative. Since Exodus begins with an enumeration of the sons of Jacob who entered Egypt during Joseph's tenure as viceroy of the land, the reader is given a laconic summary of the story of Genesis that ends with a coffin in Egypt. Moreover, the opening sequence (Exod 1:6–7) records the Israelites' proliferation, and thus refers back to Gen 12:2 where Abraham is told he will become the progenitor of a great nation. The traditional Hebrew title of the book—"Names" (שמות)—is therefore appropriate on several levels: Exodus begins with a list of names, then later reveals the name of God, and so further echoes God's promise to Abraham, "I will make your name great." In the case of the initial scenes of

---

[1] J. Hillis Miller, *Reading Narrative* (Oklahoma Project for Discourse and Theory 18; Norman: University of Oklahoma Press, 1998) 57. Miller further states, "The beginning must be both inside the story as part of its narrative and at the same time outside it, prior to it as its generative base, the father of the line of filiation, or the mothering spider from whose belly the thread is spun. If inside, then the beginning is no base, no origin. It is an arbitrary starting, like beginning a bridge in midspan, with no anchor to the shore. If outside, then the beginning is not really part of the narrative line. It is disconnected from that line, like a tower piling or abutment of no help in building this particular bridge. Any beginning in narrative cunningly covers a gap, an absence at the origin" (58).

Exodus, however, there are elements of discontinuity with Genesis as well, and the story quickly moves in a new direction: when Exodus begins, there is also a sense of an ending as the age of wandering so characteristic of Genesis is replaced by a more sedentary location in Egypt.

Balancing both the continuity and discontinuity, Helmet Utzschneider and Wolfgang Oswald provide the following summary: "A clear opening signal is the 'prologue' to the narrative in Exod 1:1–7. On the one hand, it connects back to the Joseph Story (vv. 1, 6) and to the stories of the Patriarchs and creation through the multiplication sayings in particular (v. 7). On the other hand, the prologue makes clear that all the figures of these previous narratives have died (v. 6)." The authors therefore conclude that "the narrative begins anew with new characters; the old ones are merely a memory."[2] The discontinuity is also manifested in a shift in style at the outset, as the narrative moves from more sharply etched individual characters (ranging from the scheming and sometimes histrionic Jacob to Judah, who in the end volunteers himself in an act of substitutionary atonement on behalf of his younger brother Benjamin) toward a collective representation of the teeming Israelites. Indeed, the first speaker, ominously, is not an Israelite at all, but a new king of Egypt with an insidious edge. This chapter analyzes the first two sections of Exodus 1, starting with vv. 1–7 where the growth of the Israelites in Egypt is described, and then moving on to the arrival of the new king in vv. 8–14 whose oppressive policies toward the Israelites are promulgated. The two sections are duly intertwined, as the book of Exodus begins with a genealogy of a people-group that the new king will attempt to destroy, but not succeed.

---

[2] Utzschneider and Oswald, *Exodus 1–15*, 23. Note their further remarks on 1:1–7 (p. 61), and again, their synthesis of approaches: "The synchronic analysis of the final form of the text shows how this short piece joins the book of Genesis to the book of Exodus. Diachronic analysis shows that this piece was specifically composed in order to fulfill the function of binding together two pre-existing blocks of literature. Whereas the diachronic approach points out the incoherencies that such a procedure inevitably generates, synchronic interpretation draws our attention to the linguistic and literary techniques utilized in this section in order to enable its readers or hearers to perceive the meaningful narrative continuity between the Joseph Narrative and the exodus narrative." For an incisive summary of recent scholarship and bibliography, see Konrad Schmid, "Exodus in the Pentateuch," pp. 27–60 in *The Book of Exodus: Composition, Reception, and Interpretation*, edited by Thomas Dozeman, Craig A. Evans, and Joel N. Lohr (VTSup 164; Leiden: Brill, 2014).

THE BOOK OF NAMES

Popular television shows that develop a story-arc from week to week frequently employ a simple connective technique: a pastiche from previous parts of the series, often introduced with a phrase like "as seen previously," providing the viewer with a few highlights in preparation for the upcoming episode. In the first lines of the book of Exodus there is a recap of sorts, a bridge from the previous text of Genesis and a launch into a new installment of the story. These initial verses of Exodus do not impart any fresh information to the reader, only a list of already familiar names. Yet this listing provides a cogent précis that is necessary for the extension of the story. When Jacob and his sons ventured to Egypt to join Joseph and escape the ravages of famine, it is unclear how long they were intending to stay, but in the previous chapter several passages were surveyed in Genesis that prefigure the descent into Egypt by Abraham's descendants. In Gen 50:24 Joseph tells his family that God will surely visit them and bring them up from the land of Egypt, but there is no indication when this event will take place. God's word to Abraham in Gen 15:13 reveals that his descendants would be enslaved and afflicted for 400 years in another country (cf. Exod 12:40–1). Moreover, an overriding image of Egypt in the Abraham cycle is a temporary place of survival and potential riches, but at the price of danger, seduction, and the threat of death; in short, a place of shelter with the potential for destruction hanging over it. It will later be clear that the genealogy of Exod 1:1–5 sets the stage for a reversal, as the "welcomed guests" during the era of Joseph eventually find themselves in a much less hospitable environment.[3]

> Now these are the names of the sons of Israel, the ones who entered Egypt with Jacob, each man who came with his house: Reuben, Simeon, Levi, and Judah, Issachar, Zebulun, and Benjamin, Dan and Naphtali, Gad and Asher. The total number of people born to Jacob was seventy. Joseph was already in Egypt.

For many contemporary readers, a roster of names is probably not considered the most scintillating subject matter. Carol Meyers comments on this pedestrian start to the book of the Exodus: "One of the

---

[3] Dennis T. Olson, "Exodus," pp. 27–40 in *Theological Bible Commentary*, edited by Gail R. O'Day and David L. Petersen (Louisville: Westminster John Knox Press, 2009) 28.

most gripping narratives in the Hebrew Bible—the account of the escape of an oppressed people from bondage to freedom—begins with a rather mundane listing of the Israelite tribes."[4] Other biblical books begin in a less static manner. Take the first line of the book of Ruth by comparison: "In the days when the judges were leaders, there was a famine in the land." The epoch of the judges is a most turbulent one in Israelite history, and if a famine is added in the mix, an absorbing narrative is sure to follow. Or, take the first lines of the book of Daniel: "In the third year of the reign of Jehoiakim king of Judah, Nebuchadnezzar king of Babylon came to Jerusalem and besieged it. Then the Lord gave Jehoiakim king of Judah into his hand, along with some of the vessels of the house of God." As Danna Fewell has noted, there is a dramatic irony in these sentences: Nebuchadnezzar may be under the impression that his military power and machinery have secured this victory, but the narrator undercuts that pretension with the radical disclosure that the God of Israel has handed Judah's king over to the Babylonian monarch and allowed the temple in Jerusalem to be looted.[5] The first lines of Exodus do not contain this kind of drama, and furthermore, the reader who is coming directly from the book of Genesis has already seen a longer version of this list of names in Gen 46:8–27, albeit without the next generation of sons or the wives and mothers. Nonetheless, it could be argued that by beginning in this manner the book of Exodus sets the stage for the emergence of the nation in the land of Egypt, along lines suggested by Richard Elliott Friedman:

> The book of Exodus tells the story of the birth of a nation in slavery and ends with the nation's establishment of its own center, leaders, and symbols in freedom. Genesis involves a continuous narrowing of attention from the universe to the earth to humanity to a particular family; Exodus begins to broaden the circumference of attention again as the family grows into a nation—and comes into conflict with another nation. Whereas Genesis sets the rest of the books of the Bible in context, Exodus does not set them in context so much as introduce fundamental components that will function centrally in almost all the

---

[4] Carol Meyers, *Exodus* (The New Cambridge Bible Commentary; New York: Cambridge University Press, 2005) 33.

[5] Danna Nolan Fewell, *Circle of Sovereignty, A Story of Stories in Daniel 1–6* (JSOTSup 72; Sheffield: JSOT Press, 1988) 35.

44   *An Ark on the Nile*

coming books of the Bible. Exodus introduces the nation of Israel. It introduces prophecy. It introduces law. Arguably most important of all, it introduces the theme of YHWH's becoming known to the world.[6]

From the sons of the Jacob listed in the opening verses an entire people will emerge, and so the first segment of the book operates as a preface to nationhood. In the comment of Carol Meyers quoted above, we also notice that she uses the term "tribes," since the sons of Jacob eventually become the tribes of Israel apportioned throughout the promised land. On the absence of wives and children in the listing of Jacob's 12 sons in Exod 1:1–5 there is no easy solution, but returning to the theory of Jopie Siebert-Hommes canvassed in the introduction to this study, there is an intriguing symmetry: the twelve sons named at the outset are enabled to survive, as it were, by various actions of the "twelve daughters" of Exodus 1–2 (namely, the pair of midwives, the mother and sister of Moses, Pharaoh's daughter, and the seven daughters of the priest of Midian).[7] For Siebert-Hommes, the opening segment of Exodus that itemizes the names of the sons is not incidental: "The future of the twelve sons of Israel is dependent upon one son who is indebted for his birth and existence to twelve women. Literally and figuratively, the daughters keep the liberator's head above water."[8] Of course, verse 5 reports that seventy persons came from the thigh of Jacob, so others are included in this list even without being directly named. The number 70 may connote familial completion, and glances back to the 70 nations purportedly descended from Noah and ahead to the 70 elders in Exod 24:1 "corresponding to the seventy Israelite clans."[9] Women may not be included in the first five verses, but they are certainly present in the background,

---

[6] Richard Elliot Friedman, *Commentary on the Torah, with a New English Translation* (San Francisco: HarperCollins, 2001) 167.

[7] Siebert-Hommes, *Let the Daughters Live! The Literary Architecture of Exodus 1–2 as a Key for Interpretation*, 112.

[8] Siebert-Hommes, *Let the Daughters Live! The Literary Architecture of Exodus 1–2 as a Key for Interpretation*, 134. Cf. the theoretical reflections of Said, *Beginnings: Intention and Method*, 43: "What sort of action, therefore, transpires at the beginning? How can we, while necessarily submitting to the incessant flux of experience, insert (as we do) our reflections on beginning(s) into that flux? Is the beginning simply an artifice, a disguise that defies the perpetual trap of forced continuity? Or does it admit of a meaning and a possibility that are genuinely capable of realization?"

[9] Propp, *Exodus 1–18*, 129; on Noah, see Umberto Cassuto, *A Commentary on the Book of Exodus* (Jerusalem: Magnes Press, 1967) 8. The LXX reads *seventy-five* (πέντε καὶ ἑβδομήκοντα), the tradition followed in Stephen's speech in Acts 7:14.

as vv. 6–7 indicate that after the death of Joseph there is a period of unprecedented fecundity: "Joseph died and all his brothers and all that generation. Yet the sons of Israel were fruitful: they swarmed, multiplied, and became extremely numerous, and the land was filled up with them."

Joseph's death was already reported in Gen 50:26 along with details about his embalming (חנט) and placement in a coffin. In Exod 1:6 the death notice has a structural function, akin to that in Judges 2:10, "That whole generation was gathered to their fathers, and another generation grew up after them, who did not know the LORD or the work that he had accomplished for Israel." Thomas Dozeman notes this parallel, but suggests that there is also a major difference: "The passing of a generation signifies the loss of memory and the breakdown in the continuity of tradition. In Exodus it leads to violence by Pharaoh, and in Judges it results in evil acts of worship against Yahweh."[10] The reiteration of Joseph's death also marks a change in the atmosphere of the story. Earlier in Genesis there is a concern about death from the famine, and in order to survive, the sons of Jacob venture to Egypt to buy food. Although the famine is over by the end of the book of Genesis, the family remains in Egypt, and conditions must be comfortable enough to generate such exponential growth. Moreover, scholars have pointed out that Exod 1:6 is the last occasion where the sons of Jacob are referred to as "brothers," implying that from this point onward a nation is the focus of the story, rather than a smaller family unit.[11] The beginning of Exodus is marked by a change in nomenclature that persists for the rest of the story.

The language of nationhood is appropriate when considering the report in Exod 1:7, as a string of verbs are detonated to highlight the explosive growth of Israelites after the death of Joseph and his generation. Virtually the same configuration of verbs occurs in Gen 1:28 (the divine commandment to be fruitful, multiply, and fill the earth) and again in Gen 9:1 (after Noah disembarks when the floodwaters recede; cf. 9:7), leading James Ackerman to argue that the destiny of humanity in creation and after the flood is now "in the

---

[10] Thomas B. Dozeman, *Exodus* (ECC; Grand Rapids: Eerdmans, 2009) 67.
[11] Cornelis Houtman, *Exodus I* (HCOT; Leuven: Peeters, 1993) 229.

process of being fulfilled by the descendants of Israel."¹² A lengthy passage of time is recorded with just a few words, accelerating the story to a point in time where the land—once host to only 70 members of Jacob's family—is now swarming with them. In fact, the verb swarming (שׁרץ) is first used in Gen 1:20 to depict swiftly moving creatures and rapid fertility, and later occurs in Exod 8:3 to describe the frogs that will jump from the Nile and swarm the land of Egypt. It could be that teeming growth of Jacob's descendants has a downside and could attract the wrong kind of attention, as John Durham proposes: "A shadow of what else is to come is present in the reference to the strength such numbers present, as also in the continuing biblical tension between God's promise and the threats that oppose it."¹³ As of yet there is no indication whether the general population of Egypt feels threatened in any way by the growth of the Israelites, but in the next movement of the story this numerical increase will certainly furnish a pretext for a menacing kind of initiative.

NAMELESS KING

The book of Exodus begins with a picture of Israel's growth in accordance with the divine promise to Abraham about becoming a great nation, but the announcement of that same promise also sounded warning bells about a period of affliction in a foreign land. From this link to the past in the first seven verses, the story turns to the present in Exod 1:8. The reader may have been amply prepared, but the threat to the sons of Israel seemingly comes out of nowhere, just like the new king himself in verse 8: "Then a new king arose over Egypt, who did not know Joseph." There is no mention of what happened to the previous king; in Exod 2:23 it is recorded that after a long time this new king dies, but no word of replacement there, nor here. Rather quickly, the arrival of this new king denotes the end of an

---

¹² Ackerman, "The Literary Context of the Moses Birth Story," 77. He also notes, "But through the continual allusions to the primeval stories in Genesis 1–11 we become aware of the cosmic import of these apparently insignificant events which surround Moses' early years. Through Moses and Israel, the story suggests, God will reshape or re-create the world" (75). Cf. Utzschneider and Oswald, *Exodus 1–15*, 56.

¹³ John I. Durham, *Exodus* (WBC; Waco: Word, 1987) 5.

era of comparative benevolence, and the onset of a much darker chapter. Part of the fear evoked by this new king is due to the paucity of data surrounding him, unlike Moses in the next chapters of Exodus. This nameless king forms a more immediate contrast, as the narrative moves from the genealogical certainty of the sons of Jacob to a sense of deep ambivalence with the new king of Egypt. Whether this uncertainty is best interpreted as neutral or nefarious remains to be seen.

Grand entrances by newly elected political leaders in contemporary Western democracies may be hailed in positive terms by the respective electorates, but the emergence of this "new" king of Egypt may not connote the same kind of sanguinity in Exodus 1. William Propp mentions the idea that *new* might just as easily imply inexperienced or headstrong, and cross-references the account of Rehoboam in 1 Kings 12 to make the point.[14] Political incompetence and poor judgment abound in that particular narrative of the division of the kingdom, as the 40-year-old king and his similarly aged advisors act like juveniles and treat the northern delegation with contempt. But as Solomon's successor, Rehoboam's status is uncontested (at least in Judah), and no one doubts his legitimacy in the formal sense. Murkier questions surround this new king of Egypt and the process by which he transitions to power, and a number of scholars discuss the possibility that a "new king" means rather more, that is, "most probably the founder of a new dynasty."[15] A shift in dynasty could plausibly explain why a new king would neither know about Joseph nor continue with a predecessor's policy, and a regime change would thus mark a decisive adjustment in attitude toward Joseph's family. It seems later that the new king's court has no knowledge of Joseph either, or they simply share their leader's sentiments on every policy option. There are plenty of other competing theories among scholars regarding the identity of this new king, but a more pressing issue concerns the meaning of the first word in Exod 1:8, "arose" (ויקם).[16] The action of *arising* is often benign—Hannah arose after eating and drinking in Shiloh and went to the sanctuary in 1 Sam 1:9—but the

---

[14] Propp, *Exodus 1–18*, 130.
[15] Nahum M. Sarna, *Exploring Exodus: The Origins of Biblical Israel* (New York: Schocken Books, 1986) 15; cf. Durham, *Exodus*, 7; Cassuto, *A Commentary on the Book of Exodus*, 5.
[16] Houtman, *Exodus I*, 234.

first time this verbal root occurs in the Hebrew Bible the context is decidedly violent, as it is the key action in the Bible's first murder. Cain is warned by God that sin has set an ambush at his door, and that his anger needs to be regulated. In Gen 4:8 the warning is clearly not heeded, as Cain arose (ויקם) and killed his brother Abel in an act of premeditated aggression. After Exod 1:8, the next time the same verb occurs is Exod 2:17, when Moses arose (ויקם) in defense of the daughters of the priest of Midian when shepherds came to the well and drove them away. Exactly how Moses saved the seven daughters is not our concern here, but simply that his "arising" in this context designates a combative action. Reflecting on these two uses of the same verbal form, when the new king arises over Egypt there is a possibility that aggression is involved. Further consideration will have to be postponed until his monologue in Exod 1:9–10 is interpreted, but the initial language in v. 8 does not eliminate the option of a hostile takeover or abrupt regime change rather than a smooth transition.

For an extremely powerful and influential character, the reticence and lack of further background information is striking.[17] Historians are also frustrated by the lack of a proper name for this new king, but acknowledge that the pharaohs of Genesis are not named, nor for that matter is the next Pharaoh of Exodus 5–14. Even so, several later pharaohs are named, such as Shishak in 1 Kings 11:40, who harbors Jeroboam after an assassination attempt from Solomon. Shishak also conducts an attack on Jerusalem in 1 Kings 14:25, and carries away treasures from the temple during the reign of Rehoboam, probably taking advantage of the recent schism.[18] Although Solomon had entered into a marriage alliance not long earlier in 1 Kings 3:1,

---

[17] In general terms, see J. D. Ray, "Egyptian Wisdom Literature," pp. 17–29 in *Wisdom in Ancient Israel: Essays in Honour of J. A. Emerton*, edited by John Day, Robert P. Gordon, and H. G. M. Williamson (Cambridge: Cambridge University Press, 1995) 17: "The Old Testament is full of the shadows cast by Pharaoh's sun, and the result—a mixture of admiration, distrust, envy and emulation, often at the same time—shows through in its pages, from the nostalgia of the Children of Israel in Sinai to the denunciations of Ezekiel and Jeremiah. Part of the fascination of the Joseph story for its Jewish audience must have been that it showed a poor Hebrew beating the most cultured society of the ancient near east at its own game, and there must have been many who wished that they could do the same."

[18] Jerome T. Walsh, *1 Kings* (Berit Olam; Collegeville: Liturgical Press, 1996) 209; Marvin A. Sweeney, *I & II Kings* (OTL; Louisville, KY: Westminster John Knox Press, 2007) 189.

Egypt is certainly portrayed as an unstable ally in this stretch of the Deuteronomistic History. Perhaps the most interesting Egyptian ruler is Neco, whose campaign in 2 Kings 23:29 results in the death of Josiah. In the Chronicler's narrative Neco's voice takes on a prophetic quality, cautioning Josiah in no uncertain terms to turn back and not resist God's word, lest he be destroyed (2 Chron 35:21). Josiah refuses to heed the word of the Egyptian king and dons a disguise, and promptly is killed in battle in the plain of Megiddo.[19] After assessing these other examples, it can be surmised that the very namelessness of this new king in Exod 1:8 is part of the literary design of the narrative and opens up several interpretive avenues. Anonymity among the cast of minor figures is not overly surprising, but for the king of Egypt the intentional absence of a name creates an ironic tone in his characterization. Names are provided for the two midwives later in the chapter, as well as the cities of Pithom and Rameses just a few lines from now. Carol Meyers remarks that denying the pharaoh a name is part of a larger rhetorical strategy that demeans this figure.[20] If this is the case, it will not be the last time, as the new king is foiled and undermined at numerous points in the story, not least by his own daughter in the next chapter. The absence of a name for the pharaoh here can carry a symbolic function, making this character more typical of any kind of tyrant rather than an individual bound to one particular time-period.[21] It would be misleading to suggest that this is an ahistorical narrative, but rather, there could be an attempt to make this foundational story applicable to more than one era of Israelite experience, since this new king is not the last tyrant who will oppress the descendants of Abraham.[22] Regardless, this nameless pharaoh

---

[19] On this episode and the role of Neco, see Christine Mitchell, "The Ironic Death of Josiah in 2 Chronicles," *CBQ* 68 (2006) 421-35. The reader might further compare Hophra in Jer 44:30, who is mentioned by name in Jeremiah's last oracle. King So of Egypt is only minimally sketched in 2 Kings 17:4; see Marvin A. Sweeney, *I & II Kings* (OTL; Louisville, KY: Westminster John Knox Press, 2007) 393, and Duane L. Christensen, "The Identity of King So of Egypt (2 Kings xvii 4)," *VT* 39 (1989) 140-53.

[20] Meyers, *Exodus*, 34.   [21] Childs, *The Book of Exodus*, 13.

[22] Cf. Mark S. Smith, *Exodus* (New Collegeville Bible Commentary; Collegeville: Liturgical Press, 2011) 16: "The priestly prose of Exodus is thought to have been written any time during the end of the monarchy, the exile in Babylon, or after the return to the land under Persian authority. Apart from some brief exceptions, all these periods were ones of significant testing of Israelite faith. The introduction faces these difficulties and offers an expression of encouragement and a sign of hope that

serves as a preparatory character and an anticipation of how Egypt's monarchs will be postured toward Israel in the book of Exodus.

The most significant differentiation of this new king in Exod 1:8 from his predecessors, we assume, is that he "does not know Joseph." It is unclear whether such a distinction points to his status as an outsider or operates as a synecdoche for his vicious policy shift toward the Israelites. Of course, the Joseph story is highly allusive in the Hebrew Bible, and becomes a defining narrative of triumph against the odds. For example, there are a number of parallels—from the level of individual words to larger motifs—between the Joseph story in Genesis and the release of Judah's last king, Jehoiachin, from the Babylonian prison. "Just as Joseph's release from prison and his exaltation were a prelude to Israel's original exodus from Egypt, so Jehoiachin's own release and exaltation may be interpreted as a prelude to a new exodus—only this time, out of exile and back into Judah."[23] Another example is the story of Daniel, where a young Israelite is taken from his homeland, thrives in a foreign country, has a divine gift for interpreting dreams, and eventually becomes a high-ranking official. When the new king of Exodus 1 "does not know Joseph," it might imply an Achilles heel or an underestimation of Abraham's offspring. Later policies in Exodus 1 will try to reduce the numbers of the Israelites, and fail. The new king of Exodus 1 does not know Joseph, and the pharaoh of Exodus 5 does not know the LORD (5:2), and neither understands their real adversary. In Exod 2:25 God looks upon the sons of Israel "and God knew," so the lines of conflict around the theme of *knowledge* are established early in the story.

THE KING'S SPEECH

Even more than his status or his incognizance of Joseph, the new king is characterized primarily through his opening speech, an address

the divine promise made to Abraham (Gen 17) began to be fulfilled in Egypt and will continue to come to pass despite difficult circumstances."

[23] Michael J. Chan, "Joseph and Jehoiachin: On the Edge of Exodus." *ZAW* 125 (2013) 568; cf. John E. Harvey, "Jehoiachin and Joseph: Hope at the Close of the Deuteronomistic History," pp. 51–61 in *The Bible as a Human Witness to Divine Revelation: Hearing the Word of God through Historically Dissimilar Traditions*, edited by Randall Heskett and Brian Irwin (LHBOTS 469; London: T & T Clark, 2010).

that is marked by subtlety and apprehension. Like previous pharaohs in the Pentateuch, this new king is unnamed, but there is a major point of contrast between them. Previous Egyptian potentates are always introduced *indirectly* by means of their officials or advisors. In Genesis 12 the Egyptian captains commend Sarah to Pharaoh, and she is taken into his house in v. 15. Pharaoh's formal appearance comes only later in the episode after the great plagues, when he speaks in a reactive manner, chastising Abraham and expelling him from the country. Similarly, in the Joseph narrative Pharaoh enters the storyline indirectly, first as the employer of Potiphar, then as an angry master who sends his chief cupbearer and baker to the same prison that houses Joseph. Pharaoh's first individual action comes in Gen 40:20, when he restores the fortunes of one of his servants during his birthday party, and his major actions of dreaming and his first words do not occur until the next chapter, after a lengthy buildup. In Exodus 1 there is a different literary strategy at work, because unlike previous pharaohs, the new king of Egypt has no indirect introduction whatsoever. Already, then, he is differentiated from his predecessors, and he is the one who speaks *before* any captain or official, perhaps suggesting a more insecure and malignant personality. As Brevard Childs notes, "The Egyptian king is not presented as the incarnate Son of Re, who rules with absolute sovereignty over a nation, but as a clever despot who sets about to convince his supporters of his plan."[24] If there is an uneasy feeling created by the narrator's initial description of Egypt's king—one who "arose" to power, is a new monarch, and does not know Joseph—such uneasiness is not alleviated when the new king speaks in vv. 9–10. His break with the past is sudden, and presented through a crafty and anxious address to his constituents:

> He said to his people, "Behold, the people of the sons of Israel have become more numerous and stronger than us! Come, let us deal wisely with him, lest they increase. It may be that a war will happen, and even he will be added to our enemies, and fight against us, and go up from the land!"

From a literary point of view it is notable that the new king is given the first portion of direct speech in the book of Exodus, and despite the insidiousness of his tone the speech is bursting with inadvertent

---

[24] Childs, *The Book of Exodus*, 15.

irony. For instance, I have rendered the opening moments rather too woodenly in order to stress the double mention of the term "people" (עם): the king speaks to his people about the people of Israel. So, the new king of Egypt is the first figure—even before the narrator—to label the Israelites as a people or nation with much the same status as Egypt.[25] It is through the voice of the new king, to use Terence Fretheim's insight, that the divine word to Abraham is put in perspective: "In echoing the narrator's words of verse 7 (cf. Gen. 18:18), and exaggerating the numbers, an 'outsider' highlights the fulfillment of God's promises. His acts of oppression confirm that God's word to Abraham in Gen. 15:13 was on target."[26] Glancing ahead in the chapter, there is still more Israelite growth to follow. But meanwhile, there are other echoes of Genesis texts in the speech of the new king, such as the tower of Babel incident. When the new king says, "Come (הבה), let us deal wisely with him, lest (פן) they increase," there are similarities to the deliberations of Gen 11:4, "Come (הבה), let us build a city and a tower ... lest (פן) we be scattered."[27] The builders in Gen 11:4 desire to make a name for themselves, and at the end of the episode they do: Babel (בבל), with a wordplay on the Hebrew verb "confusion." In pointed contrast, in the next chapter God says to Abraham, "I will make your name great" (Gen 12:2), and not only does this turn the tables on the tower episode, but it is this promise that is evoked in Exod 1:1–7 with the proliferation of Israelites. When shades of Babel can be detected in the speech of the Egyptian king in Exod 1:10, the reader appreciates that the builders and the new king have several common traits: like the builders, the plan of nameless king in Exodus will not ultimately succeed. Furthermore, it is long recognized that Genesis 11 becomes the founding narrative of Babylon (בבל), and given that Babylon will be an oppressive nation later in Israel's history, any allusion in the book of Exodus would certainly be

---

[25] Propp (*Exodus 1–18*, 130) presents another view for understanding the king's addressees: "This might refer to the king's advisors, or perhaps the entire people. In any case, Pharaoh is not the only culprit. All Egypt is implicated in the oppression of Israel."

[26] Fretheim, *Exodus*, 28.

[27] Ackerman, "The Literary Context of the Moses Birth Story," 81–2. Dozeman (*Exodus*, 70–1) draws a connection with Gen 41:39, where Pharaoh commends Joseph as "wise" (חכם) and the negative counterpart of the new king's speech in Exod 1:10 with the proposal to "act shrewdly" (נתחכמה), using the *hithpael* form of the verb that carries a darker nuance.

applicable to a wider audience.[28] For the time being, the new king is presented in a satirical light through this Babel connection, and implicitly undermined even at the height of his political potency.

A central contingency in the new king's speech is the threat of war, along with the alleged fear that the Israelites will somehow join with Egypt's opponents in the event of a conflict. If the new king's own path to the throne is an aggressive one, it would not be overly surprising for him to be expecting an uprising or an attack of some sort, although he does not provide any concrete details. Bracketing aside the king's rhetoric for a moment, the notion of "war" in the larger storyline deserves a comment. The new king mentions war as an urgent concern, but as Charles Isbell points out, the term war (מלחמה) is not used again until after the initial departure from Egypt in Exod 13:17 when God reroutes the people because a war might change their minds and prompt a return to Egypt: "Thus one character in the story fears they will leave Egypt because of war, another fears they will return to Egypt because of war! The issue of 'war' is not finally settled until chapter 14 when Moses seeks to allay the fear of the Israelites by promising them that 'Yahweh will war [ילחם] for them' (v.14)."[29] As far as dealing with the problem of the Israelites, Benno Jacob compares the negotiations of Balak king of Moab in Numbers 22 and his hiring of the soothsayer Balaam.[30] A quite different approach from the new king in Exodus 1, the outcome is the opposite of what each king intended: Balak unsuccessfully seeks to have Israel cursed (only to have them blessed), and the new king of Egypt seeks to curb Israel's growth by acting shrewdly, but the Israelites become even more numerous.

Examples of rhetorical skill have already been cited in this study, such as Judah's endeavor to persuade his brothers to sell Joseph as a slave in Gen 37:26-7. After throwing Joseph into a cistern, the brothers sit down to eat a meal when they notice a caravan of Ishmaelites heading to Egypt. Judah's speech begins with an interrogative, questioning their strategy of killing Joseph without netting a

---

[28] André LaCocque, "Whatever Happened in the Valley of Shinar? A Response to Theodore Hiebert," *JBL* 128 (2009) 29-41, "The end of the narrative comes with a wordplay on Babel/Babylon (not on the tower) because only the city receives a name here, in contrast to the tower, which remains anonymous."

[29] Isbell, "Exodus 1-2 in the Context of Exodus 1-14," 46.

[30] Benno Jacob, *The Second Book of the Bible: Exodus* (Hoboken, NJ: Ktav, 1992) 10.

profit. He then transitions by raising the notion of bloodguilt, before launching his proposal to sell Joseph as a slave, thereby clearing the brothers of bloodguilt and generating revenue at the same time. Judah's speech is convincing, and the brothers agree to his plan. Another instance of persuasive rhetoric is Joseph's address to Pharaoh in Gen 41:33–6. After his lengthy interpretation of the dream that explains the bizarre components of the dream and predicts the seven years of famine, Joseph switches gears and outlines an action plan. The plan is predicated on Pharaoh finding a wise man, collecting grain during the years of plenty, and creating a reserve supply in order to survive the famine. Joseph's speech is impressive in its execution, to the point that Pharaoh hires him on the spot, having been persuaded by his argument.

In Exod 1:9–10 the new king of Egypt addresses his people, and similar to Judah and Joseph, he is attempting to persuade his audience. In the previous paragraph it was discussed that in Gen 41:39–41 Pharaoh appoints Joseph as second-in-command over all Egypt, and Pharaoh does so without any consultation or approval from his officials. The new king in Exod 1:9–10, however, either lacks the stature of his predecessor or else it is a harder task that he is proposing, and thus requires a broader consensus. His address begins by stating the problem of numerous Israelites, then a rationale for why the problem needs to be dealt with in a cagey manner, and concludes with an outline of consequences if the problem of Israelite growth is not contained. It is impossible to determine if the new king is summarizing a current opinion or if this is his personal agenda, but at no point does he explain why the loyalty of the Israelites—who, after all, have been in Egypt for quite some time and owe their survival to Egypt—is open to question. Starting his speech with "behold" (הנה) may suggest that the king is drawing attention to something that has not been adequately perceived. As Gordon Davies argues, the new king "changes his countrymen's perception of appearance and reality by projecting before them a world of disturbing rhetorical couples: safety/danger; naivety/cunning; inaction/action; present/future; peace/war; weakness/power; Hebrews/Egyptians."[31] At the same time, when the new king expresses a fear that Israel

---

[31] Davies, *Israel in Egypt*, 51. He further notes, "With respect to the Egyptians, Pharaoh gains a double advantage here: by making rhetorical distinctions, his discourse grows in both realism and value preference" (52–3).

will "go up (עלה) from the land" he is unwittingly anticipating the exodus event itself later on, and his speech here sets in motion the conditions whereby Israel will indeed depart from Egypt.[32] The irony is exacerbated by a wordplay: the new king conjectures that if war breaks out, the Israelites will be added to (יסף) or join with Egypt's enemies, a pun on the name of Joseph (יוסף). So, the new king who does not know Joseph is unknowingly alluding to the words of Joseph back in Gen 50:24 when he tells his brothers that God will bring them up (עלה) from Egypt. Along with the layers of irony, it still needs to be underscored that in his address the new king does not delineate a carefully orchestrated strategy: "Instead he speaks in the hypothetical, and, without himself suggesting a plan, calls on the Egyptians to deal wisely with the Hebrews, because in his rhetorical world they endanger the future."[33] It is entirely possible that enslavement is implied in the king's rhetoric, but nothing is mentioned overtly.

The developing portrait of Egypt's new king in Exodus 1 has prompted some scholars to draw a comparison with a later figure in Israel's story, Haman the Agagite in the book of Esther.[34] Haman is portrayed as a descendant of the antagonistic Amalekites, who first battle against Israel after the departure from Egypt (Exod 17:8–16) and are placed under a curse in Deuteronomy 25:17–19. The Amalekites were supposed to have been put to the ban by Saul son of Kish in 1 Samuel 15, who spares their famous king Agag (even though he is later hacked into pieces by the prophet Samuel). In the book of Esther the main characters include Haman (a descendant of Agag) and Mordecai (a descendant of Kish), and the ancient rivalry of Israel and the Amalekites is renewed on the Persian stage.[35] When Mordecai

---

[32] John Van Seters, *The Life of Moses: The Yahwist as Historian in Exodus–Numbers* (Louisville: Westminster John Knox Press, 1994) 22. Cf. Dozeman, *Exodus*, 71: "The shrewdness of Pharaoh for the purpose of self-preservation sets in motion his own destruction and the eventual liberation of Israel, when they 'go up from the land of Egypt.'"

[33] Davies, *Israel in Egypt*, 48.

[34] E.g., Childs, *The Book of Exodus*, 13; Ackerman"The Literary Context of the Moses Birth Story," 80–1.

[35] Adele Berlin, *Esther* (The JPS Bible Commentary; Philadelphia: The Jewish Publication Society, 2001) 24–5; cf. Jon D. Levenson, *Esther: A Commentary* (OTL; Louisville: Westminster John Knox Press, 1997) 57, who suggests that names are used "from the story of Saul to highlight the significance of Mordecai and Esther's deeds within the larger history of redemption. Mordecai rises on the very point on which Saul fell."

refuses to bow before the newly promoted Haman, the outraged Agagite discovers Mordecai's identity and approaches King Ahasuerus in Esther 3:8 with a sinister proposition: "There is a certain people scattered and separated among the peoples in all the provinces of your kingdom; their laws are different from those of every other people, and they do not keep the king's laws, so that it is not appropriate for the king to tolerate them." Without getting specific about the identity of the offending people, Haman frames the matter in a way that the king must interpret as injurious to himself but has escaped his notice.[36] Having introduced this enemy that the king has been unaware of, in v. 9 Haman then unfolds his design: "If it pleases the king, let a decree be issued for their destruction, and I will pay ten thousand talents of silver into the hands of those who have charge of the king's business, so that they may put it into the king's treasuries." Compared to the new king of Egypt, Haman's genealogy and the historical rivalry provides a plausible motive for his actions, whereas the new king is surrounded by more mystery, although in both narratives Haman and the new king eventually are hoodwinked in similar ways. Most compelling for our purposes, Haman uses persuasive techniques in his speech to Ahasuerus not unlike the new king addressing his people in Exod 1:9–10. Haman is able to secure a decree from Ahasuerus that has a very real chance of destroying the Jews, and as can be seen in the next scenes of Exodus 1, the new king's words have a deleterious effect on the Israelites in Egypt.

RISE OF THE TASKMASTERS

In his speech, the new king warns of a potential crisis without giving any direct order. While it remains entirely possible that he addresses all Egypt in vv. 9–10, an argument can also be made that when the

---

[36] Haman persuades his audience about the dangers of a certain people using similar rhetorical tactics as the new king of Egypt, who likewise persuades his audience about the (hitherto unrecognized) danger of the Israelites; cf. Johanna W. H. Van Wijk-Bos, *Ezra, Nehemiah, and Esther* (Louisville, KY: Westminster John Knox, 1998) 119: "The same arguments that Haman uses can be found in a more explicit fashion in the Exodus story when Pharaoh convinces his people of the danger posed in their midst by the presence of the children of Israel (Exod. 1:9–10)."

king speaks to "his people" (עַמוֹ), he is in dialogue with his circle of advisors or military leaders.[37] Numerous scholars have analyzed the words of the new king and detected some flaws in his thinking. Phyllis Trible, for instance, senses that the king is guilty of conflicted reasoning in his speech that is laced with unintentional irony: "On the one hand, the king fears the growing number and power of the Israelites: resident foreigners who lack a leader but whose size and strength threaten the native population. On the other hand, the king finds their size and strength valuable for his building projects and so fears that 'he' may 'go up' from the land."[38] If the new king is addressing his inner circle rather than the general public, it would amount to a virtual speech-act. Indeed, the king does not explicitly outline a policy, but that is what transpires in the next lines of Exod 1:11 with the rise of the taskmasters: "They set captains of labor-gangs over them, in order to afflict them with hard work, and they built storage cities for Pharaoh: Pithom and Rameses." No subject is provided for the verb, but the plural "they" suggests that the king's advisors are responsible, and that the king has successfully presented his case: like Haman persuades Ahasuerus, so the new king has leveraged his words to maximum effect.

The main building projects of Israelite forced labor are storage cities. At the height of his influence, Joseph supervised the storage of grain during the years of plenty, and subsequently sold it during the nadir of the famine. Now there is a reversal, as the Israelites are building storage cities that are supposed to result in their depletion. Earlier Joseph made slaves of Egyptians (Gen 47:21), but now the

---

[37] Victor P. Hamilton, *Exodus: An Exegetical Commentary* (Grand Rapids: Baker, 2011) 8; Propp, *Exodus 1–18*, 130.

[38] Trible, "Difference Among the Distaff," 295. Cf. Exum, "'You Shall Let Every Daughter Live,'" 44: "Commentators have traditionally pointed out logical inconsistencies in the problem and the solution of vv. 8–14. Overpopulation is a problem, yet the pharaoh is afraid the Israelites will leave. He wants to check the population growth, yet the fact that he puts the people to work on his building projects suggests that he needs them as slave labor. Explanation of the incongruity is often sought in source-critical theories, but as the story now stands, the absurdity of the solution is only one example of the folly of Pharaoh's wisdom. It is seen again (vv. 15–22) in the decision to kill male babies, a solution that neither alleviates the present problem nor represents the logical way to control overpopulation, which would be to kill females." For Nohrnberg (*Like Unto Moses*, 243), "Pharaoh's attempt to destroy the very generation of Hebrews that he has enslaved makes very little *economic* sense and must be attributed to politics: the politics of terror."

Egyptians have made slaves of Joseph's descendants.[39] Jopie Siebert-Hommes refers to the storage cities in Exodus 1 as objects of prestige, enhanced by virtue of it being built by foreign slave labor.[40] This point can be buttressed by adding that for the first time in the book of Exodus, the term "Pharaoh" is used in the context of Israelite slave labor that is forced to produce the cities for royal aggrandizement. Glancing ahead in the story, the next time the verb *to build* is used will be Exod 17:15, when Moses builds an altar to celebrate the victory over the Amalekites. Israel is rescued from building projects that enhance Pharaoh's stature and instead are given the opportunity to construct more enduring symbols. There is a striking connection between keywords here, as the term for cities of "storage"—at least in the singular form (מסכן)—sounds like the word for *tabernacle* (משכן) that will consume the Israelites' energy in the last sector of the book of Exodus. As Victor Hamilton comments, the Exodus narrative starts with Israel building storage facilities for the new king of Egypt, but ends with them building a sanctuary for a quite different category of king: "The first building project is imposed and harsh. The second one is God-revealed and an honor with which to be involved."[41]

Exod 1:11 is not the last time that forced labor (מס) and storage cities (מסכנות) are part of Israel's experience, because as it turns out, the new king of Egypt is not the only monarch to use forced labor nor the last one to build storage cities. In 2 Sam 20:24 David appoints Adoniram as head of forced labor (מס), and despite some variations in the spelling of his name, it is conceivable that Adoniram retains this post throughout the entire reign of Solomon, until he finally is stoned to death—as mentioned earlier in this study—by the angry crowd of northerners in Shechem who bore the brunt of the forced labor during Solomon's tenure (1 Kings 12:18).[42] During Israel's own monarchic history, several kings are guilty of imitating Egyptian practices, and so the Exodus narrative becomes a foundational narrative in multiple ways, and in this instance, as an indictment of certain kinds of conduct during the united kingdom of David and

---

[39] On the text-critical issue in Gen 47:21, see Wenham, *Genesis 16–50*, 449.

[40] Siebert-Hommes, *Let the Daughters Live! The Literary Architecture of Exodus 1–2 as a Key for Interpretation*, 42.

[41] Hamilton, *Exodus*, 9.

[42] C. L. Seow, "Adoniram," in *The New Interpreter's Dictionary of the Bible*, edited by Katharine Doob Sakenfeld (Nashville: Abingdon, 2009) 54.

Solomon (who also owns storage cities according to 1 Kings 9:19). The rise of royal taskmasters in Israel, however, is rather far away in the storyline. For the Israelites in Egypt, the more immediate toil is building the storage cities of Pithom and Rameses. Like other aspects of Exodus 1, the precise location of these places enjoys no consensus among historians, but from a literary point of view they can be interpreted in other ways: "Pithom and Rameses were cities in the delta region, part of a building project of Egypt's nineteenth Dynasty. Because these cities were much more to the Egyptians than 'store-cities,' however, they are used by the narrator primarily as symbols of oppression rather than as an effort to ground the story in historical reality."[43] Moshe Greenberg also suggests that the shrewdness of the new king is evident here: "Pharaoh's cunning is revealed in the way he resolved his contradictory attitude toward the Israelites. He would turn their numbers to good use by putting them to huge work projects—whose drain on their energies could be counted on to abate their increase."[44] When they are forced to build these cities, the Israelites are *afflicted* (עָנָה), a verb used all too frequently in the context of rape, such as Gen 34:2 with Shechem's attack of Dinah, or 2 Sam 13:12 and the violation of Tamar by Amnon. To restate, God discloses to Abraham in Gen 15:13 that his descendants will be afflicted in a foreign land, but what should be recognized in the next line of the story, Exod 1:12, is that the purpose for affliction is not effective. If the plan is to force the Israelites into slavery in order to curb their growth, that plan is thoroughly frustrated by the Israelites themselves.

COUNTERPRODUCTIVE

Complying with the rhetoric of the new king, taskmasters are appointed and the Israelites are coerced into building storage cities in order to offset expansion and prevent them from departing Egypt in the event of a war. The new king invited his followers to deal

---

[43] Fretheim, *Exodus*, 28.
[44] Moshe Greenberg, *Understanding Exodus: A Holistic Commentary on Exodus 1–11*, Second Edition, edited with a foreword by Jeffrey H. Tigay (Eugene, OR: Wipf and Stock, 2013) 19.

shrewdly with the Israelite problem, but their scheme of oppression flounders in Exod 1:12 and actually has the opposite effect: "But even as they afflicted him, so he multiplied and was bursting forth, and they loathed the sons of Israel." The Israelite progeny is a double-edged reference, one that in the first instance subverts the efforts of Egypt and the new king to stifle the growth of Israel and by extension to nullify the divine promise. But further, the prolific birthrate in oppressive circumstances can also be interpreted as "a subtle acknowledgement of a female subtext" in the story.[45] Women will have a monumental role in resisting the new king's decree(s) of destruction in the next phase of the story, so the fecundity of v. 12 provides an introduction to this development. Moreover, the Israelite growth is described by a verb that normally means "to burst forth" (פרץ), nicely illustrated at a couple of points in the Jacob story. When Jacob dreams of a stairway to heaven during his flight to Aram after hoodwinking his older brother Esau, in Gen 28:14 God divulges that Jacob will inherit the promise of Abraham and that his descendants will spread out (פרץ) in every direction, and that all families on earth will be blessed. A similar nuance is found in Gen 30:43 after Jacob essentially pilfers Laban the Aramean, and his wealth is described as bursting out (פרץ). Perhaps most memorably the meaning of the verb is captured in the name of Perez, who bursts from the womb of Tamar while attempting to claim the valuable firstborn status in Gen 38:29 at the expense of his twin brother Zerah.

Taken together, these other examples of *burst forth* help illuminate the depiction of Israelite expansion in Exod 1:12 in spite of subjugation and slavery. It is this bursting growth under the circumstances that generates an abhorrence of the Israelites by the Egyptians. "Elsewhere," says William Propp, "the Bible depicts the Egyptian ruling class as obsessively xenophobic (Gen 42:9, 12; 43:32; 46:34)."[46] Propp is referring to two different kinds of texts in Genesis. The first set (42:9, 12) is Joseph's accusation of spying—in his guise as the vizier—with the tacit notion that under a pretense of buying grain the brothers were searching for a point of vulnerability in Egypt that could be exploited. In order for Joseph's accusation to work, it must

---

[45] Trible, "Difference Among the Distaff," 295.
[46] Propp, *Exodus 1–18*, 131.

have been thought plausible. The second set of texts pertains to the general attitude of Egyptians toward Israelites, certainly negative in terms of eating (Gen 43:32) and the vocation of shepherding (46:34). In the context of the Joseph narrative, such abhorrence is treated more as a cultural idiosyncrasy or arrogance, in a different category from the hostility engendered by the new king and the resultant policy of enslavement. As Brevard Childs summarizes, "the multiplication accelerated in proportion to the oppression. What is more, a revulsion fell on the Egyptians which they had not experienced up to then."[47] A pair of uses of the verb *loathe* (קוץ) in the book Numbers are instructive in this regard. When the Israelites tire of the manna during their wilderness sojourn, their complaint is registered through this same verb—they abhor (קוץ) the manna in Num 21:5—precipitating an immense crisis when God sends vipers as a punishment. Similarly, the Moabites dread (קוץ) the Israelite presence in their region (Num 22:3), prompting Balak's decision to hire the soothsayer Balaam. Like Balak of Moab, the new king of Egypt now has to react to a crisis, but the crisis is of his own making since his call to curb Israelite growth has not been achieved. "A new pharaoh," remarks John Durham, "cannot afford to be wrong."[48] In Exod 1:13-14, matters take an even darker turn:

> The Egyptians made the sons of Israel serve with harshness. They made their lives bitter with hard slavery, with cement and bricks, and all kinds of service in the fields. With every kind of slavery, they served with harshness.

Procreation in Genesis was rarely straightforward for the ancestors, but the opening section of Exodus indicates a decisive shift: "In the land of the Nile, Israel finally overcomes the sterility that had blighted the Matriarchs and Patriarchs. Moses will be the first biblical hero since Abraham conceived without difficulty."[49] But based on the Genesis precedent, fertility often carries a latent risk. As Propp further points out, in those episodes where a barren wife finally gives birth, danger often follows, as the examples of Isaac, Jacob, Joseph, or even the son of the Shunammite woman in 2 Kings 4

---

[47] Childs, *The Book of Exodus*, 16.   [48] Durham, *Exodus*, 9.
[49] Propp, *Exodus 1-18*, 130-1; cf. Hamilton, *Exodus*, 5.

variously illustrate: "the corporate 'person' Israel also belongs to this group. After the lifting of matriarchal sterility, danger (and salvation) should follow."[50] As we have already seen, the explosive growth of the Israelites in Egypt has the downside of the new king's cunning speech and the rise of the taskmasters; here in vv. 13–14 there is a further danger of increased burdens and the loathing of the Egyptians. Beyond building the storage cities, the Israelites are now forced to work with bricks and labor in the fields, making their lives bitter (מרר). There are two later occasions where the idea of "bitter" resurfaces, starting with the bitter herbs (מרים) of the Passover ritual in Exod 12:8. Carol Meyers notes that the commemoration includes this element because "eating the *maror* [lit. 'bitter things'] brings tears to the eyes and recaptures the agony of the period of oppression in Egypt."[51] Also, the term recurs as a wordplay in Exod 15:23, not long after the departure from Egypt when the people arrive at Marah (מרה) only to find that the water is bitter (מרים) and undrinkable. In different ways, therefore, the bitterness of slavery is recalled later in the Exodus story.

The least subtle repetition in Exod 1:13–14 is the root "serve" (עבד) used as both a verb and a noun, and frequently occurring in the wider book of Exodus. Such a concept is extremely important because Israel is delivered from Egyptian servitude in order to serve God. James Ackerman argues that the "monotonous, drumlike repetition" of servitude and slavery in vv. 13–14 is an intentional contrast with the terms for Israel's fruitfulness described earlier in v. 7: "On the one hand we have five verbs depicting life and fruitfulness, wrought by the quiet power of the hidden God (1:7); on the other hand, we have the fivefold stress on death-bringing service, imposed at the command of Pharaoh."[52] The colorful variation in language that highlights the Israelite fecundity is drastically contrasted with the banal repetition of the Egyptian enslavement. Ackerman labels this an *artful juxtaposition*, a literary technique used to raise a primary question in the larger narrative about which power Israel ultimately will serve: "the life giving-power of God or the death-bringing power

---

[50] Propp, *Exodus 1–18*, 131.   [51] Meyers, *Exodus*, 105.
[52] Ackerman, "The Literary Context of the Moses Birth Story," 83–4. Cf. Fretheim, *Exodus*, 30: "This root [עבד] provides one of the leading motifs in the book of Exodus (it is used 97 times!). It will also be used for the service and worship of God (cf. 3:20)."

of Pharaoh?"⁵³ Speaking of Pharaoh, his strategy takes an unexpected turn in the next installment of the story, as he turns away from his circle of advisors and addresses a quite different audience.

---

⁵³ Ackerman, "The Literary Context of the Moses Birth Story," 84. Note also the formulation in Leviticus 25:55, "... the sons of Israel are servants (עבדים) for me. They are my servants (עבדי) whom I brought out from the land of Egypt. I am the LORD your God."

3

Pharaoh's Midwife Crisis

> *I know that the LORD has given you the land, and that your terror has fallen on us, and that all who live in the land melt before you. For we heard how the LORD dried up the water of the Red Sea before you when you marched out of Egypt, and what you did to the two kings of the Amorites on the other side of the Jordan—Sihon and Og—whom you devoted to destruction. When we heard, our hearts wilted, and no courage remained in anyone because of you, because the LORD your God is God in heaven above and on earth below!*
>
> Rahab of Jericho

Images can be a crucial component of a narrative, and "regardless of whether they work denotatively as descriptive vehicles in the development of literary themes or whether they serve as the depictive medium of thematic amplification, literary images convey patterned relationships among entities and events presentationally."[1] The use of images varies enormously in Hebrew narrative, as we have already witnessed in our brief exploration of Egypt in the book of Genesis. By comparison, the images in Exod 1:1–14 are more stringent, especially when compared to the elaborate descriptions of the tabernacle or even the wilderness scenes later in Exodus. The enslavement of the people is narrated through a monochrome filter, whereas a palette of terms is deployed in the description of Israel's proliferation, highlighting the

---

[1] Phillip Stambovsky, *The Depictive Image: Metaphor and Literary Experience* (Amherst: The University of Massachusetts Press, 1988) 102. On the difference between image and metaphor, Stambovsky cites and critiques Theodore Ziolkowski, *Disenchanted Images: A Literary Iconology* (Princeton: Princeton University Press, 1977) 10: "metaphor attempts to illuminate the essence of things by exposing previously unrecognized analogies, whereas the image aims at rendering visible iconically."

theme of the ancestral promise moving closer to fulfillment in the land of Egypt. Arriving on the scene with only the murkiest of introductions, the turning point of the chapter is the new king's speech and its menacing aftermath. Although the king does not technically issue a command, his insinuation about Israel's growth posing a problem for Egypt's polity results in the appointment of taskmasters to supervise the building of storage cities, yet does not prove effective in curtailing the population increase.

Israelite growth and Egyptian failure are creatively but laconically expressed in the narrative. For instance, in Exod 1:10 the new king fears that the situation with Israel must be handled adroitly "lest they increase" (פן ירבה), but the unsuccessful policy is captured through closely worded repetition in v. 12, for even as the Israelites are afflicted, "thus they increased" (כן ירבה).[2] Also, in Exod 1:11 Gordon Davies notes a possible allusion to Gen 47:6, where Pharaoh not only offers the land of Goshen to the family of Joseph, but also encourages him to appoint anyone in his family with special aptitude as captains of livestock (שׂרי מקנה), despite the fact that shepherds are loathsome to Egyptians.[3] As an antithesis, captains of forced labor (שׂרי מסים) are appointed over the Israelites in Exod 1:11. To further Davies' point, on the one hand, placing captains of forced labor over the Israelites is an indication of how much has changed under this new king who does not know Joseph. But on the other hand, there is a destabilization of the Egyptian strategy since it fails to limit the growth. So, the more powerful captains are unable to contain the birthrate of the abhorrent (former) shepherds, enhancing the sense of loathing among the Egyptians.[4] Because the new king has not been at all successful in Exod 1:8–14, his strategy takes a more focused approach in Exod 1:16–22, the next section of the story to which our analysis now turns. Once again, however, his program will not prove efficacious, since two midwives act on behalf of Israel and against the orders of the new king of Egypt. This is not the last time that surprising allies are found in the Hebrew Bible, and in this chapter

---

[2] Cassuto, *A Commentary on the Book of Exodus*, 11.
[3] Davies, *Israel in Egypt*, 61.
[4] Another example of the verb "loathe" (קוץ) is found in Gen 27:46, when Rebekah claims to loathe the Hittite wives of Esau. Her apparent xenophobia, whether true or not, is part of a larger ploy to induce her husband Isaac to send Jacob to Laban: "I loathe (קוץ) my life on account of these Hittite daughters! If Jacob takes a wife from Hittite daughters like these—from the daughters of the land—why should I live?"

other cases are mentioned. It is certainly true that later events in the book of Exodus are more visually spectacular, especially those scenes that narrate "the conflict between YHWH and Pharaoh over the fate of Israel. It is an epic battle between kings and gods. The weapons of war are the forces of nature. YHWH summons reptiles, insects, and meteorological elements, including hail and darkness, in an initial assault on Pharaoh (Exod 7–10)."[5] But long before that climactic confrontation, and with a different Pharaoh, Israel is preserved by a rather less glamorous cast of characters, a group not as impressive in the eyes of the world but influential enough to frustrate a tyrant.

SHIFRAH AND CO.

As noted in the previous chapter, most beginnings of a sequel narrative have elements of continuity and discontinuity with the previous work. The book of Exodus begins with a recap of the 12 sons of Jacob and their descent into Egypt, thus encapsulating the later movements in Genesis and setting the stage for the next phase of the story. The discontinuity and conflict occurs early in Exodus with the rise of the new king. Of uncertain provenance, the new king who does not know Joseph speaks words that have a certain affinity with the words of accusation that result in Joseph's imprisonment in Genesis 39. Meir Sternberg describes the connection between Potiphar's wife and the new king in Exodus 1 as follows: "He projects onto the nation his own belligerence and ingratitude and treachery, apparently in cold-blooded shrewdness, as Potiphar's wife did her illicit sexuality onto Joseph, whom she knew to be all too guiltless. Once the sojourning outsider has been pronounced an enemy from within, biding his time, the emergency measures in the name of national security duly ensue, all the way to the final solution."[6] But the resulting policy does not reduce the Israelite numbers, prompting the burden of slavery to be increased with toil involving brick (לבנה) and mortar (חמר). The building supplies of Exod 1:14 echo the bricks and mortar of the Babel

---

[5] Dozeman, *Methods for Exodus*, 5.
[6] Meir Sternberg, *Hebrews Between Cultures: Group Portraits and National Literature* (Indiana Studies in Biblical Literature; Bloomington: Indiana University Press 1998) 124.

project in Gen 11:3, and in both narratives the theme of city-building looms large. Through the allusion to Babel there is a foreshadowing that the hubris of the new king is destined for ignominy, and even as his malevolence will cost many Israelite lives and produce widespread bitterness he will not stem the growth any more than the tower builders were able to reach the heavens. The builders of Babel want to make a name for themselves and the new king of Egypt is nameless, unlike Abraham and his offspring in both stories: "The anonymity of the tower builders stands in stark contrast to the genealogies that immediately precede and follow the Tower of Babel story. The progenitors of each generation are listed by name, as individuals. The builders of the tower are the exception, relegated to namelessness."[7]

A pair of proper names occur in Exod 1:15, but they are not part of the Egyptian ruling class. Instead, they are midwives who find themselves addressed by an increasingly desperate monarch: "Then the king of Egypt spoke to the Hebrew midwives, the name of one was Shifrah, and the name of the other was Puah." These two are the first named midwives in the Pentateuch, but not the first members of their profession to appear in the story. In Gen 35:17 Rachel is experiencing severe labor-pains, and the unnamed midwife speaks words of reassurance: "Don't be afraid, for this one also is a son for you!" As Rachel dies during childbirth, the midwife's words become a sort of eulogy, recalling Rachel's prayer for another son back in Gen 30:24 and also indicating that Benjamin will occupy a reasonably significant place in the story.[8] Another instance where a midwife is visible is Gen 38:27–30, when Tamar gives birth to the twins Zerah and Perez. It is the midwife who first gives voice to the outlandish scene of Zerah reaching forth his hand, only to be outflanked by Perez bursting from the womb in a frenetic bid for the rights of primogeniture. This scene not only reflects the earlier struggle of Jacob and Esau, but also anticipates a larger political tussle over the monarchy, since Perez

---

[7] Sheila Tuller Keiter, "Outsmarting God: Egyptian Slavery and the Tower of Babel," *JBQ* 41 (2013) 203–4. See further J. Gordon McConville, *God and Earthly Power. An Old Testament Political Theology: Genesis–Kings* (LHBOTS 454; London: T & T Clark, 2006) 53: "Each [story] in its own way resists the spreading of humanity, the Babelites construing this as a 'scattering' and disintegration, while Pharaoh sees the growth of Israel as a threat to his hegemony."

[8] Cf. Fretheim, "The Book of Genesis," 585.

becomes the great progenitor of Judah's kings in the line of David.⁹ Uniquely positioned owing to their obvious proximity in the birthing moment, midwives are minor characters who can utter words of direct speech that play a role in furthering plot and theme. It stands to reason that the midwives in Exodus 1 have the same opportunity, and to be sure, become even more prominent characters than their antecedents in Genesis. On the functional level, Carol Meyers notes that the two midwives "are the first in a series of female professionals who appear in the narratives, laws and sanctuary texts of Exodus."¹⁰ To extend the point, the midwives are part of a technically skilled class of women who undertake a brave delivery of the nation during the darkest period of slavery, and another class of skilled female musicians will celebrate the nation's deliverance from slavery in Exod 15:20.

The midwives of Exodus 1 serve a particular constituency, the Hebrew women, and for the first time in Exodus the term Hebrew (עברי) occurs, and it is mentioned on another half-dozen occasions in the first two chapters. One of the more complex and historically controversial terms in the text, Walter Brueggemann provides a broad outline of the socio-political resonance: "This term, with its cognates known all over the ancient Near East, refers to any group of marginal people who have no social standing, own no land, and who endlessly disrupt ordered society."¹¹ Generally speaking, when "Hebrew" is used in biblical narrative there is an *outsider* element that is highlighted in the story, either in an overtly or mildly condescending manner or to reflect the perception of a foreign character(s) in relation to Israelites. Most recently in Genesis, Gordon Davies reports

---

⁹ Alter, *Genesis*, 223. It may be noted in passing that the participle for midwife (מילדת) does not occur in 1 Sam 4:20, instead there is a plural construction: "the [women] standing over her" (הנצבות). In the context of the story—the demise of the house of Eli owing to irredeemable corruption—a collective group of witnesses to hear the dying mother's lament for the hopelessness of her son's future carries its own thematic underscoring of reversal: those standing over the daughter-in-law of Eli view the birth of a son in typically joyous terms, but the mother only voices despair. See Keith Bodner, *1 Samuel: A Narrative Commentary* (Hebrew Bible Monographs 19; Sheffield: Sheffield Phoenix Press, 2008) 49–50.

¹⁰ Meyers, *Exodus*, 37; she later writes (p. 118): "Exodus refers to female cultic functionaries (4:24–26; 22:18; 38:8) and textile artisans (35:25–26; 36:6); other biblical books mention several more (e.g., mourning women, wise women, perfumers, and prophets)." Note also the women who serve at the entrance to the tent of meeting in Exod 38:8.

¹¹ Brueggemann, "The Book of Exodus," 695.

that Hebrew (עברי) is used on five occasions in the Joseph narrative and "never by the Israelites as a description of themselves. The setting is always a confrontation of Joseph or his brothers with the Egyptians, where it either describes them as seen from the Egyptians' side or is the name by which the Egyptians call them."[12] When Potiphar's wife refers to Joseph not by name but rather as a "Hebrew" (Gen 39:14, 17) her label does not carry any positive connotations, similar to the reference in Gen 43:42 when the reader is told that eating with Hebrews is repugnant to Egyptians. The most neutral reference is Gen 41:12, when the chief cupbearer reports to Pharaoh about a young Hebrew lad's aptitude for dream interpretation, not overtly negative, but the foreign element is surely stressed in his description.

An oft-debated question in Exod 1:15 surrounds the ethnicity of the two midwives: are they the midwives of the Hebrews (i.e., likely Egyptian) or Hebrew midwives (i.e., Hebrews themselves)? Brevard Childs states that the Masoretic vocalization clearly denotes the midwives as Hebrew, but Nahum Sarna counters that the relevant phrase (מילדת העבריח) can have either meaning: midwives to the Hebrews or Hebrew midwives.[13] Faced with a measure of grammatical uncertainty, commentators almost invariably resort to the surrounding context in order to flesh out either hypothesis, and cogent arguments have been assembled for both positions. So, William Propp contends that the midwives are of Hebrew extraction because their names are Hebrew rather than Egyptian, and "their brave defiance of Pharaoh implies they are Hebrews themselves, not 'righteous gentiles.'"[14] Conversely, James Ackerman notes that numerous

---

[12] Davies, *Israel in Egypt*, 74; cf. Greifenhagen, *Egypt on the Pentateuch's Ideological Map*, 55–6: "The Hebrew etymology of עברי itself suggests someone who comes from beyond or from the other side. The introduction of the term 'Hebrew' thus introduces into the differentiation between Egypt and Israel a sense of social and economic marginalization, allowing Israel to be feared and loathed from the Egyptian perspective as an intrusive foreign element. From the Israelite perspective, the use of the term would reinforce a sense of not belonging in Egypt."

[13] Childs, *The Book of Exodus*, 16; Sarna, *Exodus* (JPS Torah Commentary; Philadelphia: Jewish Publication Society, 1991) 7. The LXX reads "midwives of the Hebrews" (μαίαις τῶν Εβραίων), indicating their Egyptian nationality.

[14] Propp, *Exodus 1–18*, 137. Note also Greenberg, *Understanding Exodus*, 22–3: "The Semitic-sounding names of the midwives are not a fatal obstacle to this view [i.e., that the midwives are non-Hebrews]. The Egyptian maid Hagar also has a name with a Semitic ring, not to speak of 'Bithya daughter of Pharaoh' (1 Chr 4:18). During the New Kingdom period there were in fact many Egyptianized Semites in Egypt, especially among the menial and slave classes." On this latter point Greenberg refers

scholars believe that the story makes better sense if the reader assumes that the two midwives are Egyptian; after all, "How could Pharaoh trust Hebrew midwives to carry out such a commission against their own people?"[15] A third alternative that might be proposed is a deliberate ambiguity, as if to highlight the midwives' loyalty that is not motivated by any patriotic designation. The new king's appeal to the midwives, as Meir Sternberg outlines, is similar to his earlier speech that suggested combining forces against a serious internal threat:

> This idea likewise arose in the tempter's opening scenario, whereby the immigrants may ally themselves with external enemies of Egypt, unless the Egyptians themselves rally around the king and strike first: common interest makes a bond on either side of the division projected, once (the "they"-alliance) athwart, once ("we") along ethnonational lines. The two-pronged, divisive–cohesive strategy now recurs with fresh twists. The ambiguity of the blood lines, far from mattering, rather implies their coming second to the battle lines; and there would also be the irony of the secret agents destroying the Fifth Column by playing Fifth Columnists within it, under the guise of active life-givers, ethnic or sympathetic. If so, in narrative terms, our backward-looking curiosity gives way to future-directed suspense: the gap about the midwives' national antecedents pales beside the forking of personal consequences across resolutions. The choice put to them lies between working themselves to death—whether as the slaves among slaves or as slaves to slaves—and exercising the power of life and death for their own deliverance.[16]

Blurring of ethnic identity will also be seen, though with a slightly different hue, when Moses is misunderstood by a fellow Israelite and then mistaken for an Egyptian by the Midianite daughters in Exodus 2. As a Hebrew in the Egyptian palace, the same question could be posed to both Moses and the midwives: where does their loyalty lie? It might be wise to keep the issue of the midwives' ethnicity open-ended for the time being; like Joseph's steward in the book of Genesis, surprising theological moves can come from unexpected places, and

---

to "the Egyptian-named soldiers with Semitic-named fathers at the time of Merneptah (*ANET*, 258d)."

[15] Ackerman, "The Literary Context of the Moses Birth Story," 85–6.

[16] Sternberg, *Hebrews Between Cultures*, 239. Cf. Exum, "'You Shall Let Every Daughter Live,'" 48–9: "In its very ambiguity, the text moves beyond nationalistic concerns to bear witness to the power of faith to transcend ethnic boundaries."

the fear of the new king of Egypt is not the only motivating force in this episode, because the fear of God will also provide a defining moment. Meanwhile, the midwives are also given proper names—Shifrah and Puah—and the fact that names are given as well as the meaning of the names has occupied the attention of commentators. There is general agreement that Shifrah means "beauty" and Puah means "girl," with the latter used in a verbal form in Isa 42:14 to depict the birth process.[17] Victor Hamilton also notes that the Septuagint has Zipporah (Σεπφωρα) for Shifrah in Exod 1:15, the same name as the wife of Moses in Exod 2:20.[18] Strikingly, two Zipporahs are pivotal in the larger rescue of Moses and Israel, as the first Zipporah intervenes with the new king of Egypt, and the second Zipporah intervenes with God in the enigmatic episode of Exod 4:24-6.[19]

Apart from the meaning of the names, the most remarkable aspect is that names of the midwives—surely characters who rank infinitely lower on the socio-economic scale in Egypt—are provided in the first place, whereas the new king is not endowed with any name in the narrative or any distinguishing genealogy. The new king's dynastic house remains a mystery in Exodus 1, whereas before long the midwives will be given houses by God. Still, the fact that only two midwives appear in this scene has troubled interpreters, prompting an array of theories: for example, perhaps the two are head of a larger guild, or perhaps the two are harshly overworked like the rest of the Israelites.[20] As it stands, the pair of midwives foreshadow another two characters who interact with Pharaoh later in the story—Moses and Aaron—replete with dissembling cross-examinations, and a power discrepancy that is exploited to full effect as the story progresses, with continual frustration until the final showdown at the water's edge in

---

[17] Cassuto, *A Commentary on the Book of Exodus*, 13-14.
[18] Hamilton, *Exodus*, 12.
[19] See Jacqueline Osherow, "Brides of Blood: Women at the Outset of Exodus," pp. 46-51 in *From the Margins 1: Women of the Hebrew Bible and their Afterlives*, edited by Peter S. Hawkins and Lesleigh Cushing Stahlberg (The Bible in the Modern World 18; Sheffield: Sheffield Phoenix Press, 2009).
[20] E.g., Jacob, *The Second Book of the Bible: Exodus*, 19; Sternberg, *Hebrews Between Cultures*, 234-5. A different view is proffered by J. P. Hyatt, *Exodus* (NCB; London: Marshall, Morgan & Scott, 1971) 60: "If the number of midwives required by the Hebrew women at this time was only two, as indicated here, the total number of Hebrews in Egypt could not have been as great as implied by Exod. 12:37 and some other passages."

Exod 14:30. Until that confrontation comes to pass, the reader can guess why the new king of Egypt approaches the midwives in Exod 1:15 for the next stage of his plan: if the midwives are professionally equipped to care for pregnant women and manage the birth process, the new king is about to exploit this proximity and convey an execution order.

LETHAL COMMAND

The initial speech of the new king of Egypt stressed the problem of Israelite growth and the threat it poses for national security. Without formally announcing the enslavement of the Israelites, the appointment of taskmasters and building of storage cities must be interpreted as an enactment of the new king's desire. Yet the growth of Israel does not decline, and the reader should assume that the enhanced burdens of bricks in the cities and labor in the fields are likewise ineffective. Turning to the midwives marks a tactical change for the new king, and a rhetorical shift as well: "The failure of the Pharaoh's plan to control the strength and growth of the children of Israel by a savage workload is made clear not by a direct statement but by his move to a secretive but murderous 'plan B.'"[21] In his first speech the king is more effusive and apparently interested in altering public opinion, but in Exod 1:16 his instructions to Shifrah and Puah are razor-sharp and include the most intimate of details: "When you act as a midwife to the Hebrew women, take a look at the stones: if it is a son, then kill him, but if it is daughter, she can live." Co-opting the two midwives gives the impression that *covertness* is the lynchpin of the new king's plan. In the framework of the larger episode his intention is to conceal his plan from the Israelites, and thus his instructions to the midwives carry such specificity. Translators differ in rendering the key term of the king's directive to the midwives, with the NRSV and numerous others opting for "birthstool," and on the basis of Jer 18:3 ("I went down to the potter's house, and behold, he was making something on the wheels") deduce that some sort of circular birthing apparatus is envisioned. More concretely, the term is a dual form meaning "two

---

[21] Durham, *Exodus*, 11.

stones" (אבנים), and so another option is a euphemism for testicles, a more abrupt rendering to be sure but perhaps in keeping with the new king's tenor. Since the new king is surely more interested in identifying the gender rather than any matter of obstetrical routine, it makes sense that he would direct the midwives' attention to some early evidence of male differentiation.[22]

The new king's interest in testicles raises the question as to why the males are targeted for death but the females are allowed to live. Destroying the males obviously depletes his slave-labor force, so the new king must be more concerned about diminishing the Israelite numbers than building up his stock of bricklayers. His worry in v. 10 is that in a time of war the Israelites might join with Egypt's enemies, so the most natural inference here is that the new king is systemically eliminating the potential soldiers who could fight against him and depart from the land. Designating males for destruction is not an isolated event in the book of Exodus, and as William Propp notes, recurs in the climactic plague later on: "the particular threat to the Hebrew males foreshadows the events of the paschal night, when all the male firstborn of Egypt are slain in retaliation." Even farther ahead, Propp comments on later happenings: "in the context of the Christian Bible, the endangerment of the Hebrew boys also anticipates the Slaughter of the Innocents prior to Jesus' birth (Matthew 2). The rescued infant savior Moses is a 'type' of Jesus himself."[23] Abram's earlier fear in Gen 12:12 is that he would be killed in Egypt and Sarai would be kept alive, so it is not overly surprising that the same pattern recurs in Exodus 1. Whether or not Abram's fears are justified is not our concern here, but rather, that he practices

---

[22] On the theory of a prenatal examination, see Scott Morschauser, "Potters' Wheels and Pregnancies: A Note on Exodus 1:16," *JBL* 122 (2003) 733: "Within the narrative logic and progression of Exodus, the royal injunction of Exod 1:16 should thus be understood as an intermediate measure in a campaign of increasing violence against the Israelites. The demand for the elimination of *unborn* males stands midway between the rigors of the corvée initially inflicted upon the adult community of Israel and the subsequent command to the Egyptian populace to commit outright infanticide." Exactly how or when the midwives are to kill the males is not outlined, so, as Cassuto (*A Commentary on the Book of Exodus*, 12) notes, it has to be inferred: "He ordered the midwives to slay the male children of the Israelites. They were to kill them, of course, secretly, in such a way that the parents and relatives would be unaware of the crime, and would think that the infant had died of natural causes either before or during birth."

[23] Propp, *Exodus 1–18*, 142.

a deception in order to survive. As we will see in a moment, the midwives likewise engage in trickery, but their motives are quite different than Abram's. The new king's speech is once again ironic, because in targeting the males he seemingly ignores the females, who in the end prove much more damaging to his program. They also prove to be his Achilles heel in the next scene, for in Exod 1:17 his orders are not obeyed: "But the midwives feared God and did not do as the king of Egypt had spoken to them: they let the boys live."

The gaping power inequity between the king of Egypt and the midwives would lead the reader to believe there is little room to maneuver within the parameters of the command to destroy the Hebrew males. Renita Weems suggests that in the new king's view women "pose no threat to national security; after all, the female midwives are conscripted into this national campaign and are sure to be, or so the Pharaoh assumes, compliant."[24] Since the new king is obviously expecting full compliance, the midwives' disobedience is all the more astonishing, motivated as they are by the *fear of God*. If they are Egyptian, their appointment could be yet another instance of subjugating the Hebrews. But a twist in the plot arrives without warning as their fear of the king is trumped by the fear of God. Martin Noth remarks that the king utters no threat, but one suspects that he does not need to.[25] The midwives' defiance is captured through a wordplay: they are instructed to "see" (וראיתן) and kill the child if it is a male, but they fear (ותיראן) God and let the boys live. As Siebert-Hommes summarizes, "In Hebrew the words for 'seeing' and 'fearing' are written with the same letters, but in a different order. Here the text offers a marvelous phonetic wordplay which serves to underline the point of the story: the midwives literally turn the whole affair inside out and upside down."[26]

There are two relevant examples of the fear of God in the book of Genesis. In Gen 22:12 Abraham is commended by the divine angel—

---

[24] Renita J. Weems, "The Hebrew Women are Not Like the Egyptian Women: The Ideology of Race, Gender, and Sexual Reproduction in Exodus 1," *Semeia* 59 (1992) 29.

[25] Martin Noth, *Exodus: A Commentary* (OTL; Philadelphia: Westminster, 1962) 23.

[26] Jopie Siebert-Hommes, "But if She Be a Daughter... She May Live!: 'Daughters' and 'Sons' in Exodus 1–2," pp. 62–74 in *A Feminist Companion to Exodus to Deuteronomy*, edited by Athalya Brenner (FCB 6; Sheffield: Sheffield Academic Press, 1994) 66.

"now I know that you fear God"—and evidently passes the test that is described in v. 1; the risk taken by the midwives in Exod 1:17, we assume, is in a similar category. Also, in Gen 42:18 Joseph—under his guise as the vizier of Egypt—tells the brothers that he "fears God," and in so doing he is vouching for his fairness and accountability. Divine fear occurs later in Exodus, just before the plague of hail. In Exod 9:20 those servants of Pharaoh who "fear the word of the LORD" take hurried precautions to bring their property indoors, but those who "do not set it in their heart" leave their slaves and cattle outside and suffer the consequences. Not long after this incident Pharaoh admits to Moses and Aaron that he has sinned, and asks for prayer while assuring them that he will release Israel. Moses acquiesces to his demand, but in Exod 9:30 adds the caveat: "But as for you and your servants, I know that you do not yet fear the LORD God." The midwives are the first group who are ascribed the fear of God in the book of Exodus, and thus anticipate later Egyptians who follow suit and act as a foil to both the new king of Exodus 1 and the later Pharaoh of the plague narrative.[27] But not just Egyptians are implicated here, as Gordon Davies and Jean-Louis Ska contend that the midwives prefigure a lesson that Israel as a nation has to learn as the departure from Egypt draws near.[28] At the height of their anxiety, with Pharaoh and his agents pursuing them frantically in Exodus 14:10-11, the people are filled with fear and complain to Moses, "Is it because there were no graves in Egypt that you have taken us to die in the wilderness?" After Israel's incomparable deliverance through the water, Exod 14:31 reports that the people saw the great power that God manifested on their behalf, and "they feared the LORD." The quality of the midwives' fear, therefore, is that they already possess what Israel belatedly learns after a long and painful ordeal, and so not only are the midwives a foil for Egyptian royalty, but they are a foil for certain elements within the community of Israel as well: "The integrity and resolution of the midwives set forth the holiness with which

---

[27] Cf. Daniel M. Gurtner, *Exodus: A Commentary on the Greek Text of Codex Vaticanus* (Septuagint Commentary Series; Leiden: Brill, 2013) 178-9: "The contrast between those who fear God and those who do not will become paramount in the encounter with [Pharaoh] and the ensuing plagues."

[28] Davies, *Israel in Egypt*, 75, citing J.-L. Ska, *Le passage de la Mer: Etude de la construction, du style et de la symbolique d' Ex 14,1-31* (AnBib 109; Rome: Pontificium Institutum Biblicum, 1986) 136-43.

the Israelites should respond to God's impending restoration of his inexorable supremacy."[29]

THE INTERROGATION

Oppression in v. 12 does not limit the growth of Israel, and now in v. 17 the midwives contribute to the expansion of Israel by defying the orders of the new king of Egypt. Scholars note that the defiance has several layers of irony, because the midwives fear the God of Israel and not the god of Egypt (i.e., Pharaoh), and the same king whose words induce the entire program of slavery is unable to intimidate Shifrah and Puah.[30] The reader of Genesis may recall Abraham's nervous defense before Abimelech, as he justifies his deception before the angry potentate because he did not expect any "fear of God in this place," and to avoid being killed he *again* passes off his wife as his sister (Gen 20:11). Yet in Egypt there *is* a fear of God, and Abraham's offspring are allowed to live. As mentioned earlier, when the new king of Egypt speaks to the midwives he did not adumbrate any consequence for disobedience, and he must have been expecting his instructions to be followed. But now in Exod 1:18 the midwives are summoned back into his presence and have to answer for their actions: "Then the king of Egypt called to the midwives, and said to them, 'Why (מדוע) have you done this thing, and let the boys live?'"

Exod 1:17 provides no clarification as to how the midwives acquire their fear of God, whether it is a natural endowment, or, like Joseph's steward, somehow received from Israelite interaction and embodied in their extraordinary act of courage.[31] It is equally unclear how the new king finds out his orders have been ignored, nor is there any temporal indicator that reveals how much time has passed. The Pharaoh in Gen 12:18 angrily summons Abram and demands an

---

[29] Davies, *Israel in Egypt*, 78. Hamilton (*Exodus*, 14) also notes the advice of the Midianite Jethro to Moses in Exod 18:21 regarding the appointment of "God-fearers" (יראי אלהים) to judicial offices.

[30] Exum, "'You Shall Let Every Daughter Live,'" 50; Fretheim, *Exodus*, 31.

[31] Sternberg, *Hebrews Between Cultures*, 244. Sarna (*Exodus*, 7) maintains that the fear of God "connotes a conception of God as One who makes moral demands on humankind; it functions as the ultimate restraint on evil and the supreme stimulus for good."

explanation—"why (למה) didn't you tell me that she was your wife?"—but similarly, there is no direct indication as to how he finds out about Sarai's marital status. One minor difference, however, is the new king's interrogative in Exod 1:17. Baruch Halpern holds the position that there are two words in biblical Hebrew for "why," one more negative (למה) and the other more neutral (מדוע).[32] So, in Exod 2:13 Moses says to the man who is in the wrong, "why (למה) are you hitting your friend?" But in Exod 3:3 Moses notices the bush that is burning yet not consumed, and turns aside to see "why (מדוע) the bush does not burn up." When the people thirst in Exod 17:3 they ask Moses "why (למה) have you brought us up from Egypt?" but when Reuel's daughters come home early in Exod 2:18 he asks them "why (מדוע) have you returned so early today?" It may be prudent not to press the difference too far, but it could be argued that here in v. 17 the king is making a request for information, perhaps even an expression of surprise, rather than issuing a stinging rebuke in the first instance. If Israel's monarchic history is any indication, royal interviews can be perilous. For instance, in 2 Sam 1:16 David verbally accosts the Amalekite who claims to have been on Mount Gilboa with King Saul: "Your blood is on your own head, since your own mouth testified against you, saying, 'I killed the LORD's anointed.'" Since David is speaking to a corpse—the Amalekite was struck down by David's men in the previous verse—it confirms our suspicion that conversing with a new king can be a nervous affair. So it is mildly bemusing that the midwives are given a genuine opportunity in Exod 1:19 to respond and provide their defense:

> The midwives said to Pharaoh, "The Hebrew women are not like Egyptian women! Indeed, they are lively—before the midwife even comes to them, they have given birth!"

For only the second time in the book of Exodus the title "Pharaoh" is used. The first occasion is Exod 1:11 in the report of the Israelite slave-labor force that built Pithom and Rameses as storage cities for Pharaoh. Replacing "the new king" with Pharaoh at that moment in the story is a signal that Israel's servitude furthers the interests of the

---

[32] Baruch Halpern, *David's Secret Demons: Messiah, Murderer, Traitor, King.* Grand Rapids: Eerdmans, 2001) 27. Note Houtman's lengthy discussion (*Exodus I*, 255–6), and his reference to James Barr, "'Why?' in Biblical Hebrew," *JTS* 36 (1985) 1–33.

state. In the context of v. 19, the title is used to frame the midwives' reply and reflect their perspective: from their point of view, they are addressing the office of the Pharaoh. The new king of Egypt is the one who commands them to kill the Israelite males, but Pharaoh is the one whom they now answer, perhaps similar to the experiences of the baker and the cupbearer in the Joseph narrative. When the midwives respond to Pharaoh, there is also a possible echo of Genesis 40, where Joseph speaks with those two Egyptian courtiers who are in prison. At the beginning of the chapter the reader is informed that the two officials "sinned" (חטא) against their master, the king of Egypt, although no specific offenses are listed (Gen 40:1). It is true that the cupbearer is restored to his former position at the end of the chapter during Pharaoh's birthday party, but the chief baker is impaled just as Joseph had grimly predicted. These events are then replayed two years later in Gen 41:10 when the cupbearer—who had forgotten Joseph—is suddenly reminded of his memory lapse when Pharaoh is handcuffed by his dream that cannot be interpreted. There is a slight shift in language, though, as the cupbearer asserts that Pharaoh was "enraged" (קצף) with his servants, leading to their incarceration. The cupbearer's experience is useful to bear in mind because the Pharaoh in Genesis 40-1 is a portrayed as a force of retribution. Whether the cupbearer and the baker are genuinely guilty is beside the point; if the Pharaoh pronounces a guilty verdict, punishment follows, and he even orders the execution of those who incur his displeasure. When the midwives respond to *Pharaoh* in Exod 1:19, therefore, the reader senses an element of fear because of the wrath and punitive measures of the earlier Pharaoh in Genesis, and owing to the disregard of their orders here in Exodus 1.

If the midwives are afraid, it is not readily apparent on the basis of their rejoinder. As Brevard Childs writes, "The response of the midwives is so clever as to have convinced not only Pharaoh, but a number of modern commentators who accept its veracity on face value."[33] It must be said that since the publication of Childs' commentary, the theories of ancient obstetrics based on the midwives' testimony before Pharaoh have not abated, which from a literary perspective make their shrewdly concocted defense all the more impressive. The syntax of their reply immediately draws attention

---

[33] Childs, *The Book of Exodus*, 17.

to their professional frustration, and they make it sound as though they are equally disappointed. The fulcrum of their case is a matter that the new king—who seems to have only a vague notion of the clinical exigencies of the birthing process—would be hard-pressed to verify. Asserting that Hebrew women are physiologically different from their Egyptian counterparts is by all accounts not a matter on which the king takes issue, especially when it is sealed with the comparison "lively" (חיה). On this term, William Propp suggests a comparison to animals: "We have already seen the Israelites compared to vermin in vv 7, 12. Oppressors typically justify their own inhumanity by explicitly or implicitly impugning their victims' humanity. A physical asset such as ease of childbirth, seen through the lens of prejudice, appears bestial."[34] The midwives are most likely spouting nonsense, and the king is satirically undermined here, for who could possibly believe such a proposition except for someone gullible and alarmingly ill-informed? Not only are the midwives ignoring the powerful king's deadly order because they fear God, but they also are implicitly ridiculing and outsmarting the new king. Earlier he had enjoined his constituents to deal wisely with the Israelites lest they multiply, but now the midwives have dealt astutely with the new king and allowed the Israelites to multiply and they themselves have escaped prosecution for treason at the same time. Through these words the midwives basically put an end to this tactic by the king, as they are indirectly telling him that he is powerless to prevent the Israelites from increasing.[35] Whether this leads to a

---

[34] Propp, *Exodus 1–18*, 140. For a theological appraisal, see Brueggemann, "The Book of Exodus," 695–6: "The reason given for such disobedience is that they 'feared God' more than they feared the new king, and for that reason they refused to participate in the state-authorized killing. When questioned about their insubordination, they do not explicitly bear witness to their faith in God. Rather, they attest to the surging power for life that is present in the Hebrew mothers, a power for life that is not known among the women of the empire. Hebrew babies, they say, are born with such vigor and at such a rate that the midwives simply cannot be present in time for each birth. In asserting their innocence, however, the midwives do not accuse the Hebrew mothers. The miracle of such births is beyond the fault of any human agent, for the fault is that of the God who will not be deterred by the new king. What counts is that Hebrew mothers are invested with dangerous, liberated power for life, which no one can deter."

[35] Greifenhagen (*Egypt on the Pentateuch's Ideological Map*, 57) suggests the midwives may have made a more tactical appeal: "The king's words in 1:9–10 show him as predisposed to such an interpretation. As Nohrnberg (1981:52) remarks: 'the lie they tell him—that the Hebrew women bear virtually spontaneously—is just the lie

new (and more sinister) policy from the king is out of their hands, for surely they have done their part: the midwives have allowed the Israelites children to live, duped the king, and saved their own lives in the bargain.

DECEPTIVE COUNTERPARTS

Beguiling the king of Egypt after contravening his direct order is serious business, but the midwives are not the only characters who embark on such actions in the Hebrew Bible. Drorah O'Donnell Setel notes that when the midwives rebel against the new king of Egypt it is part of a larger pattern of female deception, and cites the examples of Rebekah (who acts on behalf of Jacob and helps him to hoodwink Isaac in Gen 27:5-17) and Rachel (who lies to her father about stealing the *teraphim* in Gen 31:34-5).[36] To this list of female characters who deceive someone in power, one could certainly add Jael, the wife of Heber the Kenite in Judges 4, whose story takes place in the midst of an intense conflict between Israel and the Canaanites after 20 years of control exercised by King Jabin and his military leader, Sisera. Despite his technological advantage of 900 iron chariots, the prophetess Deborah predicts that Sisera will be divinely given "into the hand of a woman." Led by Barak of Naphtali, the Israelite tribal coalition routs the Canaanites, although Sisera himself manages to flee from the battle on foot. In a desperate predicament, Sisera takes refuge in the tent of Jael on account of the friendly relations between Jabin and Heber (Judg 4:17), and Jael welcomes Sisera into her tent, gives him a drink, and stands guard at the entrance after hiding him under a covering. The surprise comes in vv. 21-2, when Jael acts in a manner that Sisera could hardly have expected and that Barak is the first to witness:

---

his edict shows him readiest to believe'" (citing James Nohrnberg "Moses," pp. 35–57 in *Images of Man and God: Old Testament Short Stories in Literary Focus*, edited by Burke O. Long [Bible and Literature 1; Sheffield: Almond Press 1981]).

[36] Setel, "Exodus," 34. Citing Danna Nolan Fewell and David M. Gunn, *Gender, Power, and Promise: The Subject of the Bible's First Story* (Nashville: Abingdon, 1993) 92, Hamilton (*Exodus*, 15) notes, "It is likely that Pharaoh knows as little about labor pains and delivery of a child as Laban does about menstruation."

Then Jael wife of Heber took a tent-spike, and placed the mallet in her hand. She came to him in secrecy, and she blasted the spike into his skull, and it descended into the ground—but he was sleeping, for he was tired, and he died. Then behold, Barak, chasing Sisera! Jael marched out to meet him, and said to him, "Go, and I'll show you the man you're seeking!" So he came to her, and behold, Sisera, fallen, dead, with the tent-spike in his skull!

It could be argued that Jael's actions are different from the midwives in that she uses violence and aggressive tactics that essentially seal the victory that liberates Israel from the tyranny of their oppressor, all in keeping with Deborah's prophetic word. But Jael's conduct is similar in that her deception occurs in the context of foreign subjugation, and her deeds are ultimately loyal to Israel rather than the Canaanites, just as the midwives are loyal to Israel instead of Egypt. Jael's hospitality has a maternal ambiance, covering up Sisera (who then falls asleep), and giving him milk to drink.[37] Jael's legacy is celebrated in the song of Deborah, and her valor is memorialized in Judges 5:24 ("Most blessed of women be Jael, the wife of Heber the Kenite, of tent-dwelling women most blessed").[38] The question of motive is uncertain with Jael: whereas the midwives' defiance of the king of Egypt stems from their fear of God, there is no explicit reason stated for Jael's deception. Of course, she may well fear God and so act on Israel's behalf, but her conduct could also be politically motivated.[39] Either way, the pattern of deception by a female in a way that benefits Israel is certainly seen in Judges 4–5 with the demise of Sisera at the hands of Jael.

A more compelling example might be Rahab of Jericho in Joshua 2, where a royal order is roundly disobeyed and a carefully wrought lie is offered that saves the lives of endangered Israelite males. There is no consensus among scholars as to why Joshua sends two spies to view Jericho, nor is it clear why the two unnamed spies immediately enter

---

[37] Cf. Robert Alter, *Ancient Israel: The Former Prophets: Joshua, Judges, Samuel, and Kings: A Translation with Commentary* (New York: W. W. Norton, 2013) 129.
[38] On the Kenite connection with Moses, see Jacob, *The Second Book of the Bible: Exodus*, 509-10; Carolyn J. Sharp, *Irony and Meaning in the Hebrew Bible* (Bloomington: Indiana University Press, 2009) 103.
[39] According to Lillian R. Klein (*The Triumph of Irony in the Book of Judges* [JSOTSup 68; Bible and Literature Series 14; Sheffield: Almond Press, 1989] 43), "there is no indication that she acts under the spirit of Yahweh."

the house of a harlot (זונה).⁴⁰ On the one hand, they may want to gather information in a clandestine location. On the other hand, it is later revealed that they are young men (Josh 6:23), and presumably this is the first time they have left the camp of Israel, so a carnal motive cannot be immediately dismissed.⁴¹ The sense of ambiguity persists, as straightaway the king of Jericho finds out the exact identity of the spies and the purpose of their mission, and dispatches a message to Rahab ordering her to bring them out. Like the midwives, the reader naturally would expect Rahab to comply with the king's directive, but Josh 2:4–6 presents direct speech framed by a report of her initial actions followed by a flashback with enhanced specificity:

> The woman took the two men, and hid (צפן) them. Then she said, "It is true the men came to me, but I didn't know where they were from. When it was dark and time to shut the city gate, the men went out. I don't know where the men went. Quickly chase after them, for you can overtake them!" But she had taken them up to the roof, and hidden (טמן) them in the stalks of flax that she arranged on the roof.

Shifrah and Puah take advantage of their profession in order to finagle the king of Egypt: they pretend to disclose a trade secret and he falls for the ruse. Rahab's approach is similar with the king of Jericho: she quickly admits that visitors entered her premises, but disavows any knowledge of their identity.⁴² Her next tactic is to quite literally throw the king's agents off the scent by sending them not only out of her house but out of the city as well, along with a parting encouragement that their journey will end with the arrest of the suspected reconnoiters. But prior to her misleading of the king's messengers, she hides (צפן) the two spies, and the same verb is used in Exod 2:2–3 to describe the mother of Moses hiding her infant from the decree of the king of Egypt. The verb has a nuance of *treasure*, as

---

⁴⁰ See Sarah Lebhar Hall, *Conquering Character: The Characterization of Joshua in Joshua 1–11* (LHBOTS 512; London: T & T Clark, 2010) 28–45.

⁴¹ L. Daniel Hawk, *Joshua* (Berit Olam; Collegeville, MN: Liturgical Press, 2000) 40–1. For an alternate perspective, note Rachel M. Billings, *"Israel Served the Lord": The Book of Joshua as Paradoxical Portrait of Faithful Israel* (Notre Dame, Indiana: University of Notre Dame Press, 2013) 25–44.

⁴² Susanne Gillmayr-Bucher, "'She Came to Test Him with Hard Questions': Foreign Women and Their View on Israel," *BibInt* 15 (2007) 143: "Rahab's role is twofold: she is a prostitute and simultaneously acts as a hostess. She is only able to offer hospitality because she is a prostitute. Hence Rahab goes beyond both roles and combines them in a new and surprising manner."

though the subject is hiding an object of great value (e.g., Ps 119:11, "in my heart I treasured up your words [צָפַנְתִּי], in order that I might not sin against you"). But there is a second verb used in v. 6: as the agents leave the house, the reader is told in a flashback that Rahab had already hidden or buried (טמן) the men among the stalks of flax on her roof. For our study of Exodus 1–2 the second verb for hiding also should be kept in mind, because in Exod 2:12 Moses hides or buries (טמן) the body of the murdered Egyptian in the sand, suggesting that both Rahab and Moses are concealing evidence of their guilt from the relevant authorities. When the midwives let the male children of Israel live, the reader is told that it is because of their fear of God. A similar inference can be made about Rahab based on her lengthy speech in Josh 2:9–13, the first part of which is quoted at the beginning of this chapter. After she dismisses the king's agents, she approaches the two Israelite spies on the roof and unfurls an impressive testimony about the uniqueness of the faith of Israel and peerless qualities of their God. Rahab also, we note, makes a deal for her entire house (בית) to be saved when the Israelites invade Jericho, but this hardly obviates the theology of her speech, and it is fair to assume that this faith prompts her actions of hiding the spies from the Jericho government.[43] The reader may not be entirely sure what the two spies were expecting to find in the house of the harlot, but Rahab's conduct saves their lives and allows them to return to Joshua with a positive report in v. 24, reiterating Rahab's earlier words about all the inhabitants melting in fear because of the advancing Israelites.

REWARD AND RECALCITRANCE

As compensation for hiding the spies Rahab is singled out in Josh 6:25 after the collapse of Jericho's walls, according to the bargain struck with the spies whom she protected by deceiving the king: "But Rahab the prostitute, her father's house, and all who belonged to her, Joshua allowed to live, and she has dwelt in the midst of Israel until this day

---

[43] See also Gordon H. Matties, *Joshua* (BCBC; Harrisonburg, VA: Herald Press, 2012) 71: "Rahab, the unlikely ally, outwits the king's intelligence and foils their hopes of maintaining a position of privilege and power. In stark contrast to the king's fear, Rahab risks protecting unknown agents of a threatening power."

because she hid the messengers that Joshua sent to spy out Jericho."[44] New Testament tradition lists Rahab as part of the Davidic and messianic line (Matt 1:5), and other writings applaud her as an exemplar of faith (Heb 11:31; James 2:25).[45] Rahab's disobedience to the king of Jericho, by any measure, proves to be a fruitful move, just as Shifrah and Puah's furtive actions allow the Israelites to continue increasing. Jorge Pixley suggests that the noncompliance of the midwives to the king of Egypt provides "the first sign of an imminent insurrection." This point could be extended to Rahab's structural role, as her hiding the spies and inveigling the Jericho authorities are an indication that the overthrow of the city will be successful.[46] Like Rahab who saves her *house*, the midwives are rewarded in Exod 1:20–1, and their reward is based on their level of divine respect:

> So God was good to the midwives, and the people multiplied and became very strong. And because the midwives feared God, he made houses for them.

Scholars have drawn a connection between the episode of the midwives in Exodus 1 with the near-sacrifice of Isaac by Abraham in Genesis 22, known in Jewish tradition as the *akedah* from the unique verb used for the binding (עקד) of Isaac. When Abraham demonstrates

---

[44] Cf. Phyllis A. Bird, "The Harlot as Heroine: Narrative Art and Social Presupposition in Three Old Testament Texts," *Semeia* 46 (1989) 129.

[45] On the Matthew reference, see Raymond E. Brown, S. S., *The Birth of the Messiah: A Commentary on the Infancy Narratives in the Gospels of Matthew and Luke, New Updated Edition* (The Anchor Bible Reference Library; New York: Doubleday, 1993) 73: "We know nothing from the OT of Rahab's union with Salmon, but it had to be somewhat irregular since she had been a prostitute; and it was her initiative that made it possible for Israel to come into the Promised Land." Since there are three other women (Tamar, Ruth, and Bathsheba) in Matthew's genealogy, Brown posits (p. 591) that there may be a larger pattern: "The endeavor of Tamar and Ruth was in seeking to have a child to continue the lineage of their deceased husbands when no relative offered himself as a replacement. The endeavor of Bathsheba (the wife of Uriah) was in making certain that her son, Solomon, succeeded to the throne of his father David when another son, Adonijah, seemed about to seize the inheritance. The endeavor of Rahab was not in relation to her child (since the OT tells us nothing of her marriage or the birth), but in relation to the entrance of the Israelites into the Promised Land where the Davidic dynasty would be established. The parallelism among the women is not perfect."

[46] Jorge Pixley, "Liberation Criticism," pp. 131–62 in *Methods For Exodus*, edited by Thomas B. Dozeman (Methods in Biblical Interpretation; Cambridge: Cambridge University Press, 2010) 152.

that he is willing to go through with the ordeal, the divine angel intervenes and says, "Do not send forth your hand toward the lad, and don't do anything to him, for now I know that you fear God, for you have not withheld your son, your only son, from me" (Gen 22:12). Abraham is subsequently blessed with a reiteration of the divine promise for innumerable offspring who will possess the gates of their enemies. Both Abraham and the midwives are commended, as Esther Schor points out, for doing different things—Abraham for being willing to sacrifice his son, the midwives for refusing to kill Israelite sons—so any echo of the akedah in Exodus 1 "can only be ironic, for it demands that we contrast the midwives' act of refusal with that of Abraham's acquiescence."[47]

English translations such the NRSV and NIV prefer to render the midwives' reward as "families" instead of the more literal houses, perhaps to emphasize that Shifrah and Puah are not given physical domiciles but households of their own: just as they saved Israelite children, so they are given the gift of progeny themselves.[48] On this line of reasoning, there has been ample speculation about the midwives, probing their possible age, domestic status, infertility issues, and so forth. However, in the broader context of Exodus 1 the reader can appreciate that when the midwives are given "houses" (בתים), there is a satirical edge that can be discerned. The semantic range of the Hebrew term house (בית) not only includes dwelling or household, but also a dynastic element. For instance, in 1 Sam 25:28 Abigail asserts that God will make a house for David—the same language as used for the midwives in Exod 1:21—and in 2 Sam 7:11 God declares that he will make a house for David.[49] Both of these cases are referring to a dynastic house, not a palace or a residence as such. When the midwives are given houses, there is a biting contrast to the unnamed king of Egypt whose dynastic house is shrouded by an impenetrable

---

[47] Esther Schor, "Saviors and Liars: The Midwives of Exodus 1," pp. 31–45 in *From the Margins 1: Women of the Hebrew Bible and their Afterlives*, edited by Peter S. Hawkins and Lesleigh Cushing Stahlberg (The Bible in the Modern World 18; Sheffield: Sheffield Phoenix Press, 2009) 40.

[48] For a discussion of the masculine pronoun "for them" (להם) in v. 21, see Utzschneider and Oswald, *Exodus 1–15*, 76.

[49] Dozeman, *Exodus*, 77; Hamilton, *Exodus*, 15. On Talmudic traditions that identify Jochebed (the mother of Moses) as Shifrah and Miriam as Puah, see Scott M. Langston, *Exodus Through the Centuries* (Blackwell Bible Commentaries; Oxford: Blackwell, 2006) 18.

mist. Commentators routinely point out that the term *pharaoh* in Egyptian means "great house," as Nahum Sarna explains: "The title 'pharaoh,' uniformly used for the king of Egypt, points to the development that took place during the late 18th Dynasty when the term, meaning 'The Great House' and originally applied to the royal palace, came to be employed as a metonymy for the reigning monarch."[50] The midwives stand up to the great house—and we recall that they address *Pharaoh* in verse 19—and they are bequeathed houses for their courage. It is notable that God is directly involved here but is otherwise unmentioned for long stretches during the period of Israel's enslavement. The reader is thus aware of a thematic element that is an important dynamic within Exodus: the midwives allow Israel to live, and because Israel as a nation will later build a house of worship for God, the midwives are given houses as an anticipation of this forthcoming movement in the storyline.

If the midwives offer a glimmer of hope by withstanding the madness of the new king, it appears to be a false dawn based on the concluding line of chapter. In his first two speeches the king of Egypt sought to eliminate the growth of Israel by initially addressing all his people (resulting in the mechanism of slavery) and then more privately by directing the midwives to kill the male babies at birth. Neither of these speeches is ultimately effective, so he now moves in a different direction. The king seems to accept the midwives' report that Israelite growth cannot be stopped easily, prompting his most desperate measure to date in Exod 1:22: "Then Pharaoh commanded all his people, saying, 'Every son that is born you will throw him into the Nile, but every daughter you can keep alive.'" A different verb highlights the intensity of the king's speech: earlier he "spoke" (אמר) to both his people and the midwives, but now he "commands" (צוה) that every male child be thrown into the Nile.[51] Back in v. 9 the new king addresses "his people," but now in v. 22 there is slight extension as he issues the command to "all his people" (כל־עמו), and for Cornelis Houtman the presence of *all* in this verse emphasizes "the power and urgency of Pharaoh's order; his patience is exhausted; by means of a

---

[50] Sarna, "Exodus, Book of," *ABD* 2:697. Cf. Sternberg, *Hebrews Between Cultures*, 255; Trible, "Difference Among the Distaff," 296. A caustic element is also apparent: "the title evokes the tremendous power of the Egyptian throne just when Pharaoh loses control of the situation" (Davies, *Israel in Egypt*, 81).

[51] Cassuto, *A Commentary on the Book of Exodus*, 16. Cf. Trible, "Difference Among the Distaff," 300: "As Pharaoh hardens his word, he extends his orders."

drastic measure he wants to solve the 'problem' once and for all."⁵² This is the first occasion that the Nile river has been mentioned in Exodus. In the Joseph narrative the Nile is the spatial setting for Pharaoh's dreams, whereas now it is part of Israel's nightmare: "what for the Egyptians is a life-giving force is intended as an instrument of death for the Israelites. The significance of this act, both for Egypt's future destruction and Israel's deliverance, cannot be overstated. Water will play a central role in bringing this struggle to a close."⁵³ In all probability it is the Nile river that draws Abraham to Egypt in the first place when threatened by the famine in Canaan, but in the last verse of Exodus 1 the king decrees that the river become a channel of death for his descendants.

Some interpreters quibble about the nuances of the verb "throw" (שלך) in the context of Exod 1:22, and debate whether it means to literally toss the infants into the Nile or merely to abandon them by the edge of the river in order to die of exposure. But it should be noted that occasionally strange things happen when people are "thrown" in the Hebrew Bible. For example, Hagar "throws" (שלך) Ishmael (probably at least a teenager) under a shrub in Gen 21:15, only to have God hear the lad's voice and promise that he will become a great nation. Even more bizarrely, an unnamed man is hurriedly thrown (שלך) into the grave of Elisha in 2 Kings 13 during a funeral, only to spring to life upon touching the bones of the deceased prophet.⁵⁴ So, being "thrown" is not always the end of the story in the Hebrew Bible. But these exceptions aside, there is a more serious loophole in the new king's decree to throw the males into the river: he again grants permission for every daughter (כל־הבת) to live. The king's rationale is not stated, but maybe he believes that the women do not constitute a viable threat, or that he and his officials already "own" the women.⁵⁵ Regardless, the king is clearly unaware that the midwives have bilked him, and he has inadvertently set himself up to be double-crossed again: "had Pharaoh anticipated the effectiveness of women in thwarting this decree, he might better have commanded that all

---

⁵² Houtman, *Exodus I*, 261.

⁵³ Peter Enns, *Exodus* (NIVAC; Grand Rapids, Zondervan, 2000) 44.

⁵⁴ On the notion of throwing as a dishonorable burial, see Rachelle Gilmour, *Juxtaposition and the Elisha Cycle* (LHBOTS 594; New York and London: T & T Clark, 2014) 206.

⁵⁵ Hamilton, *Exodus*, 22. The same tactic recurs in Exod 10:10–11 when a subsequent Pharaoh gives permission for only the men to depart.

female infants be killed."⁵⁶ Since these are the last words of the new king of Egypt recorded in the narrative, there is a certain irony that his farewell address introduces the next phase in the story where all sorts of daughters—Hebrew, Midianite, and even his own royal daughter—are central actors in the plot.

---

⁵⁶ Exum, "'You Shall Let Every Daughter Live,'" 37, citing Phyllis Trible, "Depatriarchalizing in Biblical Interpretation," *JAAR* 41 (1973) 30–48. Cf. Greifenhagen, *Egypt on the Pentateuch's Ideological Map*, 62: "The Pharaoh's decree allowed the daughters to live, but daughters, including even his very own daughter, are precisely those that undo his decree." Dennis Olson ("Literary and Rhetorical Criticism," 30) also suggests that the royal syntax provides another clue: "The inverted word order and the use of the noun 'daughter' (*bat*) that occurs nine times in the rest of Exodus 1:22–2:22 highlights the critical role that 'daughters' will play in helping to unravel Pharaoh's empire in the end."

4

The Waters of Chaos

> *The best-known and most successful work to embody the idea that the future is already given is probably Sophocles' Oedipus the King. In this tragedy, and in others like it, foreshadowing is no mere artistic device. Whereas in most realist novels, foreshadowing marks the work's artifice, in the Oedipus it conveys the temporality that is supposed to govern the real world. Not fate but temporal openness proves to be the mirage, as time is shown to be essentially oracular.*
>
> Gary Saul Morson[1]

Thwarted in his attempts to decimate the Israelites either through enslavement or by means of his covert instructions to the midwives, in the final line of Exodus 1 the king of Egypt commands that every son born to the Hebrews be thrown into the waters of the Nile river, but the daughters are allowed to live. Isolating the males as his sole target must indicate that the king does not regard the daughters as a problem or an impediment. Thus without realizing it, the king is drawing attention to a major thematic element of the plot: namely, that his orders and desires are routinely undermined by various women in the story. Starting with the midwives, there is a resistance movement that discreetly gathers momentum as the

---

[1] Gary Saul Morson, *Narrative and Freedom: The Shadows of Time* (New Haven: Yale University Press, 1994) 58–9. He further notes (p. 61): "The audience recognizes this temporality while retaining the sense of past-based temporality as well. On the one hand, we contemplate the structure of the whole, and we see the signs of it as the action unfolds. On the other, we also identify with Oedipus and his experience, which, like our own, is lived without knowledge of the future. Lacking such identification with the hero, we would probably lose interest in the play."

narrative unfolds: "As so often in the Bible, God uses what is low and despised in the eyes of the world to shame and overthrow the arrogant and the strong (1 Sam. 2:1–10; Jer. 9:23; Luke 1:46–55; 1 Cor. 1:26–29)."[2] In this chapter the text of Exod 2:1–10 is considered in detail, where a two-fold group of female characters is instrumental in not only continuing the midwives' resistance, but also for setting in motion a phase in the story with implications for the entire book of Exodus and beyond. The first event to analyze is the birth of a male child, born with a death sentence hanging over him. But the manner of the boy's survival is the subject of the story at every turn, and in this chapter we will explore the mother's attempt to circumvent the decree, the sister's surprising role as a broker, and finally the participation of no less than Pharaoh's own daughter to complete the rescue (is she knowingly violating her father's orders?). Along the way, this chapter also addresses the cluster of allusions to the flood narrative in Genesis before concluding with the "naming-speech" and adoption of the lad into the Egyptian royal family. Finally, we also assess how *foreshadowing* works in this sector of the narrative: when the child is drawn out of the waters, it anticipates the drawing out of the entire people of Israel through the waters. To utilize the insight of Gary Saul Morson, the reader appreciates that the nuances of foreshadowing in the rescue of the child illustrate that the portentous events of this chapter are anything but random, pointing instead to the sovereignty of God that subvert the menacing pronouncements of Pharaoh.[3] The name of the child ultimately portends the rescue of the people, just as the name of God later revealed in Exodus 3 points to the identity of the rescuer.

---

[2] Olson, "Exodus," 28.

[3] Cf. Fretheim, *Exodus*, 35: "Pharaoh's speech is again filled with irony, particularly in its reference to the Nile. Positively, it connects with the following story, where the river provides the very setting for the rescue of the baby Moses. Again, Pharaoh provides for the defeat of his own policy in its very formulation. He ends up becoming an instrument for God's saving purposes. As elsewhere in the Old Testament (e.g., Cyrus, Isa. 45:1), God is able to work through even those who do not know God. Negatively, the policy is ironic in that it portends the way in which Pharaoh's successor and his armies will meet their end, namely, by drowning (14:26–8). Pharaoh's own decree sets a chain of events in motion that, in effect, have him signing his family's own death warrant." See also Sarna, *Exodus*, 7: "There is subtle irony in his decree, for the chosen instrument of destruction—water—will in the end become the agency of Egypt's punishment."

LEVITE FAMILY

No Israelite has specifically been mentioned to this point in the story, and instead there is a collective representation that is sketched after the report of Joseph's death. Assuming that the midwives are Egyptian—and there are good reasons for supposing so—the reader perceives the Israelites in the same manner as the king of Egypt does: as a group. But this narration style changes in the aftermath of the decree to throw the male children into the Nile, and in chapter 2 attention switches to a marriage. In normal circumstances such a detail would probably not even be reported, but here in the context of oppression and the death of children, this marriage is extremely important for the rest of the story. There are no personal names in Exod 2:1, but instead the focus is on the tribal identification: "A man from the house of Levi went and took a daughter of Levi." Despite the oppressive circumstances of slavery in Egypt, Israelite marriages still take place and thus provide the opportunity for continued expansion. No more is heard of the man: this verse is a mere seven words in Hebrew, and he virtually disappears from the narrative. We find out his name in Exod 6:20—he is Amram, and she is his aunt, Jochebed, the kind of marriage that Moshe Greenberg points out is later prohibited in Lev 20:19—but the focus for this section of the text remains squarely on the "daughter of Levi."[4] The new king underestimates the power of *daughters*, and this episode is destined to become a classic case. Still, the reader may wonder about initial anonymity and the emphasis on the Levite pedigree of the parents. Terence Fretheim suggests that priestly service is anticipated here: "It is not insignificant that Moses is of the priestly family of Levi on both parents' side (2:1; cf. 6:20). They may be unnamed here to make more prominent his connection with Levi, especially in view of his being raised in an Egyptian household and his Egyptian name."[5] In the short term, the

---

[4] Greenberg, *Understanding Exodus*, 31. Amram may be indirectly referred to again, as Greenberg (p. 43) further points out, in Exod 3:6 ("At the bush, God identifies himself to Moses as 'the God of your father, the God of Abraham, the God of Isaac, and the God of Jacob'") and perhaps by Moses himself as well in Exod 18:4 in the naming-speech of his son Eliezer, "The God of my father (אבי) was my help, and delivered me from the sword of Pharaoh."

[5] Fretheim, *Exodus*, 40. The most prominent event in Levi's career in Genesis is the attack on Shechem for his violation of Dinah (Gen 34:25), so it stands to reason that violence may occur later in the story (e.g., Exod 2:12).

withholding of names that is a hallmark of Exod 2:1–9 sets the stage for the naming-speech in v. 10.⁶ A possible wordplay can also be glimpsed: a man from the house (בית) of Levi marries a daughter (בת) of Levi, and they will soon produce the most illustrious member of the tribal house.⁷ The husband may be absent from the subsequent storyline, but his actions are nonetheless significant and should not be glossed over too quickly. The opening verb (וילך, "and he went") may seem redundant, but given the context of the king's orders Cornelis Houtman translates the opening clause as "and he dared to," implying a sense of resolve or purpose (cf. Gen 35:22; Josh 23:16). In Houtman's view, "despite the difficult time, in which marrying seemed a senseless thing to do, there was a man who dared to do just that," namely, continue to build a family notwithstanding the edict of drowning.⁸

Sarah, Rebekah, and Rachel all faced severe trials in becoming mothers of significant figures in Genesis, but not so this unnamed Levite woman who in Exod 2:2—and like all the Israelite women in Egypt by every estimate—further contributes to population growth: "The woman conceived, and gave birth to a son. She saw him, that he was good, and she hid him for three months." The reader may be inclined to think this "good" child is her firstborn, but the older siblings Aaron and Miriam show up in the narrative in due course. The careful description here is probably due to the child's unique destiny, and perhaps also that he is born under the king's brutal decree. Most mothers would probably assert that their son or daughter is "good," but scholars have detected echoes of the creation story in the specific language that is used here.⁹ When the Levite wife in verse 2 sees that her child is good, it is reminiscent of Gen 1:10–25 where on numerous occasions God sees what has been created and pronounces that it is "good" (כי־טוב). Later in the story, as it turns out, the mother's son plays a huge role in the building of the tabernacle with a host of reverberations to the creation narrative, as Jon Levenson notes: "The function of these correspondences is to underscore the depiction of the sanctuary as a world, that is, an ordered,

---

⁶ Cf. Joel N. Lohr, "Chosen and Unchosen: Conceptions of Election in the Pentateuch and Jewish–Christian Interpretation" (PhD diss., Durham University, 2007) 122.

⁷ Propp, *Exodus 1–18*, 148. See also Isbell, "Exodus 1–2 in the Context of Exodus 1–14," 40–1.

⁸ Houtman, *Exodus I*, 270.   ⁹ E.g., Enns, *Exodus*, 61–2.

supportive, and obedient environment, and the depiction of the world as a sanctuary, that is, a place in which the reign of God is visible and unchallenged, and his holiness is palpable, unthreatened, and pervasive."[10] When she recognizes that her child is good, the mother "hides" (צפן) him for three months (ירחים), and in so doing she defies the king's orders. It may be coincidental, but there is a slight assonance between the Hebrew term for months (ירחים) and the city of Jericho (יריחו), perhaps strengthening the connection between the actions of the Levite mother and Rahab. Less tenuous is the specific verb "hide," also used in Josh 2:4 when Rahab hides (צפן) the two Israelites spies and conceals them from the agents of Jericho's king. Against the interests of her monarch Rahab hides the spies, who are of great value to her because they are essential for the survival of her family. When the Levite mother hides her child in Exod 2:2, her actions are reminiscent of Rahab as she acts in defiance of a royal imperative by concealing an Israelite of great personal value to her, and, as matters develop, to the nation as a whole in due course.[11]

FLOATING SANCTUARY

When faced with the king of Jericho's orders, Rahab extemporaneously produces a plan to befuddle those seeking to apprehend the Israelite agents of espionage. Similarly, when faced with the king of Egypt's execution orders in Exod 1:15–18, the midwives came up with a solution to circumvent their instructions and bamboozle the king. Now in Exodus 2 the daughter of Levi is hiding her newborn son, but as circumstances prevail whereby she can hide him no longer, she takes an audacious next step. In Exod 1:22 the king orders that every

---

[10] Levenson, *Creation and the Persistence of Evil: The Jewish Drama of Divine Omnipotence*, Second Edition (Princeton, NJ: Princeton University Press, 1994) 86, cited in Fretheim, *Exodus*, 269.

[11] For a different application, see Casey A. Strine, *Sworn Enemies: The Divine Oath, the Book of Ezekiel, and the Polemics of Exile* (BZAW 436: Berlin: Walter de Gruyter, 2013) 2: "Concealment, argues James C. Scott, is a fundamental feature of the way in which subordinate groups resist the dominant groups that exert control over them," referencing James C. Scott, *Domination and the Arts of Resistance: Hidden Transcripts* (New Haven, Conn.: Yale University Press, 1990), and *Weapons of the Weak: Everyday Forms of Peasant Resistance* (New Haven, Conn.: Yale University Press, 1985).

male child be thrown into the Nile. In Exod 2:3 the 3-month-old Levite male does end up in the Nile—so in a sense the king's orders are followed—albeit with a subversive twist reminiscent of Rahab and the midwives: "But when she could no longer hide him, she took an ark of papyrus and coated it with mortar and pitch. Then she set the child in it, and set it among the reeds on the bank of the Nile."[12] There is no indication whether the mother is trusting the unseen hand of providence or has any larger plan when she places her child in the ark. But the reader can be sure that the mother takes great care in her preparations and chooses the right kind of material, because the same term for papyrus (גמא) in v. 3 is also used for watercraft in Isaiah 18:1-2: "Oh land of whirring wings beyond the rivers of Cush, the one that sends envoys by sea in vessels of papyrus (גמא) on the surface of the waters!"[13] Not only does the mother ensure the tiny vessel is seaworthy, but she also takes care in its waterproofing by coating (חמר) it with mortar and tar. Scholars note that the verb only occurs here in the Hebrew Bible, while the noun form that appears here also can be found in Exod 1:14 to describe the specific kind of brickwork forced on the Israelites.[14] Notably, the lad who is hidden in the papyrus ark coated with mortar and floated on the Nile is the very one who will be the key instrument in leading the Israelites out of the land of slavery and involuntary brickwork.

An exposed child on the river has evoked comparisons with other ancient Near Eastern hero accounts, and most famously, commentators frequently draw comparisons to the birth legend of Sargon, as Kenton Sparks explains: "In that story a priestess, vowed to chastity, became pregnant and was forced to bear her child in secrecy. After the child's birth, the priestess placed him in a basket and set it among the reeds at the river's edge. A water drawer found and raised the child, but it was the goddess Ishtar who gave him his big career break:

---

[12] On the Qumran variant in Exod 2:3, see Alexander Rofé, "Moses' Mother and her Slave-Girl According to 4QExod^b," *Dead Sea Discoveries* 9 (2002) 38–43.

[13] Jacob, *The Second Book of the Bible: Exodus*, 26; Utzschneider and Oswald, *Exodus 1–15*, 81. Note also Jill Middlemas, "Ships and Other Seafaring Vessels in the Old Testament," pp. 407–21 in *Let Us Go Up to Zion: Essays in Honour of H. G. M. Williamson on the Occasion of his Sixty-Fifth Birthday*, edited by Iain Provan and Mark J. Boda (VTSup 153; Leiden: Brill, 2012) 411–12.

[14] E.g., Siebert-Hommes, *Let the Daughters Live! The Literary Architecture of Exodus 1–2 as a Key for Interpretation*, 115; Exum, "'You Shall Let Every Daughter Live,'" 54.

The Waters of Chaos 95

she took a liking to Sargon and made him king of Akkad."[15] Those who are interested can certainly pursue this further, for it is entirely possible that the story of Sargon's birth is written during the reign of Sargon II. If so, it should be noted that Sargon II is ostensibly the Assyrian king who leads northern Israel into captivity in 2 Kings 17, and thus any allusion to the birth-story of Moses—who leads Israel out of captivity in Egypt—would be intriguing.[16] However, another angle will be pursued in this section of our study.

"There is increasing recognition that the pentateuchal narrative is seldom careless or arbitrary," write John Bergsma and Scott Hahn, "and intertextual echoes are seldom coincidental."[17] To this point, a number of allusions to the primeval narratives have been observed in the book of Exodus, and in v. 3 there is another. Although translations such as the NRSV render "papyrus *basket*" (תבה) for the vessel, as mentioned in the introductory chapter of this study the only other place in the Hebrew Bible where the same term is found is Genesis 6–8, the story of Noah's ark (תבה).[18] The majority of commentators

---

[15] Kenton L. Sparks, "Genre Criticism," pp. 55–94 in *Methods For Exodus*, edited by Thomas B. Dozeman (Methods in Biblical Interpretation; Cambridge: Cambridge University Press, 2010) 84; note also Childs, *The Book of Exodus*, 12–14, drawing on his earlier study, "The Birth of Moses," *JBL* 84 (1965) 109–22. For Ackerman ("The Literary Context of the Moses Birth Story," 89), the episode "does not give the impression of being an independent entity which has been casually included in an arbitrary collection of traditions surrounding his birth and early years." Cf. the careful analysis of George W. Coats, *Moses: Heroic Man, Man of God* (JSOTSup 57; Sheffield: Sheffield Academic Press, 1988) 46–8.

[16] Assuming the "king of Assyria" (מלך־אשור) in 2 Kings 17:6 is Sargon II; see J. A. Montgomery and H. S. Gehman, *A Critical and Exegetical Commentary on the Books of Kings* (ICC; Edinburgh: T & T Clark, 1951) 464–8; C. L. Seow, "1 & 2 Kings," in *The New Interpreter's Bible*, Volume 3 (Nashville: Abingdon, 1999) 253. Note also Diana Edelman, Philip R. Davies, Christophe Nihan, and Thomas Römer, *Opening the Books of Moses: Volume One of The Books of Moses* (Sheffield: Equinox, 2011) 158–9.

[17] John Sietze Bergsma and Scott Walker Hahn, "Noah's Nakedness and the Curse on Canaan (Genesis 9:20–27)," *JBL* 124 (2005) 27.

[18] Although it is confusing in standard English translations, the later "ark (ארון) of the covenant" uses a different Hebrew word (Exod 25:10ff.). The same word is used for the coffin (ארון) of Joseph in the last verse of Genesis, prompting the following comment from Alter (*Genesis*, 306): "Out of the contraction of this moment of mortuary enclosure, a new expansion, and new births, will follow. Exodus begins with a proliferation of births, a pointed repetition of the primeval blessing to be fruitful and multiply, and just as the survival of the flood was represented as a second creation, the leader who is to forge the creation of the nation will be borne on the water in a little box—not the *'aron*, 'the coffin,' of the end of Genesis but the *tevah*, 'the ark,' that keeps Noah and his seed alive." Cf. the KJV rendering of תבת גמא as "ark of bulrushes."

acknowledge an intentional allusion, and to be sure, there are some compelling similarities in the wider contexts of both episodes. Yet the differences are equally important, and provide some thematic clues for interpreting Exod 2:3 and its appropriation of the ark story. An escalation of violence in Genesis 6 leads to the unleashing of chaotic forces in the form of the floodwaters of judgment, but the ark and its contents lead to a re-creation and the possibility of salvation. The words "be fruitful and multiply" are heard after the waters recede, echoing the original mandate for creation. Turning to Exod 1:1–7, the creation language used to describe the proliferation of the Israelites suggests that the vision for creation is realized in the growth of Israel, linked as it is to the promise of Abraham. The violence of slavery imposed by the new king of Egypt hideously threatens this fruitfulness, just as the royal decree to throw the Israelite male children into the waters of the Nile is a manifestation of chaos that quite literally attempts to drown the hope of Israel:

> The decree of Pharaoh, with water as the instrument of death, is painted in cosmic terms, which, if successful, would plunge the world into chaos once again. God's creation (extraordinary growth for Israel) would be inundated in the Nile's waters. Both Noah and Moses are adrift in a watery chaos, but they are divinely chosen ones in and through whom the good creation will be preserved. *The saving of Moses is thus seen to have cosmic significance.*[19]

Recent scholarship has explored other contours of Genesis 6–8 and the schematics of the ark in order to evaluate it in the light of options other than its seaworthiness. To consider one example, the degrees of correspondence between ark of Noah and Jerusalem temple make it possible to suggest that Noah's ark is less of a boat and more of a temple that floats on the waters of destruction; in other words, a sanctuary built for buoyancy in a world of chaos. In Gen 6:16 Noah is

---

[19] Fretheim, *Exodus*, 38; cf. Brueggemann and Linafelt, *An Introduction to the Old Testament*, 82, where a slightly broader view is proposed, one that has relevance for a later stage in Exodus 15–18 and the journey to Sinai: "'wilderness' may be understood theologically and cosmically if wilderness as chaos is the primordial condition of disorder and the primordial force of anti-life that seeks to negate the life of Israel and the life of the world. Such a characterization of cosmic wilderness (chaos) is offered, for example, in Isaiah 24:1–13. The point of understanding 'wilderness' as exile and as chaos is to suggest that while the term may be rooted in the narrative geographically, it has more profound dimensions in Israel's interpretive tradition."

instructed to build the ark with three levels—lower, middle, and upper decks—with a door (פתח) on the side. In the description of Solomon's temple in 1 Kings 6:8, one prominent section of the facility has three levels with a door (פתח) located on the side. Such similarity invites Cory Crawford to conclude as follows: "That the ark, which came to rest on a mountain after the waters had returned to their ordered state, was homologized to the Temple, which was built on Mount Zion and sat 'over the flood' indicated by material water installations, should not surprise us."[20] In a compressed way, the ark that is floated on the Nile in Exod 2:3 resembles its larger counterpart, the floating sanctuary of Noah. While it would be extraordinarily difficult for the wilderness sanctuary to resemble the ark, Steven Holloway notes a temporal link between the two: "In the Hebrew Bible, the sanctuary in the wilderness was dedicated on the same day that the flood waters receded from the land of the new world (Ex 40:2; Gen 8:13)."[21] By virtue of this temporal linkage, the reader is not dissuaded from viewing the ark of Noah as a precursor to the tabernacle. If Exod 2:3 is brought into the equation, an attractive symmetry emerges: a miniature version of Noah's ark protects an Israelite who will be a major player in the construction of the sanctuary later in the book of Exodus.

Building the tabernacle and dedicating it on the first day of the first month may seem a long way off. For now, the mother sets her child in the ark and sets it among the reeds (סוף) on the edge of the Nile. Yet even this gesture is not innocuous in the larger story of Exodus, since the very term *reed* evokes a comparison with the famous Red Sea (ים סוף) later on. Increasingly, commentators are exploring this relationship. Nahum Sarna floats the possibility that the reeds in chapter 2 "prefigure" Israel's deliverance at the Sea of Reeds in chapter 15, and Charles Isbell agrees: "In both cases (chapter 2 and chapter 14), the phrase indicates a place in which life was granted when death was to have been expected."[22] It will be suggested that a

---

[20] Cory D. Crawford, "Noah's Architecture: The Role of Sacred Space in Ancient Near Eastern Flood Myths," pp. 1–22 in *Constructions of Space IV: Further Developments in Examining Ancient Israel's Social Space*, edited by Mark K. George (LHBOTS 569; London: Bloomsbury, 2013) 22.

[21] Steven W. Holloway, "What Ship Goes There? The Flood Narratives in the Gilgamesh Epic and Genesis Considered in Light of Ancient Near Eastern Temple Ideology," *ZAW* 103 (1991) 334.

[22] Sarna, *Exploring Exodus*, 29; Isbell, "Exodus 1–2 in the Context of Exodus 1–14," 48.

helpful category for interpreting this dynamic in biblical narrative is *typology*, and despite the occasional misunderstanding that surrounds the term, it is a frequently attested phenomenon in the Hebrew Bible. Adele Berlin provides a helpful working definition: "In typological interpretation, persons or events are viewed as figures that are historically real themselves, but that also prefigure later persons and events."[23] When apparently ordinary events are endowed with a much greater significance—as with the choice of a papyrus ark that directs the reader to Genesis 6–9 and allows for a connection with Exod 2:3—a typological exegesis commends itself. Consider Michael Fishbane's longer reflection:

> [C]ertain events have both a manifest and a latent dimension, a topical sequence and a deeper religious signification. Typologies serve, therefore, as the means whereby the deeper dimensions perceived to be latent in historical events are rendered manifest and explicit to the cultural imagination. For this reason, the fact that a particular event is not rendered solely in its own terms, but is rather reimagined in terms of another—a prototype—is not due to its paucity of religious significance but rather to its abundance. By means of retrojective typologies, events are removed from the neutral cascade of historical occurrences and embellished as modalities of foundational moments in Israelite history.[24]

If a typology is focused on the relationship between texts, it has a higher probability of occurring for the kind of foundational, watershed events that Fishbane points out such as Noah representing a new Adam ("who, in Gen. 9:1–9, presides over a restored world, a renewal of creation depicted in the terms and imagery of Gen. 1:26–31") or Joshua represented as a new Moses.[25] On the latter, it is striking that Joshua directs the Israelites to cross a body of water on dry ground, circumcises a new generation, and has an unexpected meeting with a daunting warrior who instructs him to take off his sandals for he is

---

[23] Adele Berlin, "Literary Approaches to Biblical Literature: General Observations and a Case Study of Genesis 34," pp. 45–75 in *The Hebrew Bible: New Insights and Scholarship*, edited by Frederick E. Greenspahn (New York and London: New York University Press, 2008) 61; Berlin engages at length with Stephen A. Geller, "The Sack of Shechem: The Use of Typology in Biblical Covenant Religion," *Prooftexts* 10 (1990) 1–15.

[24] Michael Fishbane, *Biblical Interpretation in Ancient Israel* (Oxford: Clarendon Press, 1985) 360.

[25] Fishbane, *Biblical Interpretation in Ancient Israel*, 372.

standing on holy ground.[26] As Moses led Israel to the threshold of Canaan, there is every indication that Joshua will complete the task. Ruminating on these examples in the light of Exod 2:3, it can be argued that the preservation of the child's life in the ark prefigures the preservation of the people of Israel. The one male Israelite placed among the reeds is a representative of the whole, and he in due course leads the Israelites through waters that could be their grave, as they experience the same threat of death before an unexpected life-saving intervention: "Just as Moses is placed in the סוף by his mother with the water before him and the threat of the Pharaoh behind him, so also the whole people will stand by the ים סוף with the waters before them and the Pharaoh pursuing behind them (Exodus 14)."[27] Other similarities between Exod 1:22 and Exodus 14 can be suggested, as both episodes narrate dangerous times for the Israelites with an edict of destruction hovering over them. As we have seen, in Exod 1:22 the king's command to throw the Israelite males into the water is presupposed in the mother's actions when she carefully prepares the ark for her son and places it among the reeds of the Nile. In Exod 14:5 Pharaoh abruptly changes his mind (ויהפך לבב) and, along with his officials, reverses his decision to release Israel. In fact, the manic pursuit in Exodus 14 is poetically re-accentuated in Exod 15:9–10 with some unique syntax and shades of characterization:

> The enemy said, "I will pursue. I will overtake. I will divide the spoil. My soul will be filled. I will draw my sword. My hand will dispossess him." You blasted your wind, the sea covered them, they sank like lead in the mighty waters!

Some translators render Exod 15:9 in the plural, but a case can be made for retaining the singular and interpreting it as a projection of Pharaoh's own voice, in a sequence of short sentences that indicate calculated resolve during a frantic gallop. Like Exod 1:22, there is a personal threat to destroy the Israelites in chapter 15 and a boast of

---

[26] Walter L. Reed, *Dialogues of the Word: The Bible as Literature According to Bakhtin* (New York: Oxford University Press, 1993) 55.
[27] Siebert-Hommes, *Let the Daughters Live! The Literary Architecture of Exodus 1–2 as a Key for Interpretation*, 114; cf. Exum, "'You Shall Let Every Daughter Live,'" 54; Dozeman, *Exodus*, 81: "The 'reeds' of the Nile... foreshadow Israel's impending salvation at the Red or Reed Sea (*yam-sûp*)." Note also Brueggemann, "The Book of Exodus," 699: "The baby is at the edge of the waters of freedom, there before his people."

supreme confidence that Israel will (finally) be wiped out by the Egyptian royal scabbard. Not only will Israel be killed, but also plundered in the process—as perhaps Pharaoh has every interest in retaking the innumerable articles of silver and gold that were requested from the neighbors (Exod 12:35). The poetic rejoinder of v. 10 asserts that the people of Israel are rescued by direct divine intervention, as the divine wind drowns the boasting adversary who was uttering the death threats. Exodus 14–15 recounts the surprising reversal and rescue at the Sea of Reeds/Red Sea, even as Exod 2:3 narrates the placement of the ark by the reeds of the Nile in a more reserved style, and a much quieter providence at work. When the two events are brought together, the reader grasps the larger irony of water in the story, for just as water was the king's means for destroying the future of Israel, so the waters bring Egyptian destruction in chapters 14–15 and silences the voice of Pharaoh that decreed annihilation for the people. The victory over Pharaoh and the subduing of Egyptian chaos at the Red Sea is anticipated when the child is placed among the reeds, soon to be extracted in an extraordinary sequence of events.

SISTER ACT

The papyrus ark floated on the Nile is typologically configured on the ark of Noah, a floating sanctuary that anticipates the tabernacle in the wilderness. Moreover, when the ark is placed among the reeds, it foreshadows the people of Israel at the edge of the Re(e)d Sea in Exod 13:18, poised for rescue from Pharaoh's death threat. The bold actions of the Israelite mother in Exod 2:2–3 by first hiding, then preparing, then setting adrift her son on the waters set the stage for other female characters to enter the storyline, beginning with another relative who emerges in v. 4 from the shadows of the narrative: "His sister stationed herself at a distance, in order to know what would be done to him." The anonymity of the sister is an issue that will be further discussed later in this chapter, but for now the reader might simply inquire about the sister's presence, and if her arrival in the story implies a larger plan involving the little ark in the reeds. Some interpreters have argued that the mother intentionally places the ark in a location where she knows that the ark might be taken by someone favorably inclined to the child, and to that end the sister is deployed to keep watch on the proceedings.[28] Since there is a pattern of intrepid female actions to this point in the story, the intentional placement of the little ark certainly could be argued to fit. Along these lines, William Propp notes: "There is a nice symmetry among the female characters. Moses' sister, presumably deputized by the mother to guard the basket in the reeds, parallels the princess's servant, dispatched by the princess to fetch the basket from the reeds."[29]

The idea that the sister is deputized by the mother to keep watch over the ark has several advantages, but my interpretation inclines in a different direction and suggests that the mother probably does not have a carefully wrought plan and the sister acts independently in this episode. In terms of abandonment of the child, several scholars have pointed to a parallel situation in Gen 21:14-21, where Hagar is driven out by Sarah and throws her son Ishmael under a bush when their supply of water is exhausted.[30] Among the common elements in Genesis 21 and Exodus 1-2 are affliction (Sarah banishes Hagar), the verb *to throw* (the king commands Israelite males to be thrown into the Nile, and Hagar throws her son in apparent despair), as well as weeping and a remarkable intervention that saves the child's life. Hagar's son is much older than the boy in the ark, and Gen 21:16 features her emotive outpouring and grief. There is more elaborate care in the preparation of the ark and placing it among the reeds of the Nile in Exod 2:3, but it is still a desperate act to prevent the drowning of the child by the king's decree. God is more obviously active in Gen 21:17-19, addressing Hagar with a question, a reassurance, an imperative, and a sequence of directions that culminates in opening her eyes so she can see a life-giving well of water. God remains comparatively hidden in Exod 2:3 with the ark, and even as the mother's actions are similar to the midwives—who fear God and thus disobey the king—the midwives are rewarded with houses, whereas any reward earned by this mother is held in abeyance. The mother of Exod 2:3 is heroic, and perhaps trusts in God even though it is unstated in the text. But with limited options as the ark is set

---

[28] E.g., Hamilton, *Exodus*, 20; Jacob, *The Second Book of the Bible: Exodus*, 28.
[29] Propp, *Exodus 1-18*, 153.
[30] See Dozeman, "The Wilderness and Salvation History in the Hagar Story," 28; Trevor Dennis, *Sarah Laughed: Women's Voices in the Old Testament* (Nashville: Abingdon, 1994) 98.

adrift after three months of concealment, if the mother has a larger plan it is not apparent when she then recedes into the narrative background.

Another substantial difference between the travail of Ishmael in Genesis 21 and the fate of the small ark in Exodus 2 is the sudden appearance of an intriguing minor character, the hitherto unmentioned sister of the boy who materializes without any formal introduction or elaboration. When she stations herself (ותתצב) at a distance, the verbal form suggests that it is the sister's own volition and initiative rather than an appointment by the mother. Indeed, this family trait of "stationing" will recur in the little brother's life later when Moses is positioned (יצב) before Pharaoh in Exod 8:16 and 9:13 during the early hours of the day in order to issue an imperative about releasing the people of Israel. When the sister is casually introduced in v. 4 with only her presence—watching to see what fate would befall her brother—and her relational affiliation described, there is a deep understatement since the reader has no idea how important her role will be in this episode, and again later after the events of the exodus (see Exod 15:20-1). The *niphal* form of the verb at the end of v. 4 (יעשה) does not suggest any plan or strategy, but rather implies that the sister wants to know if anything will happen. If the sister undertakes any action in the story, therefore, it will have an extemporaneous feel rather than previously rehearsed choreography. Because the mother is nowhere to be seen—which the reader might expect if a plan was in effect—the sister comes across as a free agent. When the mother does return to the storyline, it will be through the sister's efforts, and not her own. Just as the midwives enable the Israelite mothers to keep their sons through their bold and witty efforts, so the sister will broker a deal that enables this mother to likewise keep her son. Moreover, to this point in the narrative the courageous women of the story have all been reactive and act in response to the king's orders, but the sister is conducting herself in a slightly different manner that, in the end, will prove equally effective in undermining the king's deathly decrees. The king soon will feel an ironic sting, as his permission for the "daughters" to live becomes a thorn in his regal flesh. As the sister is stationed at a distance to see what is to be done for the boy, the high point of the episode follows in Exod 2:5-6:

> Then the daughter of Pharaoh came down to wash in the Nile, and her maidens were walking along the Nile's bank. She saw the ark in the

midst of the reeds, and sent her handmaiden so she could take it. Then she opened it and saw the child: behold, a lad, crying! She had compassion on him, and said, "This one is from the children of the Hebrews!"

Daughters have been crucial components of the plot of Exodus to this point—whether directly as actors in the story or indirectly through the king's repeated commands to let the daughters live—and include the mass of Hebrew mothers, the midwives, the daughter of Levi, and the sister who is watching from afar. A new phase of the story begins with an unanticipated development, as an imperial daughter arrives on the scene in Exod 2:5. There has been no mention of a royal family, but given the scant interest in even the most basic facets of the new king's pedigree—erasures that leave the reader much more in the realm of inference than certainty at every juncture—the absence of any further characteristics of Pharaoh's daughter is not unusual in any way. Consistent with the tenor of the story so far, she is not ascribed a proper name, only her brusque descent to the edge of the Nile. Her affiliation with Pharaoh is potentially ominous, since that title has been used so far in Exodus in the context of deadly policy toward the Hebrews, prompting the kinds of questions posed by Walter Brueggemann regarding the role of the princess here: "Did she willfully bathe in the very river now burdened by her father with death? What will she do when she sees the baby? Will she replicate her raging father and kill the baby?"[31] When she arrives at the river, therefore, the reader knows that she is washing in the waters that have been defiled by her father's decree, as Pharaoh's own child now bathes in the river that is used for drowning the children of Israel. In Exod 7:15 and 8:20 the later Pharaoh evidently has the same routine of washing in the Nile, and it is at this spatial setting that he will be confronted by the Israelites Moses and Aaron with divine signs and requests for liberation. So, when a member of the Egyptian royal house arrives at the Nile for cleansing, significant moments for the people of Israel ensue.

The turning-point in the scene occurs when Pharaoh's daughter notices the ark among the reeds. James Ackerman notes that once the ark is fetched, it is the perception of Pharaoh's daughter that is refracted ("behold, a lad, crying") as my rendering of Exod 2:6 tries

---

[31] Brueggemann, "The Book of Exodus," 699.

to capture in staccato fashion.[32] Her reaction to the child in the ark is compassion, the first time this specific verb has featured in the Hebrew Bible. When considering the decree of drowning, any such compassion from a member of Pharaoh's house may catch the reader off guard: "If the events were to be of a more contemporary context, the boy could be a Jewish child whom a Dutch family is hiding during World War II. In walks not merely a soldier representing Hitler and his command to exterminate, but one of his own flesh and blood. As Jonathan Sacks has said, this is 'Hitler's daughter, or Eichmann's or Mussolini's, saving a Jewish child.'"[33] Scholars often remark that the compassion of Pharaoh's daughter coupled with her "coming down" (ירד) provide a distinctly theological flavor to this scene, as though the daughter is used as an image of the divine. Cornelis Houtman points out that God will "come down in Exod 3:8 (cf. 19:11, 34:5), and that the pillar of cloud likewise descends in Exod 33:9."[34] Even if one prefers to argue that Pharaoh's daughter is presented as more of an instrument than an image of God in the story, it nonetheless has to be conceded that a powerful and surprising characterization is at work here. More often than not, the verb for *showing compassion* (חמל) is negated, as in the well-known example of 1 Sam 15:3 where King Saul is commanded by the prophet *not* to show compassion. When the daughter of Pharaoh manifests compassion for the child here, it is a specific kind of pity that strongly indicates an awareness of what is at stake: she is fully aware that any actions toward the child would be in direct contradiction to her father's agenda. If the daughter proceeds to do anything on the child's behalf, she would then be imitating the midwives who fear God and save lives despite the command of the king of Egypt.

On a more practical level, how does Pharaoh's daughter know that the child is one of the Hebrews? An early rabbinic suggestion is that circumcision is the immediate token of the boy's identity, and one that produces a distinguishing feature recognizable to most onlookers.[35] In light of the crisis over circumcision shortly to come in Exod 4:24–6, such a proposal could underscore the life-saving

---

[32] Ackerman, "The Literary Context of the Moses Birth Story," 92.
[33] Lohr, *Chosen and Unchosen*, 124, citing Jonathan Sacks, "Righteousness Knows No Racial or Religious Boundaries," *The Times* (24 May 2003) 48.
[34] Houtman, *Exodus I*, 280. Cf. Fewell and Gunn, *Gender, Power, and Promise*, 93.
[35] See Greenberg, *Understanding Exodus*, 34–5.

possibilities of circumcision (by the Levite parents) in this context. Other interpreters stress the larger narrative situation, for who else would be placed in a floatation device but a Hebrew child hidden from the king's dictates?[36] But something else happens when she identifies the child as a Hebrew, for when it is combined with her compassion, it reveals that the daughter is of a radically different disposition than her father. Furthermore, her compassion runs counter to the general consensus of Egyptians toward the Hebrew as evidenced in texts such as Gen 43:32 and Exod 1:12, where loathing and disgust appear to capture the overall mood.[37] In this case, when the daughter says "Hebrew" it reveals her opposition to and violation of her father's edict, as her words amount to a confession and potentially an inclination to act in a manner contrary to the policy of Egypt designed by her father.

If there is a momentary pause after the short exclamation of Pharaoh's daughter, the sister seizes the immediate advantage by vacating her position and decisively intervening in Exod 2:7: "Then his sister said to Pharaoh's daughter, 'Should I go and call a nursing woman for you from the Hebrew women, so that she can nurse the child for you?'" Commentators usually assume that the sister is Miriam, whose anonymity is retained in this episode as though waiting for the naming-speech that occurs in verse 10 when the scene comes to a conclusion and the sister's brokerage reaches its incredible denouement. The next time Miriam appears in the story will be near a different water's edge, commemorating the power of God for Israel's emancipation in song (Exod 15:20–1) when she is called a prophetess (נביאה). Presumably born during the dark reign of the nameless new king of Egypt, Miriam is named only when she is reintroduced in the context of her vocation *after* the rescue from the waters of chaos during the celebration of Israel. As it stands, her conduct in this episode with Pharaoh's daughter functions as an overture to her later career because her activity in Exodus 2 has a virtually prophetic edge. The sister's audacious question to the princess evinces a wisdom beyond her years. In the next verse (Exod 2:8) the sister is referred to

---

[36] E.g., Alter, *The Five Books of Moses*, 313: "The fact that this is a male child left hidden in a basket would be the clue to the princess and her entourage that he belongs to the Hebrews against whom the decree of infanticide has been issued."

[37] For Lohr (*Chosen and Unchosen*, 126), her reaction may also be perceived as "repugnant to her peers of social status."

as a "young woman" (עלמה), a term that is famously found in Isa 7:14 for a young woman old enough to bear a child; as far as her interaction with Pharaoh's daughter goes, the young woman comes across as rhetorically mature in what must be construed as challenging circumstances.[38]

In verse 4 it was noted that the sister stations herself (יצב) to watch what happens to the boy, a verb that anticipates her brothers' later actions when they station themselves near the Nile's edge to confront Pharaoh. Now in light of her actions this earlier positioning takes on added significance. Jopie Siebert-Hommes remarks on a particular use of the same verb (יצב) in Exod 14:13 when Moses exhorts the Israelites to station themselves to see the salvation of God. At either end of the story of Israel's slavery, the sister is well positioned to witness the divine salvation: "The story *begins* at the river, where Moses is found in a hopeless situation in the midst of the reeds (*swp*, 2:5). The story *ends*—for the present—at the Sea of Reeds (*ym swp*), when the whole people, all the sons, have been saved from a hopeless situation (15.19)."[39] One major difference, though, is that Exodus 2 does not have any overtly described miracle, only various actions of the female characters and the risky venture of the sister. When addressing Pharaoh's daughter in verse 7, the sister makes no introduction nor does she officially identify herself as a Hebrew.[40] The ambiguity surrounding the midwives stemmed primarily from the narration of the story: there is no clear indication of their ethnicity in the text, and hence the focus of the episode is directed to their fear of God rather than any patriotic motivation for defying the king's order. The sister deftly sidesteps any kind of self-designation, nor does she mention any relational connection to the crying infant. Instead, she directs all her words toward the princess herself with a pithy set of suggestions focused squarely on the emerging relationship between the boy and Pharaoh's daughter.

Two comments by Phyllis Trible merit reflection: "This 'sister,' whose own life the Pharaoh has spared, works to save the life of her baby brother, whom the Pharaoh has ordered drowned. Nuances in the sister's words show her as a skilled mediator."[41] First, there is a

---

[38] Dennis, *Sarah Laughed*, 99.
[39] Siebert-Hommes, "But if She Be a Daughter... She May Live!," 70.
[40] Hamilton, *Exodus*, 21.
[41] Trible, "Difference Among the Distaff," 303.

tangible irony as the sister—another example of the king's underestimation of female characters—proposes an adoption. Under this scenario, Pharaoh's own daughter will bring a Hebrew boy into her home instead of being destroyed in accordance with the royal fiat. So rather than the infant being drowned, the sister is promoting the idea that a Hebrew boy should live right under the king's nose. Second, the characterization of the sister as a skilled mediator can be expanded, for it appears that she is a rhetorical midwife even as Shifrah and Puah are literal midwives. It could be argued that the sister's vantage point—positioned "from afar"—enables her to overhear the princess and thus discern her compassion: sensing her favorable disposition, the sister unfurls her plan. Since the baby is crying, he must need to eat, hence she volunteers to find a nurse.[42] Trible also observes that the sister uses the interrogative form, thus offering to provide helpful service while deferring to the power of the princess to render the decision, and in so doing effects a successful mediation and protects her brother at the same time.[43]

THE PRINCESS OF EGYPT

When the question is posed to Pharaoh's daughter about finding a nurse, it should be noted that this is not the last time in the Hebrew Bible that an older female relative dramatically intervenes to rescue a male infant from a tyrannical purge. 2 Kings 11 features a number of similar dynamics, albeit without the involvement of a foreign superpower, when Athaliah seizes the throne of Judah.[44] The destruction wrought by Jehu son of Nimshi includes the northern and southern kings of Israel and Judah, and most memorably brings about the fall of Jezebel, thrown from a window by "two or three eunuchs" in 2 Kings 9:32. Into this vacuum steps Athaliah mother of slain Ahaziah, who solidifies her control of Jerusalem by proceeding to liquidate all the "royal seed." Athaliah's carnage leads to one of the bleakest hours

---

[42] Cassuto, *A Commentary on the Book of Exodus*, 19–20.
[43] Trible, "Difference Among the Distaff," 303; cf. Exum, "'You Shall Let Every Daughter Live,'" 55: "Her careful phrasing, 'shall I call for *you* . . . to nurse for *you* the child,' provides the idea that the princess keep the infant, and the repetition of 'for you' creates the impression that she makes the proposal for the sake of the princess."
[44] Nohrnberg, *Like Unto Moses*, 335.

in the entire history of David's dynasty, but complete annihilation is averted through a fearless sequence in 2 Kings 11:2: "Then Jehosheba—the daughter of King Joram and sister of Ahaziah—took Joash the son of Ahaziah and stole him from the midst of the king's sons who were being put to death, and placed him and his nurse in the bedroom. So they hid him from Athaliah, and he was not killed." Young Joash remains hidden in the temple precincts for six years until the high priest Jehoiada—who, according to 2 Chron 22:11 is the husband of Jehosheba—leads a popular uprising that dethrones Athaliah and installs Joash on the Davidic seat in Jerusalem.[45]

Despite some clear differences between 2 Kings 11 and Exodus 2, there also are striking points of correspondence because in both episodes an older sister-figure takes enormous risks to protect a younger male relative destined to lead the people of Israel/Judah. The motif of *hiding* is a common feature of both stories, and the element of nursing (ינק) is an essential facet of each subplot. In all likelihood Jehosheba is the daughter of Athaliah, so in both 2 Kings 11:2 and Exod 2:6–10 the subversive conduct of a princess directly counters the parent's murderous rampage. On the basis of these similarities the reader can conclude that at pivotal moments in the story of Israel, an older female relative's independent initiative carries national implications. A prominent theme in these texts is *hope kept alive* in the midst of dismal circumstances, as the promise of the nation is carried on the narrow shoulders of vulnerable infants. The two sister-figures are characterized in a slightly different manner, with the most audible difference being that Jehosheba is afforded no direct speech, whereas the sister in Exod 2:7 poses a very subtle and helpful question to Pharaoh's daughter about finding a nurse. There is also some gender reversal, as Pharaoh's daughter defies her father whereas Jehosheba defies her mother. Indeed, the mother in Exodus 2 has not been seen since she placed the ark in the reeds at the edge of the Nile, but because of the sister's brave query, she is now poised to make a reappearance in Exod 2:8–9 and will soon add *wet-nurse* to her résumé:

> The daughter of Pharaoh said to her, "Go." So the young woman went and called the child's mother. Pharaoh's daughter said to her, "Go away

---

[45] On the marriage of Jehosheba and Jehoiada as a foil to the marriage alliance between the kings of Judah and Israel, see Bodner, *The Artistic Dimension*, 164–6.

with this child and nurse him for me, and I'll provide your wages." So the woman took the child, and she nursed him.

When the midwives were summoned before Pharaoh in Exod 1:17, they proffer an excuse that the king does not question. In Exod 2:7 the sister is equally creative, but not exactly deceptive. It is true that she does not state all the facts, but she can hardly be accused of lying to Pharaoh's daughter. Whether the young woman's eager approach is appealing or whether the princess of Egypt is favorably disposed from the outset and this offer of assistance is what she wants to hear, Pharaoh's daughter signs off on the plan with a one-word imperative, "Go" (לכי).⁴⁶ A further sign of the girl's verbal effectiveness is that she obtains permission from the princess without any kind of qualification, paving the way for the final twist in the sister's intervention: she recruits the boy's mother—and her own—for the task of suckling the crying infant. The reader easily grasps the significance of the reemergence of the boy's mother into the storyline, but it is unclear if Pharaoh's daughter is aware of the relationship.⁴⁷ This gap in knowledge is one reason why ironies are abounding in the scene: the mother is now allowed to keep her child (for a season) because Pharaoh's decree is countered by his own daughter. Wages for the mother's employment are paid from the house of Pharaoh, and as mentioned earlier, in a minor way this transaction conceivably foreshadows the later plundering of Egypt by the Israelites.⁴⁸ Since the

---

⁴⁶ In the vicinity of the water's edge, Pharaoh's daughter issues a sequence of imperatives to the Israelite women about the boy, foreshadowing the boy's own imperatives to the Israelites at a different water's edge later in the story. Just as the sister and mother are compliant to the will of a superior (Pharaoh's daughter), so the boy must also obey a superior (God) in due course and exhort the Israelites to do likewise; see Peter Sabo, "Drawing Out Moses: Water as a Personal Motif of the Biblical Character," pp. 409–36 in *Thinking of Water in the Early Second Temple Period*, edited by Ehud Ben Zvi and Christoph Levin (BZAW 461; Berlin: Walter de Gruyter, 2014) 426.

⁴⁷ Cf. Utzschneider and Oswald, *Exodus 1–15*, 83: "Once again the wisdom, indeed finesse, of the Israelite women has been demonstrated, for they have let the daughter of Pharaoh unknowingly ensure that the Israelite mother is not separated from her child." Note also Gurtner, *Exodus*, 189: "Previously the (presumably destitute) mother was forced to give up her child and hope for the best, now she gets to keep him and is even paid to care for him (v. 9)!"

⁴⁸ The issue of plundering resurfaces in the book of Esther, as discussed by Sidnie White Crawford, "The Book of Esther: Introduction, Commentary, and Reflections," pp. 855–941 in *The New Interpreter's Bible*, Vol. 3 (Nashville: Abingdon, 1999) 899: Esther 3:13 "gives the content of the decree sent throughout the empire by the efficient

unnamed sister carries more influence with the princess than the all-powerful father, there are grounds for suggesting that the potentate of Egypt is satirically undermined once again by those agents whom he does not regard as a serious threat: "Three different daughters play a role in delivering Moses from death, and the word 'daughter' occurs six times in this part of the story. Certainly our attention is being drawn to the ironic connection between Pharaoh's intent to spare the daughters and the fact that a succession of daughters, the last being his own, contributes to his undoing."[49]

Ackerman's notion of Pharaoh contributing to his own undoing stems from the proviso—twice enunciated in Exod 1:16 and again in Exod 1:22—that allows the daughters to live even as the sons are doomed to destruction. It remains opaque as to why the king includes this exemption clause, but it brings to mind a comparable example in 1 Kings 1: the miscalculation of Adonijah. Clinging to the horns of the altar is an unenviable state of existence, but when he is outwitted in his quest for the throne of David by Solomon's supporters, Adonijah has few options but to plea for amnesty. He asks his brother for an oath, but his language in 1 Kings 1:51 includes an oddly pharaonic qualification: "Let King Solomon swear an oath to me today that he will not put his servant to death *with the sword*" (italics mine). In the tense atmosphere of 1 Kings 1 Adonijah might be forgiven for overlooking a trivial detail that would have been caught by any reasonably trained lawyer: he may not have been wise to add "with the sword," for there are countless other ways that an enemy can be dispatched apart from the drawn sword. Maybe Adonijah was using "with the sword" as a synecdoche for any kind of death, but clinging to the horns of the altar is not an ideal time or place to engage in the complex semiotics of literary criticism. Be that as it may, Solomon does not swear any oath whatsoever, and Adonijah in short order

---

Persian postal system. The Hebrew piles up words of destruction: 'to destroy,' 'to slay,' 'to annihilate.' All Jews are to be destroyed—men, women, children, young, old—no one is exempt. And then, the final indignity: Their goods are to be plundered. This is both a foreshadowing of events to come and a reminiscence of the paradigmatic salvific event, the exodus. At the time of the exodus, when the Jews were saved, they took the goods of the Egyptians, who gave them voluntarily in order to be saved from destruction (Exod 12:33-36)." Although the Jews are later allowed to plunder their enemies in Esther 8:11, the reader notices that such plundering does *not* occur (9:10-16). Cf. Levenson, *Esther*, 122.

[49] Ackerman, "The Literary Context of the Moses Birth Story," 95.

becomes the occupant of an early grave, paying a steep price for his qualification "with the sword" and related underestimations of Solomon's rapacity. The new king of Egypt likewise pays for his miscalculation, for just as there are other ways of dying, so there is no shortage of daughters in Exod 1:16–2:10 to wreak havoc on his malevolent designs. Still, the duration is quite different from Adonijah in 1 Kings, who fairly quickly realizes his error when Benaiah shows up in the guise of an assassin (1 Kings 2:25). The eventual undermining of Pharaoh's house takes much longer, but based on his initial paranoia in Exod 1:10 ("lest they fight against us and go up from the land") is just as lethal: "In brief, thanks to Pharaoh's daughter a man grows up and is being trained who later on will turn out to be Pharaoh's great opponent and who will make his fear (1:10) come true."[50] The king's daughter eschews his command but unhesitatingly implements the suggestion of the young Israelite woman, and so the word of the sister trumps the decree of the monarch. When the sister then fetches the mother, we note that the daughter of Levi—who recently placed her son in the reeds at the edge of the Nile—is allowed to nurse her son who was supposed to have been drowned. The undermining of the king then reaches an entirely new level in Exod 2:10 when the mother delivers the boy to the princess of Egypt according to the terms of the contract:

> The child grew up, so she brought him to Pharaoh's daughter, and he became a son to her. She called his name "Moses," and said, "Because from the water I drew him out."

The nurse given the most attention in Genesis is Deborah, the nurse (מינקת) of Rebekah, although few details are disclosed. Deborah is presumably the nurse who accompanies Rebekah when she relocates to Canaan in order to marry Isaac (Gen 24:59, but not mentioned by name), and whose death is recorded with notable specificity in Gen 35:8: "Then Deborah, Rebekah's nurse, died, and was buried under an oak below Bethel, and so it was called Allon-Bacuth (Oak of Weeping)." Any conclusions are necessarily tentative, but on the basis of these texts it might be suggested that nurses are honored members of a community and assume a kind of familial status, to the point that a reasonably elaborate funeral is noted in Genesis. On this curious

---

[50] Houtman, *Exodus I*, 290.

report about Deborah, Terence Fretheim avers that the text "provides striking testimony to the memory of a faithful servant that lives on in the community of faith. Amid all the great movements of these major ancestral figures, the author includes a note about 'little' people, who are more important in the larger story than one typically appreciates."[51] In Exodus 2, however, the contracted nurse is also the boy's mother, receiving a wage for what a mother normally does *pro bono*. But like a nurse, the mother ultimately is a provisional service-provider, and eventually delivers the lad to Pharaoh's daughter as she had previously instructed. A number of scholars suggest that when the boy becomes a son to the princess, there is a more formal exchange taking place: "The contract of wages would have likely indicated to the ancient audience that the boy had become legally adopted."[52] If the boy is legally adopted, so to speak, there is an implosion of Pharaoh's decree triggered by a member of his own household, into which a Hebrew male has now arrived. The adoption of the son in some ways reflects God's adoption of Israel, and the rescue of the lad from the waters of chaos is a precursor to the rescue of the nation at the edge of the Sea.[53]

An abundance of scholarly resources have been invested in deciphering the naming-speech of Exod 2:10, as Pharaoh's daughter provides both a name for her new son and a gloss on the meaning of the name. Starting with Eve in Gen 4:1, the maternal naming-speech is a genre of its own and widely attested in the Hebrew Bible. An apt comparison for our purposes is Hannah in 1 Sam 1:20, a formerly barren wife who miraculously becomes a mother: "When the days came around, Hannah conceived, and gave birth to a son. She called his name Samuel (שמואל) because 'from the LORD I asked (שאל) for him.'" Hannah's birth narrative occurs in the context of Israel's laborious transition to kingship, and following the contours of the type-scene of the barren wife, she delivers the nation's inaugural king-maker, the prophet Samuel. Yet her naming-speech has long bothered scholars because of the perceived dissonance between the name of the child ("name[d] of God") and the explanation of the name by Hannah (the verb *ask* is the root of the name *Saul*). The apparent

---

[51] Fretheim, "The Book of Genesis," 586.
[52] Lohr, *Chosen and Unchosen*, 124, citing Childs, "The Birth of Moses," 113–14.
[53] Cf. Propp, *Exodus 1–18*, 154: "one might regard Pharaoh's daughter as symbolizing God himself, who rescues Israel from the waters and claims him as his son."

confusion has led some to posit that a naming-speech for Saul—whose birth is otherwise unrecorded—has mistakenly found its way into this pericope.[54] It could be countered, however, that Hannah's naming-speech is tightly integrated into the larger storyline, as her stress on *asking* forms a segue to the people asking for a king in 1 Samuel 8, a request that the elders of Israel direct to her own son, Samuel. From the outset, therefore, Samuel the prophet and Saul the king are intertwined in the narrative, and this naming-speech of the triumphant mother forms an introduction to the birth of kingship in the nation. Although Hannah's discourse in 1 Sam 1:20 is only one example, it is possible to infer that maternal naming-speeches can be an important index for the character of the mother as well as the role of her offspring in the forthcoming plot.[55]

Like Eve and Hannah, Pharaoh's daughter bestows a name on her newly acquired son that helps illumine her character and hint at looming plot developments. The absence of any proper name so far in Exodus 2 lends a climactic air to the naming-speech of Moses (משה). Recent events of finding the lad and drawing him from the river are summarized in the explanation of the name, further illustrated in a poetic text such as 2 Sam 22:17, "He sent from on high and

---

[54] Note the discussions in P. Kyle McCarter, *I Samuel: A New Translation with Introduction and Commentary* (AB 8; Garden City: Doubleday, 1980) 62–6; and Robert Alter, *The David Story: A Translation with Commentary of 1 & 2 Samuel* (New York: Norton, 1999) 6.

[55] A more subtle example—where it could be argued that the naming-speech is intentionally elided—is Bathsheba in 2 Sam 12:24, at least in the *qere* of the Masoretic Text: "David comforted his wife Bathsheba, went to her and lay with her. She gave birth to a son, and she named him Solomon. And the Lord loved him." The reason David comforts Bathsheba is because of the recent death of their son, an unnamed child who dies on account of David's transgressions that procure the murder of Uriah and cover-up of the prior adultery. If the name Solomon (שלמה) means "his replacement," then it would be natural to infer that the new son is understood by Bathsheba to be a substitute for the deceased child (cf. Steven Weitzman, *Solomon: The Lure of Wisdom* [New Haven: Yale University Press, 2011] 6–10). Even so, in light of Solomon's future career as the replacement for David on the throne of David—an office secured in no small way by the deft politicking of Bathsheba herself in 1 Kings 1–2. When viewed from this broader perspective, the mother's naming without any accompanying speech turns out to be rather more than one may have expected, and highlights Bathsheba as an intriguing character in the drama just as it anticipates Solomon's eventual path to the throne as David's successor in the heated cauldron of the Jerusalem court.

took me, he drew me out (משה) from the mighty waters."[56] Since the princess is not the one who actually pulls the boy out of the water—in Exod 2:5 she sent her maidservant to fetch the ark—the naming-speech may be a more capacious testimony. Cornelis Houtman suggests that when Pharaoh's daughter asserts that she drew the boy out of the water, it "was in effect her way of saying that she had gone against the order of her father."[57] If this is plausible, the naming-speech itself is an act of defiance in the same vein as the midwives in chapter 1 or the mother of the boy defying the king's edict in chapter 2. By delivering the boy from the perils of the Nile, the princess not only rescues him but also "models for Moses his forthcoming role. The daughter of Pharaoh aligns herself with the daughters of Israel. She breaks filial allegiance, crosses clan lines, and obliterates racial and political differences."[58] From her point of view, the name enshrines the memory, but for the reader the name also looks ahead. It was noted earlier that naming-speeches are not particularly easy to translate or immediately understand; indeed, if I had to render Gen 4:1, it would be "I have forged a man with the LORD" (קניתי איש את־יהוה). On such challenges, Benno Jacob's caution is appropriate: "Whenever a Biblical name is followed by the phrase 'then (she) spoke,' the explanation is not intended to be etymological. It is a phonetic explanation meant to remind of a particular event." Jacob concludes: "Parents have never been interested in etymology."[59] As it turns out, the name Moses can be interpreted as a sophisticated hybrid wordplay that has two distinct but interwoven linguistic fields:

---

[56] Brueggemann ("The Book of Exodus," 700) notes that the wider poetic context of 2 Sam 22:17 (cf. Ps 18:16) includes other verbs of deliverance and salvation, and hence the verb to "draw out" is "used with reference to God's mighty acts of rescue. What may be a royal Egyptian name is transposed by the proposed etymology into Israelite praise for deliverance. Thus the rescue of little Moses from the waters anticipates a larger rescue to be wrought through the power of Moses." Cf. Ilana Pardes, *The Biography of Ancient Israel: National Narratives in the Bible* (Berkeley: University of California Press, 2002) 17: "Moses is a national leader whose history blends with the history of the nation. He is one of many Hebrew babies persecuted by Pharaoh. His story, however, is marked as the exemplary account that sheds light on the collective birth story as it prefigures the deliverance of the nation as a whole from bondage."

[57] Houtman, *Exodus I*, 268.

[58] Lohr, *Chosen and Unchosen*, 130, citing Trible, "The Pilgrim Bible on a Feminist Journey," *Princeton Seminary Bulletin* 11 (1990) 238.

[59] Jacob, *The Second Book of the Bible: Exodus*, 32.

an Egyptian word for "born/son" and a Hebrew verb "to pull out." Nahum Sarna provides a detailed overview:

> The Hebrew name is of Egyptian origin. Its basic verbal stem *msy* means "to be born," and the noun *ms* means "a child, son." It is a frequent element in Egyptian personal names, usually but not always with the addition of a divine element, as illustrated by Ahmose, Ptahmose, Ramose, and Thotmose. Two papyri from the time of Ramses II mention officials named Mose.... The Narrator puts a Hebrew origin for the name into the mouth of the Egyptian princess; unbeknown to her, it foreshadows the boy's destiny. By means of a word play, the Egyptian Mose is connected with Hebrew *m-sh-h*, "to draw up/out (of water)." The princess explains the name as though the form is *mashui*, 'the one drawn out,' a passive participle, whereas it is actually an active participle, "he who draws out," and becomes an oblique reference to the future crossing of the Sea of Reeds.[60]

Apart from aesthetic delight, one of the central functions of a wordplay in the Hebrew Bible is that it can signal to the reader an impending reversal of fortune.[61] By means of this (adopted) son drawn from the waters and rescued from drowning by the princess, the Egyptian royal house will experience a stunning reversal when the boy who survived the waters of the Nile leads his people through the Red Sea and the later Pharaoh is drowned. More than an individual deliverance, the nation of Israel will be rescued, and thus the extraction of Moses becomes a paradigmatic anticipation of what God will do for the descendants of Abraham: extracting them from the chaos of slavery in order to begin a long journey through sand and stone toward the ancestral promise of their homeland. The wordplay on the name of Moses operates as a preface to a larger drama: "Although an appellation relating to 'birth' and 'life' (as with the Egyptian one) would be most fitting for the narrative and follows logically from an analysis of the episode's plot and characterization, the narrator hooks a meaning upon the root that foreshadows the life of this somewhat ambiguous child. As one

---

[60] Sarna, *Exodus*, 10. For an anticipation of the dual movement toward Sinai, see Mark S. Smith, with contributions by Elizabeth M. Bloch-Smith, *The Pilgrimage Pattern in Exodus* (JSOTSup 239; Sheffield: Sheffield Academic Press, 1997) 228: "both Moses and Israel were viewed as moving from the threatening waters to the mountain. In Moses' case these waters are the waters of the Nile while for the Israelites they are the waters of the Reed Sea."

[61] Wilfred G. E. Watson, *Classical Hebrew Poetry* (JSOTSup 26; Sheffield: JSOT Press, 1986) 246.

who was 'drawn out,' he also will 'draw out,' in the impending contest between the forces of Pharaoh and Israel's descendants at the Exodus event."[62] The naming-speech at the conclusion of the scene also draws the reader back to the beginning of the episode in Exod 2:1. Before the bestowal of the proper name Moses, the Levite ancestry of the child is provided, so it may not be a stretch to suggest that the Levites themselves will play a role in extracting Israel from chaos, drawing the people from the waters of tyranny by maintaining the sanctuary as a reminder of how God continues to subdue the waters of chaos. The naming of Moses therefore encapsulates the wider plot of the story in a number of creative ways. But on a more somber note, several commentators mention a later naming-event by an Egyptian authority figure.[63] Long after the liberation from Egyptian slavery—at the twilight of the kingdom of Judah—Pharaoh Neco dethrones Jehoahaz from the Davidic seat in 2 Kings 23:24 and replaces him with Eliakim. However, upon installing Eliakim Neco renames him Jehoiakim in an act of muscle-flexing hubris (cf. Nebuchadrezzar's renaming of Zedekiah in 2 Kings 24:17). Yet the naming of Moses belongs to a different category, not least because his parents are not recorded as bestowing any name, so Exod 2:10 is not an attempt to rebrand as with Eliakim/Jehoiakim or even perhaps Joseph in Gen 41:45 (given the name Zaphenath-paneah). When Pharaoh's daughter names the child it is one more act of defiance in this sector of Exodus, and inexorably points to the future inundation of Egyptian leadership in the waters of chaos in an ironic reversal of the attempt to drown the hope of Israel. The princess takes the side of the oppressed in this story, much like her adopted son will do in the next phase of the narrative.

---

[62] Paul E. Hughes, "Moses' Birth Story: A Biblical Matrix for Prophetic Messianism," pp. 10–22 in *Eschatology, Messianism, and the Dead Sea Scrolls*, edited by Craig A. Evans and Peter W. Flint (Studies in the Dead Sea Scrolls and Related Literature; Grand Rapids: Eerdmans, 1997) 21. For another angle on the naming, see Nohrnberg, *Like Unto Moses*, 135: "The birth story is otherwise largely determined by its mediation of the Hebrew/Egyptian polarity found in the child's dual extraction: Moses is alternatively and alternately Moshe. In Hebrew, he is drawn out of Egypt. In Egyptian, he is born of the Hebrews. Moses' singularity is his duality, a Hebrew Egyptian and an Egyptian Hebrew. The interface points to the almost constitutive role the royal house will have in Moses' vocation."

[63] Hamilton, *Exodus*, 23; Jacob, *The Second Book of the Bible: Exodus*, 34.

5

Criminal Charges

> *Like Othello killing the malignant Turk, the violence of the Egyptian provokes the reciprocal violence of Moses; but as with Othello at the end of his play, it is also a violence against something in himself. For to violence Moses has added stealth. He looks both ways, murders in secret, and hides the body, in effect "man-steals" it. Moses seems to break the sixth commandment, but also eight, nine, or ten, if we think of them as forbidding the furtive or dishonest action. Moses is similarly compromised by the second episode, where he tries to stand back from abuses, rather than fall into repeating them. But Moses cannot get away with murder, without also flying from its scene—yet even after his getaway to Midian, the scene of violence comes back to him.*
>
> James Nohrnberg[1]

The machination of the midwives allowed for further Israelite expansion in Egypt, but it is a temporary measure that is soon obviated by Pharaoh's pronouncement of death by drowning for every Israelite male in the final sentence of Exodus 1. Yet in spite of this menacing decree, the next chapter begins with a Levite father's quiet defiance and evident determination to continue the growth of his own family in oppressive circumstances, even as his new son is born under a death sentence. The father is not formally heard from again in the episode, but the Levite mother assumes a central role when she

---

[1] Nohrnberg, *Like Unto Moses*, 166. The reference is to *Othello* 5.2; for one example of how the scene has been performed in the past, see Marvin Rosenberg, *The Masks of Othello: The Search for the Identity of Othello, Iago, and Desdemona by Three Centuries of Actors and Critics* (Berkeley: University of California Press, 1961) 66.

protects her child from drowning by preparing a waterproof papyrus ark. As discussed at length in the preceding chapter, Exodus 2 is the only other place where the word *ark* (תבה) appears in the Hebrew Bible outside of the Noah story in Genesis. By means of this allusion the reader associates the violence in the days of Noah with the slavery imposed by the king of Egypt, and the rescue of Noah foreshadows initially the rescue of the boy, to be followed in due course by the rest of Israel. More than a boat, Noah's ark is a floating sanctuary that bears a striking resemblance to a later Israelite worship installation, and so in Exodus 2 it is fitting that the child floating in an ark will play a major role in planning and building the sanctuary in the wilderness that enables Israel to spiritually navigate the waters of chaos after liberation from Egypt.[2] Indeed, when the mother places the infant among the reeds of the Nile river where he is subsequently retrieved by Pharaoh's daughter in a stunning reversal of expectation, the events operate as a foretaste of the nation's rescue by God at the edge of the Re(e)d Sea by the hand of the very child hidden in the ark. In Exod 2:4 the boy's sister was perched at a distance watching the events transpire. It appeared to be merely an incidental notice until her moment in the story comes after Pharaoh's daughter extracts the lad and perceives some clue as to his Hebrew identity. On the one hand, when the princess says, "From the children of the Hebrews is this one," it inaugurates a debate over identity in the story that becomes a crisis in Exod 2:14–15 as we will shortly see. On the other hand, the exclamation of the princess is a cue for the sister to seize the moment, and, with a well-timed question, the amazing narrative of the boy's unlikely survival approaches a climax: the young woman is duly commissioned to recruit a nurse—her and the boy's mother as it happens—and eventually when he is returned to the princess he is called *Moses*, a hybrid nameplay fusing the Egyptian term for born/son with a Hebrew verb "to draw out." The rescue and naming of Moses ("he who draws out") can be interpreted as a paradigm for the rescue of Israel, both in the immediate horizon of the book of Exodus and beyond, as Walter Brueggemann concludes:

---

[2] Gabriel Josipovici, *The Book of God: A Response to the Bible* (New Haven: Yale University Press, 1988) 98: "The building of the Ark by Noah provides us with what is perhaps the closest parallel to the later making of the elaborate tent."

The last phrase of v. 10 sounds and anticipates the desperate petitions and the glad thanks of Israel for the many rescues made in its life... This is a people who always live under the threat of chaos, always about to be inundated by the chaotic waters, helpless lest the Lord of chaos act and intervene. Thus the story of Moses is paradigmatic for Israel's life and faith. It not only anticipates the exodus narrative, but it also resonates with the deepest spirituality of Israel, a practice of plea and praise, of need and hope.[3]

Any such liberation and praise, however, will need to be kept in a holding-pattern for the time being, as the various scenes in Exod 2:11–15 illustrate, and to where our attention now turns. As the rescue of the infant foreshadows the eventual rescue of the nation, so some early incidents in the adult life of Moses anticipate some of the vicissitudes of his career as Israel's leader in the days ahead. But compared to the previous scenes of the ark and its retrieval, the next scenes in vv. 11–15 are much less charming as the grim realities of slavery and ill-treatment return as the central frame in the narrative point of view. Moses quickly emerges as the main character of the story, and in this section of the narrative there is a movement from the palace of Egypt to his liminal status as an exile in Midian. This geographical shift is precipitated by two related incidents: Moses' murder of an Egyptian and his tense confrontation with a fellow Israelite, followed by Pharaoh's discovery of his crime. In terms of the characterization of Moses, the significance of these scenes is perhaps crystallized in his question to the Israelite in v. 13: "why would you strike your neighbor?" It could be argued that this (unresolved) question lingers over the entire narrative, and given the preponderance of legal material later in the career of Moses, this question posed to the one "in the wrong" will be probed. Moreover, the flight to Midian is also analyzed at length, as it seems to be a major setback in the story, and resembles a frustrating moment down the road in Exod 5:23 when Moses himself complains to God: "From the time I went to Pharaoh to speak in your name, he has brought evil to this people, and you have certainly *not* delivered them!" So it may be true that the buoyancy of the previous episode in Exod 2:1–10 is followed by a more somber interlude in vv. 11–15, but by no means should this material be overlooked, especially when Moses sits down

---

[3] Brueggemann, "The Book of Exodus," 701.

by a well at the end of v. 15. Since several other biblical figures similarly have a fortuitous encounter at a well of water (Gen 24:11; 29:2; cf. 1 Sam 9:11; John 4:4–26), there is cause for modest optimism in the story, and the reason for sanguinity is introduced as this chapter draws to a close: the well of water sets the stage for a *typescene* that operates as a sign whereby God's past promise is poised to be reactivated in the storyline.

GROWING PAINS

When the Levite mother delivers her son to Pharaoh's daughter, presumably he is weaned and a reasonably young child. But the next section of the story in Exod 2:11a begins with a rapid acceleration to the adult life of Moses: "In those days Moses grew up, and he went out to his brothers, and saw them with their heavy burdens." Bypassing the younger period of Moses' life, Scott Langston reports that "the biblical author left a vacuum that subsequent readers have filled to a variety of purposes."[4] Using diverse forms of media such as the novelistic canvas or modern cinema, there is no shortage of speculative attempts—both contemporary and ancient—to fill this lacuna by reconstructing or imagining the early life of Moses in the Egyptian royal court.[5] Some questions are intriguing: does Pharaoh ever find out about his daughter's activity, and is he aware that Moses—the name could act as a convenient cover—is actually a Hebrew drawn from the water in defiance of his edict? Despite the

---

[4] Langston, *Exodus through the Centuries*, 35.

[5] For discussions of topics such as Thomas Mann's *The Tables of the Law* and films such as *The Prince of Egypt*, see Brian Britt, *Rewriting Moses: The Narrative Eclipse of the Text* (JSOTSup 402; London: T & T Clark, 2004). Ronald Hendel (*The Book of Genesis: A Biography* [Princeton: Princeton University Press, 2013] 7) has an illuminating quotation from Frank Kermode (*The Uses of Error and Other Essays* [Cambridge, MA: Harvard University Press, 1991] 4): "The history of interpretation, the skills by which we keep alive in our minds the light and the dark of past literature and past humanity, is to an incalculable extent a history of error.... The history of biblical interpretation will provide many instances of fruitful misunderstanding. It arises because we want to have more of the story than was originally offered, or we want to see into the depths of that story. We have always been pretty sure that the literal sense is not enough, and when we try to go beyond it we may err, but sometimes splendidly."

enticing diversion offered by such inquiries, for the purposes of this study it will be submitted that the reader's energy is best directed at what happens in v. 11, events that quickly become a turning-point in the story. A lack of interest in the youthful experiences of Moses is implied by a repetition of the verb "grew up" (ויגדל): the boy grows up in v. 10 and is brought to the princess for adoption, and "grows up" again in v. 11, where the story now continues.[6] Furthermore, it was suggested above that the early life and career of Moses are typologically configured to represent some of the experiences of Israel as a nation, so it is hard to understand how any prolonged exposition of his adolescence could advance such a literary trope, other than to satisfy the curious. Having said that, Moses must be aware of his Hebrew provenance—it is uncertain how exactly he knows about his ethnicity, but circumcision may be a factor—because he ventures out of the palace to "his brothers." Given the mother who nursed him and the princess who rescued him, the reader ought not to be overly surprised that Moses knows that the Hebrews are his brothers, and seeing them suffer under heavy burdens must awaken or heighten his empathy. The same term for heavy burdens (סבלות) is used earlier in Exod 1:11 at the outset of Israel's enslavement to describe the level of oppression. Not only does Moses witness their burdens, but in the second half of the verse (Exod 2:11b) he sees something else that alters the story dramatically:

> Then he saw an Egyptian man striking a Hebrew man, from his brothers.

A pair of thematic verbs is strategically deployed in the two halves of Exod 2:11, one that glances forward and the other that reflects back. First, when the older Moses "goes out" (יצא) from the Egyptian court to his brothers, it is preliminary to the larger "going out" of Israel to come: "In Exodus 3:10–12 the same verb is used three times when Moses, in the critical event at the burning bush, is commanded to bring Israel out of Egypt. Before he can lead others out of Egypt, however, it is necessary for him to go out from the royal court, and

---

[6] Cassuto, *A Commentary on the Book of Exodus*, 21. Cf. Michael Fishbane, *Text and Texture: Close Readings of Selected Biblical Texts* (New York: Schocken Books, 1979) 65: "Time is telescoped, actions are highly stylized, and Moses is portrayed from the start as linking his personal fate to that of his people."

finally, to flee from the land of Egypt."⁷ While there are a host of challenges and stumbling blocks still to come, this movement in a minor way represents the first step of departure. Meir Sternberg agrees that Moses' going forth "cunningly" stands for the people destined to go forth, but much has to transpire before any corporate departure: "Not only is the prophet still to be called, but his aliveness to peoplehood nonexistent and the prefigurative or typological nexus loose at best, soon indeed undone. His, even as a one-man affair, is a very restricted 'exodus,' since it implies an exploratory 'going out' from one's habitat toward the outside world, nothing like a break without any thought of return."⁸

The critical break with Egypt is much harder and takes much longer than anyone might expect—both for Moses personally and the Israelites corporately—but the process ostensibly is set in motion with the second thematic verb in Exod 2:11, "to see" (ראה). When Moses goes out to his brothers, he *sees* an act of violence against a Hebrew, and this verb was a keyword in the previous episode of Exod 2:1–10. When the Levite mother saw (ראה) that her son was good, it prompted her actions of preparing the ark and then placing it among the reeds of the Nile in defiance of the king's decree. When Pharaoh's daughter saw (ראה) the ark and discovered the Hebrew child, it led to her act of disregarding the edict of her father by rescuing and adopting the boy. Now in Exod 2:11 Moses sees the violence perpetrated against his brother, and likewise will be tempted to act in a way contrary to the will of Pharaoh.⁹ More specifically, he sees an unnamed Egyptian *striking* a Hebrew man. A fairly common verb that can be found approximately five hundred times in the Hebrew Bible, the next episode where the verb "to strike" (נכה) is used will be Exod 3:20, when God provides an assurance to Moses: "I will send forth my hand and I will strike (נכה) Egypt with all my wonders that

---

⁷ Ackerman, "The Literary Context of the Moses Birth Story," 98; cf. Utzschneider and Oswald, *Exodus 1–15*, 89: "Moses' personal departure from the hegemonic Egyptian milieu to some extent prefaces the departure of his people from Egyptian slavery."

⁸ Sternberg, *Hebrews Between Cultures*, 341. Since the verb also occurs in Exod 2:13, Davies (*Israel in Egypt*, 138) states: "The double יצא is thus a kind of 'non-Exodus,' and Moses' escape an 'anti-liberation.' It is a flight from the past rather than an advance towards its fruition, a necessity brought on by powerlessness and carried out in the ambivalence of irony."

⁹ Cf. J. Gerald Janzen, *Exodus* (Louisville: Westminster John Knox Press, 1997) 23.

I will perform in their midst, and after that he will send you out." God's striking of Egypt can later be interpreted as a form of retribution for the cruelty of slavery and its corollaries; although no reason for the beating nor any other details are given in the present context, there is no reason to think this is an isolated incident, even if physical aggression has not been described explicitly before. This is not the last time such violence occurs either: Egyptians beat Hebrews in Exod 5:14 when the Israelite supervisors responsible for ensuring the daily quotas are "struck" if the requisite number of bricks (without straw) is not supplied. In the immediate context of Exodus 2, the physical abuse of the Egyptian is significant because "the fate previously intended for the newborn males is now being visited upon adult males."[10] On the two occasions when Moses is *seen* by his mother and Pharaoh's daughter, he is the object of compassion; now he *sees*, and his emotive yet calculated reaction to the beating of the Hebrew proves equally momentous to the overall storyline.

STRIKE OUT

In recent scenes Pharaoh and his accomplices "emerge as less than the powerful overlords they presume to be," but in this next installment of the story no women are present, and no power is subverted as in earlier episodes involving the midwives, the Levite mother and sister, or the princess of Egypt.[11] As mentioned above, the details of the physical abuse meted out by the Egyptian are sparse, with no cause or vocational rank ascribed. On the identity of the assailant, William Propp cites Rashi's inference that one of the corvée masters first introduced in Exod 1:11 must be the perpetrator: "This may be so," Propp responds, "but the aggressor is called simply 'an Egyptian man.' The author is not primarily depicting the relationship between slaves and their bosses, but between Israel and Egypt."[12] From Moses' point of view, the Egyptian man is attacking one of his brothers, and

---

[10] Ackerman, "The Literary Context of the Moses Birth Story," 99.
[11] Melissa Jackson, *Comedy and Feminist Interpretation of the Hebrew Bible: A Subversive Collaboration* (Oxford Theological Monographs; Oxford: Oxford University Press, 2012) 79.
[12] Propp, *Exodus 1–18*, 166.

this relational dynamic is what prompts him to furtively respond to the power inequity in Exod 2:12:

> He turned this way and that, and saw that no one was around. So he struck the Egyptian, and hid him in the sand.

Various theories have been proffered as to why Moses turns and looks around earnestly before launching his counterstrike. Robert Alter duly notes a long-standing tradition that Moses is glancing around to see if anyone else is set to intervene, and therefore he will not have to.[13] This proposal is well-meaning enough—Alter describes such a reading as somewhat apologetic—but the more probable deduction is that Moses searches around in preparation for his own deed: are there any witnesses to the crime he is about to commit? If the interpreter follows this line, it implies a measure of premeditation, and that when he strikes, it is with lethal intent. When the midwives acted against Pharaoh and the Egyptians, it was through deception, but Moses turns the tables: "Whereas previously violence was implicit in the oppression of Israel and in the genocidal policies of the Pharaoh towards the Hebrews, here the differentiation between Egyptian and Israelite/Hebrew is explicitly drawn in blood. And the victim, interestingly, is not an Israelite or a Hebrew but an Egyptian."[14] It should be underscored at this point that Moses "sees that no one was there" (וירא כי אין איש), and the reader is certainly entitled to take this seriously, as Moses is known for his keen eyesight (e.g., Deut 34:7, "Moses was one hundred twenty years old when he died: his eyes had not gone dim and his vigor had not fled").[15] In all likelihood, Moses was looking around for another Egyptian who would either sound the alarm or likewise intervene to save his fellow Egyptian like Moses was saving the Hebrew. With a sad irony, Moses therefore misses what should be the real source of his anxiety, the beaten Israelite who may well betray him in the end or reveal the secret. In other words, the text makes it clear that there is only one witness to Moses' crime, an important notion that we will return to below.

In practical terms, it can be assumed that Moses buries the body of the slain Egyptian to cover up the evidence of his crime. The action of

---

[13] Alter, *The Five Books of Moses*, 314.
[14] Greifenhagen, *Egypt on the Pentateuch's Ideological Map*, 63–4.
[15] On the identical phrase (וירא כי אין איש) occurring in Isa 59:16 as a probable justification of Moses, see Greenberg, *Understanding Exodus*, 38.

hiding carries with it some residual effect from the earlier episode where Moses himself was hidden, and perhaps into the present moment as well where he is still conceivably hiding something from Pharaoh: this murder to be sure, but also perhaps his Hebrew identity (or willingness to identify with the Hebrews over and against the Egyptians). In Chapter 3 of this book it was noted that the particular verb used for Moses' hiding/burying (טמן) the corpse is also found in Josh 2:6 in the flashback description of Rahab's hiding the two spies from the Jericho authorities. Concealing the spies is clearly a guilty act, and scanning several other uses of the same verb in the primary history of Genesis–2 Kings, some common traits emerge. In Gen 35:4 Jacob buries the foreign gods found in the family circle as though ridding the community of its accumulated guilt in harboring such deities before continuing their journey. Achan son of Carmi admits to contravening the ban in Josh 7:21 by hiding plunder from the invasion of Jericho in the ground under his tent, and after his confession the stolen articles are recovered and the thief faces a steep penalty. Finally, the four lepers of 2 Kings 7:8 had walked into the Aramean camp in order to surrender during the siege of Samaria, only to find the camp deserted and intact. Hardly believing the cache they have discovered, the lepers frantically hide valuable items before the pricks of conscience set in, and they report their findings to the royal palace. In each of these cases where *hiding* occurs there is a knowing violation or act of defiance; when Moses buries the body in the sand, he joins this company of characters who all have something to hide from their superiors. Yet there is no guarantee of success when hiding or burying something. Rahab gets away with it and survives the invasion of Jericho, and the four lepers become unsung heroes in the story of 2 Kings 7. But Achan son of Carmi disturbingly does not depart the narrative unscathed, as he and entire family along with their possessions are destroyed in Josh 7:24–5. In the case of Moses, the act of hiding can be partially understood as an element of his maternal inheritance: "Both Moses and his mother hide something from Pharaoh. She is doubly successful because her child ends up taking refuge in the oppressor's own court. Moses fails to the same degree because it is another Hebrew who threatens him by abusing information that he saved a fellow-sufferer from assault."[16] Although the midwives are

---

[16] Davies, *Israel in Egypt*, 131.

not recorded as hiding any particular object from Pharaoh, Moses is now in their company as far as acting against Pharaoh and the mechanisms of slavery. But as we will discuss below, Moses might be able to conceal the evidence, but his crime will still be found out even if the body is never recovered.

From ancient to modern times, a dizzying array of interpretations surround Moses' killing, ranging from heroic adulation to moralistic condemnation to puzzled ambivalence, interpretations that alternate between justifying the use of violence to disappointment with the outburst of temper.[17] Because the text is virtually silent on the matter—if the narrator passes any judgment on the deed in Exodus 2, it is nearly impossible to find—interpreters have valiantly striven to fill the gap. But if the reader appreciates that the text is intentionally terse, there are two kinds of highly provisional conclusions that can be submitted. First, the reader should not expect that Moses' action will lead to a slave revolt, and any liberation for Israel will not come through a popular uprising or similar acts of violence. In fact, it is notable how *unsuccessful* the murder is, and it accomplishes little in the larger scheme of the story. Commentators have routinely maintained that the striking by Moses anticipates the plagues against Egypt to come, but there are also some substantial differences between the later divine signs and this clandestine action of murder and hiding. Second, through the action of striking the Egyptian and rescuing the assaulted Hebrew, several of Moses' character traits are communicated to the reader. Consequently, his initial appearance as an opponent of injustice is a positive harbinger of his judicial role in the nation.

Less positively, this is not the last time that striking (נכה) is associated with Moses: in Numbers 20:1-13 there is an controversial occurrence where Moses is once more the subject of the verb *to strike*. During the long march in the wilderness en route to the promised land after the departure from Egypt and setting out from Mount Sinai, the people gather in opposition and complain to Moses about the lack of water in the desert. Along with Aaron, God instructs Moses to speak (דבר) to a certain rock, and it will pour forth its

---

[17] Note the surveys and discussions in Langston, *Exodus through the Centuries*, 35-7; Coats, *Moses*, 49-50; Louis H. Feldman, "Josephus' Portrait of Moses," *JQR* 82 (1992) 285-328. On the actions of Moses as a centerpiece of Stephen's speech in Acts 7 and in different ways in Hebrews 11:24-8, see Childs, *Exodus*, 33-40, and "Moses' Slaying in the Theology of the Two Testaments," pp. 164-83 in *Biblical Theology in Crisis* (Philadelphia: Westminster, 1970).

water and therefore meet the demands of the community. The conduct of Moses in Numbers 20:10-11, however, is slightly different from God's orders: "Moses and Aaron assembled the community at the face of the rock, and he said to them, 'Listen up you rebels, should we bring out water for you from this rock?' Then Moses raised his hand, and he struck (נכה) the rock with his staff twice, and an abundance of water came forth, and the congregation was satisfied, along with their livestock." Despite a satisfactory finale after yet another instance of grumbling amidst the scarce resources, the episode proves less beneficial for Moses himself, because striking the rock disbars him from the promised land: "The LORD said to Moses and Aaron, 'Because you did not trust in me enough to sanctify me before the eyes of the Israelites, therefore you will not bring this assembly into the land that I have given them.'"[18] No consensus has been formed as far as interpreting the striking of the rock in Numbers, but a case can be made that striking the Egyptian in Exodus 2 has some eerie similarities. Again, there is no outright condemnation for the murder given by the narrator, but if the act of temper anticipates the striking of the rock in Numbers, then it stands to reason that the violence does not lead to a successful outcome. Striking the Egyptian is also enveloped in some irony, since Moses and Pharaoh now have something in common: "Although Moses seeks to liberate Hebrews, his first act as an adult is a violent murder performed in secret, recalling the private instructions of Pharaoh toward the midwives."[19] Pharaoh's attempted infanticide fails in its larger purpose, and the murder by Moses arguably does not accomplish much that is positive in the larger framework, even if the Hebrew slave that is bludgeoned in Exod 2:11 may have cause for gratitude.

FRATERNAL STRIFE

Leah's third son through Jacob is born in Gen 29:34, and his long-suffering mother calls him Levi (לוי) in her optimistic naming-speech:

---

[18] On the translation and implications of *trust*, see Adriane Leveen, *Memory and Tradition in the Book of Numbers* (Cambridge: Cambridge University Press, 2008) 53-4. Compare Exod 17:1-7 where Moses *is* commanded to strike the rock, and does so.

[19] Dozeman, *Exodus*, 87.

"Now this time my husband will be joined (לוה) to me, for I have borne him three children."[20] As a character, Levi bursts into prominence through acts of stealth and violence in Gen 34:25-9 when Simeon and his younger brother Levi visit retribution on the son of Hamor and the Shechemites for the rape of their sister Dinah.[21] Murdering the Shechemites while they are still in pain from the surgery of circumcision raises the ire of Jacob, who upbraids Simeon and Levi by pointing to his vulnerable status in the region and the potential fallout from their massacre. Ignoring this public-relations fiasco, the brothers respond with a question that underscores the larger issue of justice at stake ("Should our sister be treated like a harlot?" [הכזונה יעשה את־אחותנו]), and this query is never answered by Jacob and thus lingers even as the episode draws to a close. It is hard to know to what degree this question and the brothers' conduct influences Jacob's tribal prognostication in Gen 49:5-7, but his speech is fraught with reference to violence, the sword, anger, curse, and ferocity. It may not be a stretch to infer that Moses inherits this incendiary temperament in the presence of injustice—it should also be noted that the sons of Levi put 3,000 to death in Exod 32:25-9 in the aftermath of the golden calf debacle—and there are some parallels between the reaction of Levi to Dinah's treatment and the strike of Moses on the Egyptian attacker of his brother.[22] Both Levi and Moses are responding to an injustice committed against their kin, and both act as enforcers for the defenseless by killing the perpetrator. But in

---

[20] Cf. Numbers 18:2, "Also bring with you your brothers of the tribe of Levi (לוי), your ancestral tribe, in order that they may be joined (לוה) to you, and serve you while you and your sons with you are in front of the tent of the covenant."

[21] Hamilton, *Exodus*, 30: "In so acting, Moses is repeating his ancestral heritage."

[22] Cf. John R. Spencer, "Levi," *ABD* 4:424: "The militaristic activities of Levi have often posed a problem for scholars, as they attempt to relate the warlike Levi with the assumed irenic priests, the Levites. However, if one takes into consideration the fact that Levi's military actions are always in defense of Yahweh and the correct worship of Yahweh, the fact that the 'sons of Levi,' the priestly Levites, often performed militaristic activities such as guarding the tent of meeting, and the fact that Hittite parallels in the ancient world indicate that it is not unusual for priests to carry on martial activities, then it is no longer troublesome to connect Levi and the priestly Levites. Indeed, it is the fervent defense of Yahweh which is the consistent and characteristic role of Levi and his descendants." Note also the more detailed studies of Mark Leuchter, "The Fightin' Mushites," *VT* 62 (2012) 479-500; and Joel S. Baden, "The Violent Origins of the Levites: Text and Tradition," pp. 103-16 in *Levites and Priests in Biblical History and Tradition*, edited by Mark Leuchter and Jeremy M. Hutton (Ancient Israel and Its Literature 9; Atlanta: Society of Biblical Literature, 2011).

the context of Canaanite political dynamics, Jacob takes issue with the attack by reminding Simeon and Levi that they are at a numerical disadvantage and could be obliterated if a military coalition is gathered against them. In the context of Egyptian slavery Moses seeks to defend his fellow Hebrew, but given their marginal status James Nohrnberg suggests that homicidal confrontation is not an ideal tactic: "Outside of any formal judicial structure or vocation, Moses begins his ministry by acting to police a world polarized into aggressors and victims; but his private intervention on behalf of abused parties only shows that the protection he offers is as much the protection he needs."[23] Since the next scene in Exod 2:13 continues the theme of violence with a startling inversion, it strongly implies that Moses' intervention created more problems than it solved, even if his motives were laudable:

> Then he went out on the second day, and behold, two Hebrew men fighting! He said to the guilty one, "Why are you striking your neighbour?"

Assorted reasons could be proposed for why Moses ventures out on the next day, since once again the laconic narrative provides only the barest of hints. A repetition of the same verb *go out* (יצא) may imply the same spatial setting as the previous day, as though he is returning to check out the crime scene.[24] Whether he is making sure the evidence of his murder remains hidden in the sand or if he is searching for another injustice to redress is not specified, nor is there any indication that he again plans to passionately intervene against further Egyptian brutality. Regardless of why Moses goes out again the day after his murder of the Egyptian assailant, there is a sense of utter bewilderment that is presented in the narrative. The visual perspective of Moses is refracted in v. 13 by means of the הנה particle that captures his viewpoint on the unfolding scene. Once more I have followed the venerable KJV in translating the particle as "behold," and although no English rendering is wholly adequate, in the context of Exod 2:13 this syntactical form "introduces a totally unexpected development" and his evident surprise at the sight of two brawling Hebrews.[25] For the second time in Exodus 2 a character's internal

---

[23] Nohrnberg, *Like Unto Moses*, 165.
[24] Houtman, *Exodus I*, 301: "The place where it happens is apparently the same as that in the earlier scene."
[25] Sarna, *Exodus*, 11; cf. Childs, *The Book of Exodus*, 30.

visual angle is presented in the story: first in Exod 2:6 when Pharaoh's daughter has an emotional reaction to the crying baby in the ark, and now with Moses as the narrative conveys his shocked response at the spectacle of his two kinfolk acting aggressively toward each other.[26] Moses may have been hoping that something changed—however modestly—after his intervention the day before, or if he was searching for another act of injustice to counter, his surprise is palpable: "Here is another act of oppression, the more heinous because victim and aggressor are compatriots."[27]

On the previous day when the Egyptian was beating the Hebrew, the reader can guess that a larger power inequity was at work: whether there was a punitive reason for the beating or if it was merely a random act of cruelty, the Hebrews are slaves, and periodic beatings from the overlords are quite likely a regular occurrence. In this next scene with the two Hebrews, though, there is no reason given as to why they are engaged in a *mêlée*. The particular verb that is used for fighting (נצה) is not overly common in the Hebrew Bible, but it seems to be a serious term that "denotes more than a quarrel which remains restricted to a verbal dispute; it is a scuffle that leads to or involves hitting the other; if no one interferes chances are great that one of the parties involved will kill the other."[28] A comparable case is 2 Sam 14:6 where the same verb is used for a fight among two brothers, as depicted by the allegedly bereaved mother in the presence of the king: "Your maidservant had two sons, but they fought (נצה) with each other in the field and there was no one to tear them apart. One struck the other, and he killed him." It should be said that 2 Sam 14:6 is part of a larger fiction concocted by Joab—who employs the wise woman of Tekoa in order to coax King David into bringing back Absalom from his northern refuge in Geshur and thus curtail further mischief from the handsome prince—but the verb for fighting is surely used in an accurate and realistic way to describe a struggle

---

[26] Davies, *Israel in Egypt*, 127: "Narratively, he comes upon the Hebrews fighting in the same way as the princess discovers the boy in the basket: והנה accompanies inward-scanning focalization and introduces free indirect discourse that uses a nominal construction headed by the subject. The event is described emphatically and synchronically just as Moses himself experienced it. Soon we learn too of his fears and further thoughts (v. 14)."

[27] Propp, *Exodus 1–18*, 167.   [28] Houtman, *Exodus I*, 302.

Criminal Charges 131

that ends in the death of one of the combatants.[29] If the reader had hoped that the oppression of slavery would create some solidarity among the Israelites, such hopes—and Moses is evidently feeling the same way—are dashed: "The promises in Genesis made us hope that the more the Egyptians oppressed the Hebrews, the more they would increase (1:12a–c). But nothing has prepared us for the image of Hebrews fighting each other."[30]

The physical intervention with the abusive Egyptian the day before did not include any verbal preliminaries from Moses, and no direct speech is recorded in Exod 2:11–12. But now with his own kinfolk he opts to persuade with words rather than force. Again, the exact cause of the altercation among the two Hebrews may not have been disclosed at the beginning of v. 13, but a clearer picture emerges by attending to the subject of Moses' address: instead of speaking to both parties in a general way, he begins with a specific appeal to the one *in the wrong* (רשע). The particular term used here also appears in accounts that involve some sort of legal dispute or quasi-judicial proceeding, and ironically, a helpful explication comes from the later Pharaoh in Exod 9:27. In the context of escalating signs and consistent recalcitrance, a massive hailstorm strikes the land of Egypt except for the region of Goshen where the Israelites reside, prompting Pharaoh to summon Moses and Aaron and offer the following confession: "I've sinned this time. The LORD is righteous and I and my people are the ones guilty of a crime (רשע)." A later legal example in the so-called Book of the Covenant in Exod 23:7 is also illuminating: "Keep your distance from a false charge, and do not kill the innocent or the righteous, for I will not acquit the guilty one (רשע)." These examples are helpful in understanding the nuances of the term, but it still does not answer the pressing question of Exod 2:13, "How did Moses know who was right or wrong?"[31] The important point may be that the discernment of Moses is the focus of the scene: he observes the situation and is able to determine the initiator of the fight or the one who is otherwise malfeasant. When he speaks, he directs his

---

[29] For a detailed overview of the allusion to the Cain/Abel fracas and of 2 Sam 14:1–20 reflecting the simmering rivalries among brothers in the Davidic court, see Larry L. Lyke, *King David with the Wise Woman of Tekoa: The Resonance of Tradition in Parabolic Narrative* (JSOTSup 255; Sheffield: Sheffield Academic Press, 1997).
[30] Davies, *Israel in Egypt*, 126.
[31] Jacob, *The Second Book of the Bible: Exodus*, 38.

address to the criminal, and by already making a judicial decision it foreshadows his legal role in the nation later in the story.

To the Hebrew in the wrong, Moses asks a question that never receives a direct response, and in a sense this question acts as a prologue for the legal material to come in the book of Exodus. Moses' inquiry is reminiscent of Pharaoh's interview with the midwives in Exod 1:18, when he asks them why (מדוע) they have let the Hebrew boys live. It was tentatively suggested earlier that the interrogative form employed by Pharaoh contains a request for information; alongside his anger he is also perplexed as to what has happened. When Moses addresses the guilty Hebrew, however, he uses a different word: "Why (למה) are you striking your neighbor?" Since he has already assessed that this Hebrew is in the wrong, Moses is hardly making a request for information. His question is a rebuke, and an opportunity for the guilty party to relinquish or at least acknowledge the deviant behavior. In Exod 5:4 Moses hears the same kind of question from the later Pharaoh, who refuses to acquiesce to their request for a three-day festival in the wilderness and accuses them of distracting the Israelite slaves: "Moses and Aaron, why (למה) are you causing the people to leave their work? Go to your burdens!" In both of these instances the question is loaded with rhetorical force, as Moses and Pharaoh are expressing a high degree of dissatisfaction with their respective interlocutors. Furthermore, Moses asks the guilty Hebrew why he is striking his neighbor/friend (רע), and this term connotes a relational bond that—at least in the mind of Moses—should rise above a petty squabble. It is as though he can understand why a Hebrew would be tempted to strike out against an Egyptian, but given the violence they must suffer as slaves to the Egyptians, why would even more abuse be piled on from among their own community? Assuming that the one "in the wrong" has started the fight, the use of *friend* enhances the rebuke, and it is not surprising that the theme of neighborly relations is a common occurrence in the legal portions of Exodus.

Robert Alter notes that the first spoken words of a major figure in biblical narrative can operate as a defining moment of characterization.[32] Combined with his opening actions of leaving the royal house

---

[32] In his discussion of Saul's first words ("Come, let's go back" [לכה ונשובה]) spoken to his servant after the futile search for his father's lost donkeys in 1 Sam 9:5, Alter (*The David Story*, 47) comments as follows: "According to the general principle of

and combating the Egyptian hostility, the first speech of Moses—"a reproof to a fellow Hebrew and an attempt to impose a standard of justice"—certainly locates his character within the sphere of social justice and legal affairs.[33] Some larger threads can be drawn together at this point: just as the beginning of Exodus foreshadows the larger plot of deliverance and Israel's national journey, so the opening moments of Moses' career in Exod 2:11–14 anticipate the fluctuations and challenges of his personal journey as Israel's leader and spokesperson. As will soon be apparent, his intervention in the altercation of the two Hebrews does not turn out as he may have wanted, and in my view this presages something important: yes, Moses will confront the daunting power structures of Egypt, but more grief will ultimately come from *within* Israel than from Egypt or any other foreign potentate or army. The brawl in Exod 2:13 signals that many more judicial issues will follow, as rivalries and fights within the community of Israel will create no shortage of headaches for their leader.[34] Though it would be premature to press this claim too far, the reader may suspect that in some ways Moses will be more successful in confronting and subverting Egyptian power structures than getting the Israelites to exhibit basic neighborly and covenantal care, both here and in the immediate future.

MURDER MYSTERY, PART I

In the not too distant future Moses will resist God's commission on the grounds that he is not a good speaker, specifically that he is "heavy

---

biblical narrative that the first reported speech of a character is a defining moment of characterization, Saul's first utterance reveals him as a young man uncertain about pursuing his way, and quite concerned about his father. This concern, especially in light of the attention devoted to tense relations between fathers and sons in the ensuing narrative, is touching, and suggests that the young Saul is a sensitive person—an attribute that will be woefully submerged by his experience of political power. But as this first dialogue unfolds, it is Saul's uncertainty that comes to the fore because at every step he has to be prodded and directed by his own servant."

[33] Alter, *The Five Books of Moses*, 314.
[34] Smith (*The Pilgrimage Pattern in Exodus*, 229) compares "the threat to Moses' life from Pharaoh's decree of death against 'Hebrew' newborn males (1.22)" using water, with "the threat of death posed to Moses' life from the Israelites (17.4)" also involving a crisis of water.

of mouth and heavy of tongue" (Exod 4:10). But based on his first words in Exod 2:13, the reader may suspect that he is being slightly disingenuous when he also tells God that he has never been a "man of words" (איש דברים) and is therefore unfit for the task of leading Israel out of Egypt. It is possible that the absence of success with his first speech engenders a lack of confidence, and so he later complains not of a speech impediment but rather a sense of frustration that his words do not produce the intended effect. Statistically, it is true that Moses is not a man of many words in this episode. Apart from a brief inner speech at the end of v. 14, Moses does not speak again until v. 22 when he calls his son Gershom, a naming-speech that underscores his sense of alienation. As it turns out, the criminal who aggressively responds in Exod 2:14 has a higher word count than all of Moses' combined utterances in Exodus 2. This unnamed Israelite strikes Moses with his words in v. 14 even as he is striking his neighbor with his fists, a verbal lashing that must be understood as equally painful:

> But he said, "Who placed you as a man who is captain and judge over us? Are you thinking about killing me just as you killed the Egyptian?" Then Moses was afraid, and he thought, "Surely the matter has become known!"

Moses' question to the criminal in v. 13 carried a rebuke, but it is deftly sidestepped as the criminal only responds in v. 14 with obfuscating questions that deflect attention back to Moses and away from himself. When Moses identifies him as the "one in the wrong" in the previous verse, the nature of the response indicates that Moses correctly decided who is the guilty party.[35] Not only does the unnamed Hebrew sound evasive and culpable in his reply, but he has a fairly sharp wit as well, it must be said. If Moses was expecting the welcome of a modest folk hero from his compatriots, that is far from the case, and instead he is greeted with a tone of resentment and suspicion. The word choice is not incidental, because when the Hebrew asks if Moses is a "captain" (שר) over them, it is the same term used in the designation for the Egyptian taskmasters in Exod 1:11, "suggesting that perhaps the Hebrew views Moses as an Egyptian."[36] It might be

---

[35] Jacob, *The Second Book of the Bible: Exodus*, 39.
[36] Dozeman, *Exodus*, 88. In Exod 1:11 "captains of forced labor" (שרי מסים) is the label for the taskmasters.

argued that this question—or insinuation—sets in motion a debate about identity that will persist in both the early and later phases of Moses' leadership, even to the point where he is misidentified as an Egyptian in the next installment of the story (Exod 2:19). Herbert Marks observes that "disguise and the doubling of identities are prominent features of the succeeding episodes," and the hybrid name of Moses now invites suspicion whereas previously it may have protected his life.[37] The criminal Hebrew, at any rate, exploits a perceived ambiguity as to the true loyalty of the adopted son of Pharaoh's daughter: Moses certainly has not been a captain of oppression or in any way adding to the burden of slavery, but his living apart from his kin can be interpreted as a form of complicity, and venturing out to his brothers and watching them at their tasks (and rescuing one of them) only invites criticism from the criminal. The reader might assume that the criminal is expressing a private question or a personal opinion rather than a more widely shared doubt about whose side Moses is on, but there may be some antipathy that he is raised in the affluence of the palace while they are building store-cities for Pharaoh. Yet Moses' upbringing is hardly his fault, and in fact his acquaintance with the inner workings of the royal administration arguably prepare him for later confrontation with the Egyptian court. So it may be tempting to write off the questions as the ranting of a criminal, but accusations leveled against Moses are an oft-recurring motif in Exodus and other parts of the Pentateuch. In my view the guilty Hebrew is an anonymous character who is represented as much more than an individual: to be sure he has a characterization of his own, but he also represents those voices of criticism frequently heard in the narrative. As one example from farther afield, in Numbers 12 Miriam and Aaron lodge a complaint against Moses for his Cushite wife. Scholars debate the identity of this wife and whether Zipporah or another woman is referred to here.[38] My point is not to resolve this issue, but rather to say that the

---

[37] Herbert Marks, "Biblical Naming and Poetic Etymology" *JBL* 114 (1995) 31.

[38] For a convenient overview, see Terence E. Fretheim, "Numbers," in *The Oxford Bible Commentary*, edited by John Barton and John Muddiman (Oxford: Oxford University Press, 2001) 119: "This text concerns the authority of the Mosaic tradition in view of rival claims regarding divine revelation; it may reflect later power struggles among priestly groups (cf. Num 16). Challenges to Moses as a unique spokesman for God are brought by his sister and brother (though God alone hears them, v. 2?). The stated basis for the challenge is that Moses had married a Cushite woman. Cush usually refers to Ethiopia (if so, this would be Moses' second wife; so the LXX), but

criminal Hebrew in Exod 2:14 introduces the *outsider* debate that curiously resurfaces in due course. Consequently, the questioning here presages that the eventual task of liberating Israel has now become doubly difficult, as Moses will be challenged to deliver the Israelites from Egyptian slavery, and from themselves as well.

Asking Moses who set him as a captain over the Hebrews is a loaded question because of the associations with slavery, but it is augmented by the word *judge* (שׁפט) in v. 14. This term has an ironic element in light of Moses' future as the judge of Israel, but it also is reminiscent of a rather grim episode in Genesis where the same word is similarly framed in an accusatory manner. Residing in the city of Sodom, Abraham's nephew Lot harbors two divine visitors to the city and tries to appease the assembled mob who demand their bodies. Rejecting Lot's offer of his two virgin daughters in order to safeguard his visitors, the crowd sarcastically turns on Lot in Gen 19:9, "This one has come as a sojourner, but he acts like a judge (וישׁפט שׁפוט)!"[39] In both of these cases the outsider is charged with imposing a moral standard but lacking the official capacity to do so. It is more of an insult in the case of Moses because he is not an outsider, and in fact has left the apparent security of the palace on two occasions and demonstrated his insider status: first he protects an Israelite life from an Egyptian beating, and now he prevents one Hebrew from harming another. Like the townsfolk of Sodom, the guilty Hebrew in this altercation accuses Moses of unauthorized judging but in reality is masking his own iniquity. Furthermore, there are echoes of Joseph's brothers in this scene as well, as their incredulity is expressed through a pair of scathing rhetorical questions ("Are you really going to reign over us? Are you really going to rule over us?") that are powerfully

---

here it probably refers to a Cush in northern Arabia (see Hab 3:7). If so, she would be Zipporah, a Midianite (10:29; Ex 2:15–22)." See also Peter Machinist, "The Meaning of Moses," *Harvard Divinity Bulletin* 27 (1998) 14: "Incidentally, the label that Aaron and Miriam pin on Moses' wife, 'Cushite,' has the effect of making her even stranger to an Israelite settled in Palestine, since it normally refers to the Ethiopians, a people much farther away from Palestine than the Midianites."

[39] Hamilton, *Exodus*, 30. On the importance of the plural in Exod 2:14 ("over *us*"), see Gurtner, *Exodus*, 192–3.

inverted when Joseph does govern over them in Egypt (Gen 37:8).[40] As with Joseph, the angry question posed to Moses is a preface to a long period of exile that actually results in Israelite lives being saved, but evidently this lesson has been forgotten: "Like Joseph's kin, yet without extenuating circumstances, they have in a fashion 'sold' to Egypt the brother who came looking for them. Patriarchal history repeats itself to gloomy effect in the national, or denationalized, framework."[41]

If the first question from the fighting Hebrew casts aspersions on Moses, it also acts as a segue to a second and even more provocative question, as he drops a bombshell and asks if Moses is thinking about killing him just like he killed the Egyptian! This stunning disclosure must catch Moses off guard as it does the reader, for it is not clear how the guilty Hebrew could possibly know about the murder and the corpse in the sand. As we recall, Moses takes considerable precaution by looking around for any witnesses. How the guilty Hebrew discovers this hidden truth is certainly a mystery, and the most plausible explanation is that the rescued Hebrew of v. 11 has broadcast the news. Perhaps the victim is grateful and thus shares the events of his escape from the Egyptian assailant with his compatriots, and it is not inconceivable to suppose that the story "goes viral" and quickly circulates amongst the slaves. The guilty Hebrew, however, intends to use this knowledge as leverage in his dialogue with Moses, and the reader senses a kind of blackmail at work.[42] When Moses glanced around in Exod 2:12 we assume he was concerned about getting caught by the Egyptians, but he should have been equally apprehensive about his own people finding out, such as this Hebrew who raises his sinister inquiry: "Moses discovers that some of his own people can act insidiously as informers to the oppressive authorities."[43] Cynical or caustic questions will often be heard during Moses' long tenure of

---

[40] Nohrnberg, *Like Unto Moses*, 168; cf. Enns, *Exodus*, 71 for a comparison of the false accusations.

[41] Sternberg, *Hebrews Between Cultures*, 347.

[42] Nohrnberg, *Like Unto Moses*, 167: "For the Hebrew indicates that Moses failed to kill in secret and is in a position to be blackmailed. But the Hebrew's taunting murmur—must Moses now do to him as he did to the Egyptian?—also constitutes an epiphany: Moses could kill the Egyptian because no one was looking, for he looked both ways first (Exod. 2:12). Yet someone was looking. This is the revelation to Cain, and it makes a murderer into a fugitive."

[43] Sarna, *Exodus*, 10; cf. Olson, "Literary and Rhetorical Criticism," 37.

leadership, and so the guilty Hebrew again introduces a pattern that soon becomes familiar. As Alter notes, "These words of the brawler in the wrong not only preface the revelation that Moses' killing of the Egyptian is no secret but also adumbrate a long series of later incidents in which the Israelites will express resentment or rebelliousness toward Moses."[44] In later questions there is an unusually high frequency of *death* or related morbidity, as texts such as Exod 14:11 ("Is it because there are no graves in Egypt that you have taken us to die in the desert?") or 17:3 illustrate on either side of the departure ("Why have you brought us up from Egypt to die of thirst, along with our children and cattle?"). When the Hebrew in v. 14 asks if Moses is thinking of killing him, it is typical of the kind of Israelite complaints involving starvation or the lack of graves that will punctuate their journey out of Egypt and toward their ancestral home. In the meantime Moses does not respond to either of the questions directly with his interlocutor, and instead of any outward response there is only an inward deliberation of fear. To further an observation of Gordon Davies, there is a contrast with the midwives: they fear God (ירא) and act in defense of the Hebrews, whereas Moses has defended a Hebrew and is now afraid (ירא).[45] To be sure, the revelation of the murmuring Hebrew triggers a crisis that is poised to get much worse for Moses.

MURDER MYSTERY, PART II

Moses is afraid that his secret has become known, and in the next scene of the story he is about to learn that his worst fear is realized. The reader is unsure if Moses is scared about prosecution for the murder of the Egypt or about some other item that might become public knowledge. Moreover, is Moses concerned about the Egyptians in general learning about his crime, or Pharaoh in particular learning

---

[44] Alter, *The Five Books of Moses*, 314. Note also Meyers, *Exodus*, 44: "one of the Hebrews challenges his authority to intervene, thus adumbrating the difficulties Moses will face later in establishing himself as a credible leader."

[45] Davies, *Israel in Egypt*, 132. "But the dissent of the murmuring Hebrew," says Nohrnberg (*Like Unto Moses*, 166-7) "could make it painfully clear to one that Moses had put the fear of Moses into the offender, but not the fear of God."

that he is more of an Israelite than a member of the royal court? Along with the body in the sand, Moses might be concealing his identity or sympathies with the oppressed Hebrews. For the second time, Pharaoh seeks to kill Moses: once as an unnamed infant along with the other Hebrew males in Exod 1:22, and now as an adult in Exod 2:15.

> Then Pharaoh heard about the matter, and he sought to kill Moses. So Moses fled before Pharaoh, and dwelt in the land of Midian, and he sat down beside the well.

The most likely scenario is that the rescued Hebrew has divulged the story of his rescue, with the result that a much wider circle of people are now acquainted with the actions of Moses. But the news must have traveled far and fast if Pharaoh is now aware of recent events. By any measure this is a dramatic shift: it is understandable that the Hebrews have learned about Moses' intervention, but how does the report reach the ears of the king? A similar mystery is found later in 1 Kings 11 when Jeroboam is covertly appointed to replace Solomon by the prophet Ahijah of Shiloh. Even though Ahijah finds Jeroboam on the road and accosts him "when the two of them were alone in the field" (1 Kings 11:29), Solomon somehow finds out and "sought to kill" Jeroboam in v. 40. Since there are manifold similarities between Solomon's tyranny and that of Pharaoh, it would not be too bold to suggest that both kings have surveillance networks and informants who provide these kinds of data. We are not sure exactly how Pharaoh finds out, but he seeks to kill Moses, and though the lineaments of his plan are not disclosed, there is a clear sense of his anger and intention. Peter Enns comments that Pharaoh's murderous impulse toward Moses may seem extreme under the circumstances, and while this might be one more example of an irrational outburst or capricious act, it is also conceivable that "his strong reaction may be evidence that he is well aware of Moses' Hebrew birth, or that Moses' act of murder actually betrays his true national allegiance."[46] If Pharaoh's wrath is kindled by the questionable loyalty of Moses, it should be noted that in Exod 4:24 God will seek to put Moses to death

---

[46] Enns, *Exodus*, 82. Cf. Greifenhagen, *Egypt on the Pentateuch's Ideological Map*, 64: "Having been rejected in his attempt to identify with the Hebrews, now Moses also has his Egyptian identity repudiated, for the Pharaoh seeks to kill him (2.15a)."

using similar language as here in 2:15. The issue in Exodus 4 surrounds circumcision as a mark of identity, and once more Moses will be rescued by alert actions of a woman but not before a strenuous ordeal: "To be treated as an enemy by Yahweh, in the same way that Yahweh is going to treat Pharaoh and the Egyptians, is a terrifying experience that pushes one to define one's identity in relation to Yahweh."[47] In Exod 2:15 Pharaoh attempts but is unable to kill Moses. This is not the first nor the last time that Moses is able to escape the murderous designs of the king of Egypt, but he will have other forces to contend with in due course.

"The first story of Moses as an adult," writes Thomas Dozeman, "is a tale of failed leadership."[48] It is hard to vehemently disagree with this assessment, and indeed, it is just the start of a legion of challenges and discouragements that Moses will face. The inauspicious beginning to his Israelite leadership is replayed in Exod 6:9 after the initial setbacks in the interviews with Pharaoh, when God provides him with an emphatic oracle of assurance that is not absorbed by receptive hearts: "When Moses told this to the Israelites, they would not listen to Moses, their spirits crushed by cruel bondage."[49] In Exod 2:15 it may appear that Moses has been defeated now that Pharaoh seeks his life, but he manages to flee and survive—which surely counts as a modest success—and by avoiding the reach of Pharaoh's tentacles he anticipates Israel's victory in Exodus 14. But for the moment Moses' flight from Egypt marks a new era in both his career and the larger storyline: "the action of getting up and moving off and the separation of someone from a group as here in 2:15 can mark the end of a narrative segment."[50] There is also a shift in territory and spatial setting, and the choice of Midian as Moses' destination is intriguing. Walter Brueggemann points out that there is no reason provided for this particular locale: "We are not told anything about Midian, except that it is not Egypt. It is evidently a pastoral society, and it is free of the dangers, threats, and abusiveness

---

[47] Athena E. Gorospe, *Narrative and Identity: An Ethical Reading of Exodus 4* (BIS 86; Leiden: Brill, 2007) 195.
[48] Dozeman, *Exodus*, 86.
[49] Jon D. Levenson, *Resurrection and the Restoration of Israel: The Ultimate Victory of the God of Life* (New Haven and London: Yale University Press, 2006) 191.
[50] Shimon Bar-Efrat, *Narrative Art in the Bible* (JSOTSup 70; Sheffield: Almond Press, 1989) 142-3, cited by Davies, *Israel in Egypt*, 123.

Criminal Charges 141

of the Egyptian kingdom."⁵¹ A confederation of five semi-nomadic tribes ranging over a wide expanse beyond the eastern arm of the Red Sea, the eponymous ancestor of the Midianites "is said to be a son of Abraham by Keturah. This reflects an early history of close and friendly relations between Israel and the Midianites."⁵² The connection of Midian as a descendant of Abraham is probably insufficient grounds for claiming that Moses chooses to take refuge in the land of Midian, but it does not sound particularly ominous either. James Nohrnberg notices a slight irony here, because "the name Midian in the Keturah story merely advises us that any rivals to Isaac were 'pensioned off' (Gen. 25:6): it does not suggest a place where the patriarchal identity might be symbolically renewed, or the patriarchal career symbolically reenacted."⁵³ For this study a key point of connection is the travail of Joseph in Genesis 37 when he is sold as a slave by his brothers to a caravan of merchants and subsequently purchased by Potiphar: "But the Midianites sold him into Egypt, to Potiphar the eunuch of Pharaoh, captain of the bodyguards" (Gen 37:36).⁵⁴ The Midianites play a role in bringing Joseph into Egypt and selling him as slave, and now the place of Midian becomes a formative site for preparing Moses to bring Israel out of slavery in Egypt.⁵⁵ As we will also soon discover, when Moses enters the land of Midian the links with Genesis are by no means over.

---

⁵¹ Brueggemann, "The Book of Exodus," 703.
⁵² Sarna, *Exodus*, 11–12; cf. Gen 25:1–4, "Abraham took another wife, whose name was Keturah. She bore him Zimran, Jokshan, Medan, Midian, Ishbak, and Shuah. Jokshan was the father of Sheba and Dedan. The sons of Dedan were Asshurim, Letushim, and Leummim. The sons of Midian were Ephah, Epher, Hanoch, Abida, and Eldaah. All these were the children of Keturah" (NRSV). See also Greifenhagen, *Egypt on the Pentateuch's Ideological Map*, 66: "Archaeologically, Midian has been identified with a sophisticated culture that arose in the Late Bronze Age in the northern Arabian peninsula east of the Arabah [citing George E. Mendenhall, 'Midian,' *ABD* IV: 817]. However, the biblical narrative is more interested in Midian as a foil for Israelite identity."
⁵³ Nohrnberg, *Like Unto Moses*, 155.
⁵⁴ On the spelling מדנים as opposed to the expected מדינים, see Joel S. Baden, *The Composition of the Pentateuch: Renewing the Documentary Hypothesis* (New Haven: Yale University Press, 2012) 252.
⁵⁵ Enns, *Exodus*, 82: "The Midianites brought the patriarch Joseph to exile in Egypt; Moses winds up with the Midianites after his exile from Egypt."

NEAR THE WELL

The flight to Midian is a desperate measure, but nonetheless an effective move, as there is no evidence that Moses is pursued. By contrast, at a much later stage in the story Pharaoh and his colleagues do opt to madly pursue the fleeing Israelites in Exod 14:5: "It was reported to the king of Egypt that the people had fled, and Pharaoh and his servants turned their heart against the people, and they said, 'What is this we have done? For we have released Israel from serving us!'" Since no such pursuit is reported for Moses' solo flight to Midian, he arrives apparently unmolested as a fugitive, but safe. William Propp notes that there is an efficacy to this flight in the longer term: "unbeknownst to Moses, his flight from Egypt to meet Jethro and Yahweh at Mount Horeb foreshadows the emigration of the entire Hebrew nation."[56] In the short term, however, there is a more pressing significance in Moses' departure to Midian, because upon arrival "he sits down near the well (וישב על־הבאר)" in the last clause of Exod 2:15. Far from the sense of an ending, this seemingly incidental detail actually marks a radically new beginning for Moses, because when he sits down by the well he is following in the footsteps of a pattern established earlier in the book of Genesis: a "maiden at the well" type-scene.

Since the pioneering work of Robert Alter's *The Art of Biblical Narrative*, scholars are increasingly researching various kinds of type-scenes in the Hebrew Bible and the New Testament.[57] Numerous categories have been identified or postulated, such as the type-scene of the call of the prophet, the storm at sea, or the divine council.[58]

---

[56] Propp, *Exodus 1–18*, 169.

[57] Alter, "Type-Scenes and the Uses of Convention," pp. 47–62 in *The Art of Biblical Narrative* (New York: Basic Books, 1981). A useful theoretical discussion, recent survey of secondary literature, and examples that range farther afield can be found in Koowon Kim, *Incubation as a Type-Scene in the 'Aqhatu, Kirta, and Hannah Stories: A Form-Critical and Narratological Study of KTU 1.14 I–1.15 III, 1.17 I–II, and 1 Samuel 1:1–2:11* (VTSup 145; Leiden: Brill, 2011). Note also Robert H. O'Connell, "Proverbs vii 16–17: A Case of Fatal Deception in a 'Woman and the Window' Type-Scene," *VT* 41 (1991) 235–41, and Pamela Lee Thimmes, *Studies in the Biblical Sea-Storm Type-scene: Convention and Invention* (San Francisco: Mellen Research University Press, 1992).

[58] E.g., Brian Britt, "Prophetic Concealment in a Biblical Type Scene," *CBQ* 64 (2002) 37–58; George Savran, "Theophany as Type Scene," *Prooftexts* 23 (2003) 119–49; Min Suc Kee, "The Heavenly Council and Its Type-scene," *JSOT* 31 (2007)

A particularly well-known example is the type-scene of the "barren wife," with each episode sharing a set of common characteristics: an aged husband married to a barren wife, the announcement of the end of sterility from an authority figure in the story, and the birth of a child of destiny as the narrative unfolds. The first recognized instance of the barren wife type-scene is Sarah in Genesis, whose sterility is mentioned several times (Gen 11:30; 16:1–2). The announcement of a forthcoming birth is given to Abraham and Sarah on more than one occasion (Gen 17:19–21; 18:9–15), reaching a climax with the birth of Isaac through whom the promise to Abraham continues (Gen 21:1–3). Although debated by scholars, other instances of the barren wife type-scene include Rebekah in Genesis 25, the mother of Samson in Judges 13, and Hannah in 1 Samuel 1, all of whom are infertile but proceed to give birth to sons who play an important role within the unfolding storyline, and all of whom are somehow connected with God's promise to Abraham that through his offspring every other family on earth will be blessed (e.g., Gen 12:1–3).[59] A barren wife type-scene can also be found in the New Testament, in Luke 1 involving Zechariah the priest and his aged wife Elizabeth. The angel Gabriel speaks to Zechariah during his shift in the temple, and announces that a son will be born. After several detours in the episode such as Zechariah's astonishment and disbelief, John is born and certainly develops into a major character in the various gospel narratives.

The type-scene of "the maiden at the well" is also a well-attested example, and when Moses sits down near the well in Exod 2:15 the reader immediately recognizes the significance of the spatial setting. Our discussion will be continued in the next chapter of this book, but by way of introduction it should be noted that several instances of this type-scene can be located in Genesis. The elements that comprise this category of type-scene can be summarized as follows: a potential hero is journeying away from home, and in the course of his travels encounters a well of water where a maiden is nearby. Almost

---

259–73; Jeffrey Stackert, *A Prophet Like Moses: Prophecy, Law, and Israelite Religion* (New York: Oxford University Press, 2014) especially pp. 73–5.

[59] On the Samson episode, see Benjamin J. M. Johnson, "What Type of Son is Samson? Reading Judges 13 as a Biblical Type-Scene," *JETS* 53 (2010) 269–86. In my view the Shunammite woman of 2 Kings 4 also belongs in this category; see Bodner, *Elisha's Profile in the Book of Kings*, 77.

invariably there is a conflict of some kind, followed by a sense of resolution and a festal meal that allows the relationship between the potential hero and the maiden to move to a higher level.[60] Similar to the barren wife scenario, the type-scene of the maiden at the well has a larger purpose than merely finding a bride for the protagonist of the story: it is to further the promise to Abraham. An obvious case is Jacob in Genesis 29, who is fleeing from the wrath of Esau after tricking his father into giving him the blessing.[61] Jacob encounters a well of water in the vicinity of his uncle Laban's home, and there he meets Rachel and some not-overly hospitable shepherds who perhaps resent his single-handed removal of the stone that guards the mouth of the well. Rachel then takes Jacob home to meet her father, and even though the actual marriage does not take place until seven years later—with Leah unexpectedly included in the bargain—the type-scene is nonetheless complete. A more complex version is found in Genesis 24, when Isaac—represented by Abraham's servant—is betrothed to Rebekah, who is likewise discovered at a well. Perhaps the most subtle variation is Genesis 38, where the main character Judah encounters the future mother of his children—his own daughter-in-law disguised by a veil—in the most dubious circumstances: "Tamar, hoping to have a child by Judah, waylays him by the entrance to Enaim, which means 'twin wells,' and as a result gives birth to twins."[62] More will be said about this kind of type-scene in the next chapter, but at this point the reader senses that Moses' flight from Egypt concludes on a less disastrous note. When Moses sits

---

[60] Utilizing the work of Alter and other scholars, I have discussed these categories in Keith Bodner, "Go Figure: Narrative Strategies for a New Generation," pp. 9–24 in *Go Figure! Figuration in Biblical Interpretation*, edited by Stanley D. Walters (Princeton Theological Monograph Series 81; Eugene OR: Pickwick, 2008). Note also the five elements listed by Michael W. Martin ("Betrothal Journey Narratives," *CBQ* 70 (2008) 505–23): "1. The groom-to-be travels to a foreign country. 2. He meets a young woman or young women at a well. 3. Someone draws water. 4. The woman/women rush home with news of his arrival. 5. A betrothal is arranged, usually in connection with a meal" (p. 507). Martin suggests an expanded schema later in the article. On the well of water as a fusion between a "popular singles' spot" and a symbol of fertility, see Sabo, "Drawing Out Moses," 417–18.

[61] Both Jacob and Moses have to flee because of a death threat, and as Utzschneider and Oswald (*Exodus 1–15*, 92) aptly observe, with Jacob having deceived Esau and (perhaps) Moses having deceived Pharaoh: "Moses thereby acquires characteristics of the patriarch Jacob."

[62] Janzen, *Exodus*, 24; see also Jonathan Kruschwitz, "The Type-Scene Connection between Genesis 38 and the Joseph Story," *JSOT* 36 (2012) 383–410.

down near the well in Midian, he joins this particular group of his ancestors in Genesis who have portentous experiences at a well of water, and as will be revealed in the next chapter, Moses' future now appears in a much different light than when Pharaoh was seeking his life at the beginning of v. 15.

6

The Stranger in Midian

> *Those five verses (2:11–15) not only manifest but multiply all the elements that Aristotle deems essential to the finest (e.g., Oedipus's or Iphigenia's) tragic plot: the crime within the family, the peripety between happiness and unhappiness, the ignorance-to-knowledge anagnorisis. For good measure, all run at two levels, the public and the private, the observable and the subjective, the vocal and the silent. The drama interior to the nation gets interiorized in the narration itself, because anchored fast in the mind of the hero (who suffers the crimes, arrives at the discoveries, enacts and/or undergoes the reversals of fortune) to an extent unforeseen by the outward-directed Greek* Poetics.
>
> Meir Sternberg[1]

Moses' recent experiences are comparable to the tribulations of Joseph in the book of Genesis, not least because both have a narrow escape from either the waters of the Nile or the empty cistern.[2] But more poignant is the suffering they both endure from unexpected sources: "He is rejected, not as a child by his parent, but as a young man by his wicked half brothers. He is exiled from the tribe at just the age he should be joining it."[3] James Nohrnberg is here referring to Joseph in Genesis 37, but he could well be describing the experiences of Moses in Exod 2:13–14, and as will be discussed later in this chapter, the similarities between Joseph and Moses continue. However, the connections with Genesis are not limited to Joseph. It was noted previously that at the end of v. 15 Moses sits down by a well in

---

[1] Sternberg, *Hebrews Between Cultures*, 348.   [2] Hamilton, *Exodus*, 24.
[3] Nohrnberg, *Like Unto Moses*, 143. On Moses' passion for justice that results in his exile, see Walter Houston, "Exodus," in *The Oxford Bible Commentary*, edited by John Barton and John Muddiman (Oxford: Oxford University Press, 2001) 70.

Midian, and this otherwise innocuous action triggers an association with the type-scene of the maiden at the well: "A well, whose water fertilizes the earth and sustains animal and human life, becomes a symbol of the children expected from marriage (compare the Song of Sol. 4:15 with Prov. 30:15–16). Thus the well becomes a sign of hope and good news. So when we find Moses at a well where women come to water their flocks, our pulses should quicken with hope."[4] In this chapter we will explore the various events of Exod 2:16–23, including the type-scene and later incidents in the land of Midian such as Moses' marriage and the naming-speech of his newborn son. Exodus 2 concludes with a divine perspective on the anguish of Israel, and our analysis considers interpretive options as the story is poised for a momentous new phase.

THE GROUP OF SEVEN

Among the aesthetic delights of the type-scene are the creative variations that are experienced by the reader: within a reasonably fixed set of elements, each particular scene has its own distinctive configuration. Compared to Jacob's encounter at the well in Gen 29:1–14, one can immediately grasp that Isaac's type-scene has a unique component, namely that the protagonist—Isaac himself—is nowhere present at the well in Genesis 24 and others do his bidding. Moreover, Rebekah's nuanced role implies that she will be a prominent character in the story, borne out when she later colludes with her younger son Jacob to hoodwink blind Isaac in Genesis 27. Betrothal type-scenes are by no means limited to the Pentateuch, and an arresting example is found in 1 Sam 9:11–14 early in the career of Saul. On a search for his father's missing donkeys, Saul and his servant encounter a group of maidens on their way to draw water. The requisite ingredients for the type-scene of the maiden at the well are present, but the resolution palpably lacks any relationship with a potential bride or a customary meal. Saul meets Samuel in place of a maiden—hardly an attractive prospect given the prophet's antipathy to kingship in general and Saul of Benjamin in particular—who leads him to an ominous high place

---

[4] Janzen, *Exodus*, 24.

redolent with sacrificial imagery. This lack of resolution leads Robert Alter to posit that 1 Sam 9:11–14 is an aborted type-scene: "Instead of a betrothal feast, there will be a sacrificial feast that adumbrates a rite of coronation. The destiny of kingship to which Saul proceeds will lead to grimmer consequences than those that follow in the repeated story of a hero who finds his future bride at a well."[5] Readers can appreciate that a central purpose of the episode is to foreshadow Saul's bleak destiny as Israel's inaugural monarch, and the aborted type-scene prefigures Saul's aborted kingship.

Equally creative and more elaborate is the book of Ruth, which arguably inverts the familiar motifs by making the main character a female and substituting the well in the field with receptacles "that the young men (נערים) have filled with water" (Ruth 2:9). The overall result is a story that has layers of irony, as the main character Ruth becomes the ancestress of the great King David—who himself does not experience a betrothal type-scene owing to his multiple marriages (e.g., 1 Sam 25:42–4; 2 Sam 3:2–5, 5:13, 12:11, 19:5)—and also because Israelite males are drawing water for a foreign woman. Perhaps the latter picture suggested itself to the writer of John's gospel in the New Testament since many of the conventions of the betrothal type-scene are evident in John 4. Naturally there are unique contours to this episode, not least because there is no interest in marriage in the scene; having had five husbands already, the Samaritan woman is in need of a different kind of relationship altogether. But if a larger purpose of the betrothal type-scene is linked to the promise to Abraham—through whose offspring every other family on earth will somehow be blessed—then John 4 exploits the type-scene imagery to understand its messianic fulfillment in this conversation. Indeed, in John 4:39 the reader is told, "many of the Samaritans from that town believed in him because of the woman's testimony," and thus her conversion creates a ripple effect that culminates in v. 42 with the words of the townspeople: "We no longer believe just because of what you said; now we have heard for ourselves, and we know that this man really is the Savior of the world."[6] Taken together, these betrothal type-scenes exhibit creative variations while retaining a common set of characteristics. When Moses fled to Midian in Exod 2:15 his future may have appeared rather desolate, but the presence of

---

[5] Alter, *The David Story*, 48.
[6] Note the longer discussion in Martin, "Betrothal Journey Narratives," 520–3.

a well now links him with the ancestral promise, and v. 16 introduces a troupe of important new actors on the stage:

> Now the priest of Midian had seven daughters, and they came to draw water and fill the troughs to water their father's flock.

The reader may not realize it, but the priest of Midian—who in v. 18 is given the first of several names—becomes a reasonably prominent figure in the Pentateuch.[7] This Midianite is the first priest officially mentioned in Exodus; Moses is from a Levite family, soon to develop into Israel's foundational priest, and now he comes into contact with a priestly family after fleeing from Egypt. Here the Midianite is unnamed, but William Propp observes that the syntax of the verse highlights the priest: "By opening with a parenthesis, the writer signals that it is the priest who is of most interest, not his daughters. And by keeping him temporarily nameless, the author makes Reuel's identity a subject of mild suspense, like that of the foundling in 1:22–2:10."[8] To be sure, this priest of Midian will have an abiding influence on Israel's priestly traditions, but for now, says Walter Brueggemann, "his only function is to be the father of seven daughters."[9] In itself, having such offspring is a prolific enough achievement, though it gives scant insight into the priest's character. The priest is obviously the owner of a healthy number of sheep as well, and Moses is certainly not aware of it, but this flock will provide him with later employment. Leading these sheep "to the far side of the desert" (אחר המדבר) in Exod 3:1 paves the way for Moses' life-changing encounter at the burning bush where he will be commissioned to lead Israel out of Egypt.[10] Also, the presence of this Midianite as the first priest mentioned in the book of Exodus triggers the memory of the first priest in the book of Genesis, the enigmatic Melchizedek who appears in the narrative after Abram recovers his nephew Lot (Gen 14:18). Although the interpreter should be cautious

---

[7] For a convenient listing, see Durham, *Exodus*, 22: "Indeed, his priestly vocation is more clearly remembered than his name. For while Moses' father-in-law is consistently said to be a priest of Midian, his name is variously given as Reuel (v 18), a name assigned also to the father of Moses' father-in-law in Num 10:29; Jethro ('His abundance,' 3:1, 18:1, 2, and throughout the chapter); Jether ('Abundance, Preeminence') and Jethro in a single verse (4:18; Jether is apparently a textual slip in MT); and Hobab ('Loving, Embracing One,' Num 10:29; Judg 4:11)."

[8] Propp, *Exodus 1–18*, 171.

[9] Brueggemann, "The Book of Exodus," 703.

[10] Cf. Smith, *The Pilgrimage Pattern in Exodus*, 192.

here, Melchizedek is pictured as a spiritual ally and mediator who provides welcome hospitality to Abram, but he is also an outsider who is not at all marginalized in the text.[11] Thus, the role of Melchizedek is a favorable antecedent for the priest of Midian here, and in a modest way prepares the reader for the characterization of the priest of Midian. Of course, any comparison begs the question as to the relative orthodoxy of this Midianite priest: "If Reuel/Jethro is a priest, what god does he serve? Since he resides near Mount Horeb (3:1, 18), confesses Yahweh's greatness (18:10–11) and leads Israel in sacrifice (18:12), the biblical authors probably considered him a Yahweh-worshipper."[12] Melchizedek appears to receive a passing grade both from Abram and other biblical writers, so it would seem that the same grade should be awarded to this priest of Midian as well.

Usually the betrothal type-scene has one leading female actor, as Rebekah illustrates in Genesis 24 or Rachel in Genesis 29. An exception is Saul in 1 Sam 9:11–14, where a group of young women (נערות) are going out to draw water as Saul and his servant stop them and ask for directions. "The reply of the young women is notable for its garrulousness," notes Robert Alter, and to be sure, the voice-structure of 1 Sam 9:12–13 is replete with excitement and awkward syntax, as though the maidens are all speaking at once and vying for the attention of the handsome Saul.[13] Even in this case, however, the number of maidens is not specified, and at any rate the type-scene does not arrive at a favorable resolution for Saul. With Moses in Exod 2:16 the signs are more positive, as the number "seven" must be interpreted as an encouraging portent. Furthermore, the multitude of young women in the Saul episode probably indicates a sense of competition, with numerous voices clamoring to be heard. The seven daughters of the priest of Midian, by contrast, silently go about their work. There is no individuation, as in the cases of Rebekah (the reader is told about her outward appearance and virginity) or Rachel (who likewise is beautiful, and the genealogical affiliation with Abraham is carefully adumbrated).[14] The absence of individuation centers attention on the number *seven*, which surely carries a stereotypical

---

[11] On Melchizedek in Genesis 14 (and other references in Psalm 110 and Hebrew 5–7), see Fretheim, "The Book of Genesis," 438–42.
[12] Propp, *Exodus 1–18*, 171.   [13] Alter, *The David Story*, 49.
[14] Davies, *Israel in Egypt*, 146: "More interestingly, the girls in Exodus 2 are not reported to be beauties or relatives of the male protagonist, like Rebekah (Gen. 24.15–16) and Rachel (Gen. 29.10, 17)."

significance as it does in passages such as 1 Sam 2:5 or Ruth 4:15, and in this present context of Exodus it "may symbolize matrimony and procreation."[15] On a more practical level, the number seven indicates that Moses will be hard-pressed to fail in this type-scene: he may have had a difficult run of form lately, but given the pool of candidates at this well in Midian, there is a high probability of success. Glancing ahead, it should be said that Moses will succeed in this matrimonial endeavor and not speak a single word of direct speech in the process. Consequently, we can once more appreciate that the journey of Moses anticipates the journey of Israel, for the people will likewise flee from Egypt and find their covenant partner in the land of Mount Horeb—the mountain of God—where Moses soon will shepherd his new father-in-law's flock.

Since no particular daughter is distinguished in any way in v. 16, the emphasis falls on the collective affiliation of the women with the priest of Midian. This in turn echoes another point of connection with Joseph in Egypt: after the appointment by Pharaoh, his upturn in fortune is sealed in Gen 41:45 with a wife: "Asenath daughter of Potiphera, priest of On." Both Joseph and Moses are named, though in slightly different ways, by a member of the Egyptian royal house: Moses is of course named by Pharaoh's daughter, but along with a wife Joseph also is given a new name—Zaphenath-paneah—in Gen 42:45 by Pharaoh after his elevation as vizier of Egypt. As we have already discussed, the Midianites deliver Joseph to Egypt, and now Moses is poised to marry into a Midianite priestly family after escaping from Egypt. In Exod 2:16 the Midianite girls are drawing water, and one of the seven will soon draw Moses, as it were, but in a quite different way than the daughter of Pharaoh. Prior to any marriage, there is another event to consider while Moses is still a bachelor, as some villainous characters arrive at this rather popular well in Midian. Moses has been rescued by women on more than one occasion up to this point—the two midwives, his mother, his sister, and Pharaoh's daughter come to mind—but in Exod 2:17 he now has the opportunity to return the favor and rescue the seven daughters:

> Then the shepherds came and drove them out, but Moses arose and saved them, and he watered their flock.

---

[15] Propp, *Exodus 1–18*, 171.

In other betrothal type-scenes shepherds have been part of the supporting cast. In Gen 29:4–8 Jacob enters into dialogue with the local shepherds of Haran, and while they may not be overly friendly, they are certainly not hostile like the group of shepherds who arrive at the well in Midian. Disputes over water, a precious and often scarce resource, are not unheard of in the book of Genesis, and shepherds have been present in previous episodes of hostility. For example, the servants of Isaac in Gen 26:19–21 have a set of quarrels with local herdsmen over wells and water-rights, contentious moments that are inscribed in the names that Isaac bestows on the wells: "Esek" from the root meaning *argument*, and "Sitnah" from the root meaning *adversary*. Consequently, when the shepherds arrive on the scene in Exod 2:17 there is some precedence for conflict. According to Brevard Childs, the violence of the shepherds is matched only by their rudeness and abominable lack of chivalry: "In a few strokes the writer pictures the deliberate ruthlessness of the shepherds. They wait until the women have finished the tedious work of drawing water and filling the water troughs before driving them away with force."[16] It is unknown whether this is the first time the shepherds are guilty of such aggression or whether this happened before, but the difference is that Moses is present on this occasion, and presumably is watching the scenario unfold. The reader recalls Moses observing an injustice previously, when he was roused to action at the sight of the Egyptian beating his fellow Hebrew in the context of Israel's slavery, and was willing to commit murder in order to defend the victim.

Apart from the question of whether the shepherds launch a premeditated strike on these vulnerable women at the well, their action introduces an important verb for the book of Exodus. The shepherds "drive out" (גרש) the sisters, and this is the first of several times the verb is used in the confrontation narrative with Pharaoh. In Exod 6:1 Moses complains to God that ever since he spoke to Pharaoh there has been nothing but trouble, but God responds by declaring that Pharaoh will be compelled to drive out (גרש) the Israelites from the land, and that they will be brought out of slavery to the land given to their ancestors. The climactic use of the verb occurs in Exod 12:39 on the night of Passover: "They baked the dough that they brought out from Egypt as unleavened cakes, because it had not been leavened, for

---

[16] Childs, *The Book of Exodus*, 31.

they were driven out (גרש) of Egypt and could not linger nor prepare supplies for themselves." In the more immediate future, the same root (גרש) occurs in the naming-speech of Moses' firstborn son. As we will analyze below, the word is the centerpiece of Moses' first recorded speech since leaving Egypt and is used to define his liminal status. But it is also significant that the word (גרש) first occurs in the context of the shepherds, a gang that Cornelis Houtman describes as "loutish profiteers."[17] Far from a marginal or an isolated incident, the attack of the shepherds is tightly integrated in the larger thematic unfolding the story. In my view these shepherds are also subtly configured to represent the taskmasters and officials of Egypt who leverage their position of strength for manipulative ends. Assuming that the shepherds wait until the daughters draw the water before driving them away, then the shepherds too are guilty of exploiting the labor of a weaker group. Also, the Egyptian beating the Hebrew in Exod 2:11–12 takes advantage of a power inequity, but as we recall, there was a nearby observer who intervened and ended the abuse. Similarly, the upper hand of the shepherds in Exod 2:17 is only temporary, as they are confronted by a stranger who proves to be a dangerous and formidable opponent. The Egyptians also enjoy the upper hand over Israel, but in due course a stronger hand compels them to drive out (גרש) the group they have long mistreated.

In all likelihood the Egyptian beating the Hebrew earlier in Exodus was not aware he was being watched, and in the same way the shepherds may not notice that a stranger is present when they drive away the seven daughters of the priest of Midian from the well. But just as the shepherds are configured to represent Egypt as they aggressively drive away the girls, so Moses prefigures God's salvation of Israel when he arises against them. The use of the specific verb "arise" (קום) underscores such a representation, for it echoes and inverts the earlier action of the new king of Egypt: in Exod 1:8 the new king who arises over Egypt begins the oppression of Israel, but now Moses arises to confront the shepherds and anticipate Israel's eventual deliverance. Gordon Davies comments that the same verb is used for both Moses and Pharaoh at a pivotal moment of transition in Exod 12:30–2 that marks the outset of Israel's collective movement out of Egypt:

---

[17] Houtman, *Exodus I*, 310.

> And Pharaoh rose up (ויקם) in the night, he and all his servants and all Egypt and there was a great cry in Egypt, for there was not a house where one was not dead. And he summoned Moses and Aaron by night, and said, "Rise up (קומו), go forth from among my people, both you and the people of Israel; and go, serve YHWH, as you have said. Take your flocks and your herds, as you have said, and be gone..."[18]

The idea of Moses prefiguring God's action on behalf of Israel does not end with the verb arise, but also with the next significant verb, one that looms large in the Hebrew Bible: he "saved them" (יֹשִׁעַ). Some standard English versions have a different construal here, for translations such as the NRSV's "came to their defense" does not quite capture the larger *tenor* of Moses' action within the larger storyline.[19] Although it occurs over two hundred more times in the Hebrew, the verb "to save" only occurs once more in Exodus, but it is used in 14:30 to convey the ultimate victory in the narrative: "The LORD saved (יֹשַׁע) Israel on that day from the hand of the Egyptians, and Israel saw the Egyptians dead on the edge of the sea." Victor Hamilton notes that nominal forms of the root are used on either side of the deliverance: first in Exod 14:13 where Israel is instructed to stand firm and see the salvation (יְשׁוּעָה) of God despite their doubt and panic, and then again in the opening lyrics of the Song of Sea (15:2) to memorialize the event, "The LORD is my strength and my song, and he has become my salvation (יְשׁוּעָה)."[20] The combined effect of these three uses of the root ensures that the audience and reader understand that victory on that day is solely due to God's ineffable involvement. In a much smaller but similar way, the seven daughters are also saved from the shepherds when an outsider intervenes. God will save Israel from the exploitation of Pharaoh and bring the people through the waters of the Red Sea, and as an anticipation Moses here saves the girls from the brutality of the shepherds and waters their flock. Among other things, the action of watering the flock serves to introduce what will become a familiar motif for Moses during his leadership career. After all, this is not the last time Moses will be involved in a water dispute, for not long after bringing Israel through the waters of the Red Sea—and singing the lyrics quoted above—there is the grumbling at the bitter waters of Marah (Exod 15:22–7). It could be maintained

---

[18] Davies, *Israel in Egypt*, 157, his translation.
[19] Brueggemann, "The Book of Exodus," 703.
[20] Hamilton, *Exodus*, 34.

that the rescue of the seven daughters at the well marks a turning-point for his leadership, for just as he waters their flock, so later he will be called on to provide water during Israel's long journey in the wilderness.

FRIEND OF THE FAMILY

For the third time in recent memory Moses intervenes when he perceives an injustice. First he killed the Egyptian beating a Hebrew, followed by his attempt to reason with a Hebrew who was striking his neighbor. Both of those two interventions could be described as problematic, so it is curious that his rescue of the girls in v. 17 is narrated in such understated terms. There is no mention of how he saves the seven daughters, nor any attempted negotiation, or of striking, or hiding bodies in the Midianite desert. William Propp avers that Moses' "calm demeanour after the incident stands in marked contrast to his furtive behaviour after the earlier conflicts."[21] Since Moses did not receive much gratitude for his earlier interventions in Egypt, it is not overly surprising when the seven daughters wordlessly depart. In the betrothal type-scene, one of the usual conventions is the maiden(s) rushing home to bring news of the arrival, and the actions of Moses surely merit some sort of report.[22] Rebekah encounters the servant of Abraham at the well in Gen 24:15–25, and after their dialogue and her energetic watering of the camels she runs home *after* virtually inviting the man to the house by informing him that there is plenty of straw and fodder. There is no parallel invitation here, and Moses presumably sits back down at the well after they depart. Eventually the women do return to invite Moses home, but it is a leisurely unfolding that begins in Exod 2:18 through the agency of their father, in what turns out to be an engaging sequence of dialogue:

---

[21] Propp, *Exodus 1–18*, 175. Greenberg (*Understanding Exodus*, 39) further suggests that Moses' "good deed appears to be wholly disinterested," especially compared to Jacob who first sees the lovely Rachel (and hears that she is a relative) and then single-handedly moves the large stone and waters the flock.

[22] Berlin, "Giving Birth to a Nation," 313: "One difference about this scene is that here the man defends the women and waters their flocks, thus giving prominence to the hero, Moses."

So they came to Reuel their father, and he said, "Why have you so quickly come back today?"

As mentioned, the priest of Midian is known by several different names in the Pentateuch and the Deuteronomistic History, and perhaps this is an indication that different earlier sources or disparate traditions were combined at a later date to form the present text. Even so, John Durham notes the anomaly of the name Reuel (רעואל) here, because apart from this instance, "Jethro is the sole name assigned to him in the Book of Exodus."[23] The exact solution may remain elusive, but as it stands there is an intriguing wordplay, since the name Reuel apparently means "friend/neighbor of God." The first part of the name occurs earlier in the confrontation between the two Hebrews, when Moses asks the one in the wrong, "Why are you striking your neighbor (רע)?" Moses is rejected and insulted by his fellow Hebrew after posing this question earlier in the chapter, but is about to be shown considerable hospitality by this non-Israelite priest, who will extend the neighborly courtesy lacking from his own people. Moreover, the name "neighbor of God" works to theologically define this priest of Midian, who certainly comes across as friendly to the faith of Israel. While he is a neighbor of Israel on the literal plane, his theological congruence becomes formally evident after the emancipation from Egypt. He and his son-in-law Moses also develop a lasting bond, as illustrated when they are reunited in Exod 18:7 and "each man asked about the welfare of his friend (רע)." Because "Reuel" is the first of several names listed, it quite plausibly is used to foreshadow important characteristics about the relationship between this priest of Midian and the stranger who has arrived.

The father's question (מדוע) about the early return of his daughters betokens genuine curiosity at this change in schedule.[24] Like Pharaoh questioning the midwives in Exod 1:18, Reuel issues a query about this adjustment to his daughters' normal work routine. Commentators wonder if the father's question indicates that shepherds' attacks have happened before, or whether it points to higher efficiency and a shorter work-day on this occasion. So, Nahum Sarna opines that Reuel's question "suggests that the girls regularly experienced such maltreatment at the hands of the male shepherds," while Umberto Cassuto writes of the father's surprise "that they came sooner than the

---

[23] Durham, *Exodus*, 22.   [24] Brueggemann, "The Book of Exodus," 703.

tyranny of the shepherds normally permitted them to do."²⁵ The reader is aware that on this day the seven women do not have to refill their troughs because Moses gets involved, and it gives reason to pause: if the father had not asked, would the daughters have ever disclosed the remarkable presence of the stranger at the well? But the father does ask, and the daughters dutifully answer in v. 19 and explain why they have arrived home early: "They said, 'An Egyptian man rescued us from the hand of the shepherds, and he *even* did the drawing for us and watered the flock!'" For the second time in Exodus 2 an attempt is made to determine the ethnicity of Moses: Pharaoh's daughter immediately identifies him as a Hebrew male in 2:8, but now he is misidentified *as* an Egyptian by the seven daughters. Pharaoh's daughter is correct, but the daughters of Reuel will have to revise their opinion as events proceed.

Most audiences would no doubt appreciate the entertaining irony of the girls' confusion about Moses: the character who is about to be commissioned to wreak havoc on Egypt is thought *to be an Egyptian himself*. But there are other, more nuanced points of significance with Moses being referred to as an Egyptian here. In a sardonic manner, the guilty Hebrew was insinuating *who are you* to play the role of a judge, casting aspersion on Moses as a Hebrew who has been raised by the Egyptian overlords: "In the preceding episode, Moses has clearly identified himself with the Hebrews and has visibly set himself against Egypt. Now, however, he has enough remaining marks of his royal station that this is how he appears to the daughters. This identification is telling, because it suggests that Moses is at a liminal moment in his life, moving to a new identity."²⁶ It is not obvious how the seven daughters distinguish the stranger as an Egyptian, although clothing and speech are common theories and certainly not by any means a stretch of the imagination (even if there is no recorded

---

²⁵ Sarna, *Exodus*, 12; Cassuto, *A Commentary on the Book of Exodus*, 25. Cf. Ackerman, "The Literary Context of the Moses Birth Story," 104: "The dialogue between the puzzled father and the excited girls is a gem. As in the conflict sequence, the scene is very brief; but the closeup effect of the thirty-second exchange achieves a strong impact. The father is surprised that the flocks have been so quickly watered. Why? Moses did not force-feed them! This can possibly mean that the conflict between the girls and the shepherds had been a recurring one, and the daughters had consistently been forced to wait for whatever water was left after the shepherds' flocks had drunk their fill."

²⁶ Brueggemann, "The Book of Exodus," 704.

discourse with the seven daughters). If Moses is wearing distinctively Egyptian apparel or speaks with an accent that causes the misidentification, it recalls another such error during the career of Joseph.[27] As the ravages of famine are felt in Canaan, in Gen 42:6–10 the brothers of Joseph travel to Egypt in order to present themselves before the vizier of Egypt to purchase grain. Later in the episode it is revealed that Joseph is using an interpreter (v. 23), and of course at the time of his promotion (Gen 41:42) Joseph is clothed with garments of fine linen and has the gold chain placed around his neck. As with the seven daughters, the clothing of Joseph and the speech (or concealment thereof) naturally convince the brothers that they are dealing with a native Egyptian, and these cases of mistaken identity are one more connection between Joseph and Moses. For both figures the error is made when each is acting in a judicial capacity, as it were, but for Moses there is a slightly darker hue. He may be acting as a judge in Midian, but James Nohrnberg suggests that this outsider status of Israel's most famous lawgiver will remain: "Midian is only a stopgap for another country, and Moses will not ever enter the actual sovereign territory of Israel; but that is just why he is able to project its legislation, that is, from an ideal standpoint outside it."[28]

Apart from the daughters' forgivable blunder about the identity of their champion, the verb they use is a potent one in the book of Exodus: "he rescued (נצל) us." Once more the NRSV's construal might be questioned—"An Egyptian helped us against the shepherds"—implying more of a team effort wherein Moses lends a hand or proffers some assistance, a polite gesture but not quite capturing the force of the Hebrew verb. Two vivid pictures in the poetic oracles of Isaiah give a better sense of the verb and are useful to compare. Isa 5:29 provides a graphic depiction of an invader who is characterized as a lion, a predator who appears daunting and without mercy: "It growls, seizes prey, carries it off, and there is none to rescue (נצל)."[29] An unambiguously negative picture, the prophetic text highlights the unenviable fate of those who have no rescuer. The other text to compare is Isa 31:5, "Like flying birds, thus will the LORD of Hosts defend Jerusalem. He will defend and rescue (נצל), passing over and

---

[27] Hamilton, *Exodus*, 36.   [28] Nohrnberg, *Like Unto Moses*, 172.
[29] On the leonine imagery, see H. G. M. Williamson, *A Critical and Exegetical Commentary on Isaiah 1–27*, Volume 1: *Commentary on Isaiah 1–5* (ICC; London: T & T Clark, 2006) 407–8.

enabling escape." This oracle paints a much more positive picture, as the inhabitants of Jerusalem are secure because God engineers the rescue of the city from the invader. In Exod 2:19 Reuel's daughters inform their father that they have been rescued by "an Egyptian man" with the same use of the verb for God's rescue of Jerusalem from the invading army in Isa 31:5. In the configuration of this scene at the well in Midian, the rescue of Moses anticipates God's rescue of Israel from the tyranny of Egypt; in fact, the same verb occurs twice in Exodus 3 to underscore this point. From the burning bush God announces to Moses in 3:8 that a forceful and unilateral extraction will take place: having seen and heard the affliction of the people, God has now come down to deliver (נצל) them from the hand of the Egyptians and bring them to a land flowing with milk and honey. "In rescuing the Midianite women," says Carol Meyers, "Moses prefigures Yahweh's saving deeds."[30] The seven daughters of Reuel testify that the stranger delivered them *from the hand* (יד) of the shepherds, and God declares in Exod 3:8 that Israel will be delivered *from the hand* (יד) of the Egyptians. When the rescue is complete and the Egyptian army has been inundated by the waters of chaos, in Exod 14:31 the people of Israel see the "great hand/power" (יד) that God exercises over Egypt and they place their trust in God and Moses his servant.[31]

A second use of the verb *rescue* (נצל) is found in Exod 3:22, though in this case it is used in the *piel* form where it carries the more particular meaning of "despoil" or "plunder." In this context God is unveiling to Moses how the people of Israel will depart from Egypt. After a series of miraculous signs, God will cause the Egyptians to be favorably disposed toward Israel and submissively respond to requests for gold and related valuables: "And you will plunder (נצל) the Egyptians."[32] The verb is used in the same way in 2 Chron 20:25 after Jehoshaphat and the residents of Judah score an unlikely victory over a coalition of foreign armies. It turns out that the coalition forces destroy each other, and after Jehoshaphat and his citizens notice the vast array of dead bodies they gather the spoil, and they plunder (נצל) until they can carry nothing else away. As for the assurance of plunder

---

[30] Meyers, *Exodus*, 45.
[31] Isbell, "Exodus 1–2 in the Context of Exodus 1–14," 49–50.
[32] On the LXX reading, see Joel S. Allen, *The Despoliation of Egypt in Pre-Rabbinic, Rabbinic and Patristic Traditions* (Supplements to Vigiliae Christianae 92; Leiden: Brill, 2008) 64.

in Exod 3:22, the fulfillment takes place in 12:36 exactly as forecasted: "The LORD granted the people favor in the eyes of the Egyptians, who gave them what they asked for, and they plundered them." The seven daughters of Reuel sound grateful enough, and Thomas Dozeman notes that their disposition stands in contrast to the earlier Hebrew—who does not label Moses' intervention as a rescue but instead asks if Moses is going to commit another murder—completely missing the larger implication of what Moses has done and what his actions represent for the future of Israel: "Salvation as a rescue is not free of violence. It signifies deliverance from a threatening situation. Yahweh promises such liberation for Israel in 3:8 and 6:6. It takes place on the night of Passover."[33] Not only does Moses deliver the women from the hand of the shepherds, but he *even* draws water for them. The daughters' speech employs the infinitive aspect of the verb (דלה דלה), and as my translation tries to capture, this syntax reflects their excitement and perhaps the rarity of the occasion.[34] Moses himself is drawn from the water and protected from a tyrant, and now he draws water after rescuing the seven daughters from the shepherds, and this is not the last time water will be involved in his career: from the Red Sea to the waters of Meribah and finally striking the rock that results in disbarment from the promised land, water is part of Moses' experience from start to finish.[35]

THE NEXT GENERATION

Near the end of the betrothal type-scene of Genesis 29 Rachel hurries home to inform her family about Jacob. Laban hears this news in v. 13 and likewise rushes out to meet the newcomer, and so begins a

---

[33] Dozeman, *Exodus*, 90.

[34] For Utzschneider and Oswald (*Exodus 1–15*, 95), Moses makes a considerable impression on the women: "The narrative rather humorously lets this shine through by having the daughters exaggerate certain nuances of Moses' deed" (e.g., the "energetic" drawing of the water).

[35] Cf. the longer reflection of Sabo, "Drawing Out Moses," 409: "Moses, perhaps more than any other biblical character, is intimately associated with water. It plays an important role in his birth story, and also, in an odd and oblique way, his premature death. In between, water shows up at important stages in his life: his chance meeting with the seven Midianite daughters at a well, his encounters with Pharaoh on the Nile, the parting of the Suph-Sea, and his search to provide water for the Israelites in the desert. A web of thematic and linguistic ties links these episodes together."

complicated relationship between Jacob and his uncle/father-in-law Laban. Moses too will have a close association with his father-in-law, but without the disingenuousness that typifies the interactions between Laban and Jacob. Moreover, when Laban hastens to meet Jacob after hearing about his arrival, it sets the tone for an adversarial relationship where one character is consistently seeking an advantage over the other. In Exod 2:20 Reuel could be accused of manifesting impatience with his daughters, but only because he is interested in showing hospitality to their rescuer:

> He said to his daughters, "So, where is he? Why is it that you abandoned the man? Invite him so that he can eat bread!"

Reuel had previously inquired why the women came home so early, as though it was an unforeseen turn of events. But if his first question in v. 18 is a request for information, his rhetorical questions—including the interrogative למה—here in v. 20 are a mild reprimand. Not only is the priest of Midian keen to extend hospitality, but as the father of seven (presumably eligible) bachelorette daughters, the prospect of lowering his number of dependents by one is perhaps not lost on him. Either way, Reuel's agitation certainly lends some color to his characterization, and might be compared to another annoyed character in the Pentateuch. In Numbers 22 the foreign soothsayer Balaam is hired by Balak king of Moab. En route to curse Israel, Balaam's journey is temporarily suspended by a divine angel standing in the path with a drawn sword. The angel is perfectly obvious to his donkey but not to Balaam, who beats his donkey on several occasions. Finally laying down, Balaam's repeated abuse elicits this comment from his animal in Num 22:28: "What have I done to you, that you have struck me these three times?" Within the surrounding context, the donkey is endowed with greater perspicuity than the powerful characters in story, and thus the donkey becomes a foil for Balaam and the others. Just as the donkey is configured as a foil, so Reuel becomes a foil for the Israelites because he is keen to honor the rescuer of his daughters whereas the Hebrews seem less inclined. For Terence Fretheim there is an ironic contrast between the foreign priest and the lack of welcome by Moses' own community: "Israel does not appreciate his acts of justice on its behalf; the Midianites welcome it. Israelites engage in accusations of Moses; the daughters of Reuel publicly sing his praises. Those who stand within the community of faith are abusive; those without faith in Israel's

God exemplify genuine relationships."[36] Further down the road Moses will experience moments of hostility from his own people as well, so the urgency of Reuel to invite "the Egyptian" home proves to be another difference between the two receptions of Moses.

> Moses was pleased to stay with the man, and he gave his daughter Zipporah to Moses. She gave birth to a son, and he named him Gershom, for he said, "I have been a sojourner in a foreign land." (Exod 2:21–2)

With the betrothal type-scene drawing to a close, the invitation to partake of a meal at Reuel's table is evidently extended to a longer-term residency. In Jacob's case (cf. Gen 29:14; 31:38), he too stays for an extended period with Laban, an arrangement that leads to a host of dubious machinations, with Laban acting as a measure-for-measure *alter ego* of the conniving Jacob himself. The only comparable incident between Moses and his father-in-law would have to be Exod 4:18, when Moses seeks permission to leave after receiving the divine commission to lead Israel out of Egypt. Yet Moses' actual request is reticent to say the least: "Please let me go so that I may return to my brothers who are in Egypt, so I can see if they are still alive."[37] The purported rationale for returning to Egypt may be technically true in the broadest sense, but there is a startling omission of any details from the recent theophany, such as the burning bush or God's audible voice and announcement of Moses' call to lead Israel out of slavery and into their own land after a lengthy confrontation with Pharaoh replete with signs and wonders. Instead of sharing his divine commission, Moses provides his father-in-law with the extremely vague objective of determining if his fellow Hebrews remain alive in Egypt. Yet if Moses is being shifty or evasive, it hardly compares to Laban (who begins to fleece Jacob within 30 days of his arrival) or Jacob (who rarely gives up an opportunity to profit at Laban's expense).

---

[36] Fretheim, *Exodus*, 44. For the contention that Exodus 2 is structured to reveal such contrasts, see Davies, *Israel in Egypt*, 155: "Like the repetition that helps create it, the symmetry of this passage is both internal and external. Its parts stands to each other in the ways we have seen. But, as a whole, its plot also bears on the last episode as its inverse: success not failure; foreigners not his people; a welcome not a rejection; entrance into a new relation of marriage not flight from the old one, adoption. In the first, the Egyptian is the enemy who oppresses; in the second, Moses is called an Egyptian as he offers help against the oppressor. Moses flees his home; he finds a home."

[37] Cf. Childs, *The Book of Exodus*, 101: "Commentators have continued to puzzle over the fact that Moses does not communicate to Jethro his real reason for leaving."

Jacob does not even inform Laban that he is leaving for Canaan in Gen 31:20, and quite literally "steals his heart." The interpreter might even want to exonerate Moses here by arguing that his perceived inadequacies are what prevent him from disclosing to his father-in-law the real reason for returning to Egypt—or the danger to which he is exposing his wife. So apart from this one aberration in Exod 4:18—under extenuating circumstances it must be said—the association between Moses and Reuel is on a higher plane than Jacob and Laban, and their cordial relationship is anticipated by Reuel's guileless hospitality.

After the initial invitation to a meal, Moses is "pleased" (יאל) to remain with the priest and his family in v. 21. Whether the pleasure partially comes from the fact that Reuel has seven daughters is not stated, but in short order Zipporah ("bird") becomes the wife of Moses. No reason is given as to why Zipporah—as opposed to one of her six sisters—becomes the wife, nor if she is the firstborn of Reuel or the one who desires Moses the most. But she certainly is not plagued with barrenness, unlike the other participants in the betrothal type-scenes such as Rebekah and Rachel. Without any reported difficulty, Zipporah gives birth to a son whom Moses names *Gershom*. This naming-speech represents Moses' first spoken words since leaving Egypt, and as is argued, it here underscores his liminal status in Midian.[38] In light of Zipporah's overall characterization, it is notable that Moses the father names their son, hinting that in general Zipporah will be a background figure in the narrative. The birth of her second son Eliezer is not actually recorded prior to his arrival in Exod 18:4. He too is named by Moses ("For the God of my father has been my help, and rescued me from the sword of Pharaoh"), and although his name does not provide any concrete evidence regarding the time of his birth, it does suggest that Moses is expressing gratitude for making it to Midian as a fugitive. The scene where Eliezer is first introduced is strange, with some commentators asserting that Moses divorced his wife. Thomas Dozeman states that the language would

---

[38] As Davies (*Israel in Egypt*, 151) notes, the seven daughters speak considerably more than Moses: "The women's talk is set against his taciturnity. He says only one thing, at the end: 'A sojourner have I been in a foreign land.' In the last pericope Moses became trapped between the juridical language in which he parroted Pharaoh and the rhetorical question by which the Hebrew tricked him. In the moral sense, he lost the power of speech."

formally permit the interpretation of divorce (cf. Deut 22:19), but the context seems to indicate otherwise.[39] My point is that Zipporah is again a background figure, with much more attention on the relationship between Moses and his father-in-law instead of husband and wife. Moreover, it is perhaps appropriate that Zipporah, like Moses, is misidentified: the text is not overly clear, but it is possible that she is labeled a Cushite in Num 12:1, and so like her husband, she has an outsider status that is never fully removed and is challenged by the community of Israel.[40]

For all the hospitality Moses enjoys as the guest of the priest, Midian itself has a rather ambivalent status in the rest of the Pentateuch. The reader may have been prepared for such a contingency, for as F. V. Greifenhagen notes, Midian is a close relative of Israel "and yet as a branch of the family rejected as a bearer of the promises to the ancestors. In other words, according to the genealogical ideology of Genesis, Midian will eventually be a dead end for Moses."[41] Indeed, transporting Joseph to Egypt marks the Midianites (and the Ishmaelites for that matter) as temporary mediators, and therefore in Moses' career Midian is a provisional site in preparation for his role in the continuity of the promise to Abraham through Israel. But tensions increase between Israel and the Midianites, almost inversely proportionate to the relationship between Moses and his father-in-law. As Greifenhagen further observes, Moses receives advice and guidance from his priestly father-in-law when Israel is located in the desert (Exodus 18), but "later Midian refuses to join Israel (Num. 10:29–32),

---

[39] Dozeman, *Exodus*, 402. Cf. Fretheim, *Exodus*, 195–6: "it is not known when or why Moses' family had been separated."

[40] E.g., Naomi Graetz, "Did Miriam Talk Too Much?" pp. 231–42 in *A Feminist Companion to Exodus to Deuteronomy*, edited by Athalya Brenner (FCB 6; Sheffield: Sheffield Academic Press, 1994) 235: "In Numbers 12, it is not clear who is the Cushite woman, and whether Miriam's case against Moses is just or not."

[41] Greifenhagen, *Egypt on the Pentateuch's Ideological Map*, 65–6. Cf. Ronald Hendel, "The Exodus in Biblical Memory," *JBL* 120 (2001) 618: "The life of Moses spans the geographical opposition of Egypt and Israel. Born in Egypt, he flees to Midian and returns to Egypt at Yahweh's behest to lead Israel in its escape from Egypt. He leads the people back to the holy mountain, and thence through the desert to the land of Israel. As in the transition from slavery to freedom, Moses has already experienced the passage out of Egypt, making it appropriate for him to lead the rest of the people in their passage. Moses' death on the threshold of the Promised Land, after viewing the whole land, leaves him betwixt and between, neither in Egypt nor in the Promised Land. Moses' geographical movements mark him as a mediator in the spatial transformation of the people."

and the involvement of Midian in Israel's participation in idolatrous fertility rituals at Peor leads to Israelite hostility towards Midian (Num. 25). Finally, one of the last acts of Moses is to command the extermination of the Midianites (Num. 31)."[42] Consequently, the downturn of Midian squares the focus on the character of Reuel rather than his ethnicity, and on his action as the priest comes along at the exact right time for the career of Moses. In this sense Reuel has parallels to Pharaoh's daughter—who may also be characterized as a foil for her father—creating the impression that certain foreigners enter the story at integral moments for the survival and prosperity of Moses. Zipporah also enters the group, as she too makes a decisive contribution to Moses' future. Like the midwives, she intervenes to save an Israelite life and shows herself in Exod 4:24–6 to be quick-witted and cool under pressure in the process:

> Now it came to pass at the lodging place on the way that the LORD met him and sought to kill him. So Zipporah took a flint and cut off her son's foreskin. She touched it to his feet, and said, "Surely you are a bridegroom of blood to me." Then he relented from him. Then she said, "Indeed, a bridegroom of blood!" on account of the circumcision.

Among the most bizarre and cryptic episodes in the Pentateuch if not the entire Hebrew Bible, the interpretation of this passage is well beyond our present scope in this study.[43] Acknowledging that the text contains some profound enigmas, my interest here is focused primarily on the contribution of Zipporah as one more foreign character whose timing and apparent courage are extremely valuable to Moses, if not to the people of Israel as well. The episode in Exod 4:24–6 occurs after Zipporah has departed from her father's house, and takes place after God gives directions to Moses for speaking to Pharaoh: since Pharaoh refuses to let Israel go, his firstborn son will be killed (v. 23). But before any conversations with Pharaoh, Zipporah plays a major role in the crisis involving her firstborn son, because at the stopping-point along the way she is forced to perform some emergency surgery. If circumcision here is connected with Israelite identity, Zipporah intervenes to secure her son's identity as an Israelite

---

[42] Greifenhagen, *Egypt on the Pentateuch's Ideological Map*, 66.
[43] For a detailed overview and recent review of scholarship, see John T. Willis, *Yahweh and Moses in Conflict: The Role of Exodus 4:24–6 in the Book of Exodus* (Bern: Peter Lang, 2010).

under the covenant (Gen 17:9–14). There is an irony here, since Zipporah earlier confuses the Israelite identity of her future husband—mistaking Moses for an Egyptian—yet now her rapid response ensures an escape from this dangerous nocturnal scene, and circumcising her son marks him as a descendant of Abraham.

Not only does Moses survive the ordeal in large measure because of his wife, but there is also a new angle on the name of their firstborn son, Gershom (גרשם). Based on the naming-speech of Moses in Exod 2:22, the name is presumably a compound from the terms "sojourner" (גר) and "there" (שם).[44] While the geographical reference conceivably refers to Midian, the name could also point to the uncertain status of Moses in Egypt, eventually prompting his flight when Pharaoh discovers his Israelite provenance. For Athena Gorospe, the ambiguity as to which place Moses refers to when naming his firstborn "underscores the lack in Moses of a real sense of belonging to any group, whether Israelite, Egyptian, or Midianite."[45] But the name of Gershom also resembles the verb "drive out" (גרש), anticipating Israel shortly being driven out from Egypt. Like the name of the father (the name "Moses" foreshadows Israel being drawn out of the waters of the Red Sea), the name of the son also looks ahead to God's intervention. Gershom is imperiled in the episode of Exod 4:24–6, but his mother—who herself was saved by Gershom's (future) father after the shepherds drive her away from the well—is able to mitigate the divine wrath, and continue the family's journey to Egypt that results in Israel being driven out.[46] Furthermore, there are grounds for suggesting

---

[44] Cf. Utzschneider and Oswald, *Exodus 1–15*, 95–6.

[45] Gorospe, *Narrative and Identity: An Ethical Reading of Exodus 4*, 162.

[46] J. P. Fokkelman, "Exodus," pp. 56–65 in *The Literary Guide to the Bible*, edited by Robert Alter and Frank Kermode (Cambridge, MA: Belknap Press, 1987) 60: "The name of his son Gershom contains a pun which anticipates Israel's departure from Egypt: Pharaoh 'shall surely thrust you out hence altogether [*garesh yegaresh*].'" On the naming of Gershom and the characterization of Moses, see Harold Bloom, "Moses" in *The Book of J: Translated from the Hebrew by David Rosenberg, Interpreted by Harold Bloom* (New York: Grove Weidenfeld, 1990) 244: "We have learned already, from his useless revenge against the Egyptian, that Moses is intemperate though wary. Here we see again that he is courageous and, in the naming of his son (Ex. 2:22), wholly dedicated to the fate of his people. But he has qualities in plenty that argue against his suitability to lead a people out of bondage and exile: anger, impatience, and a deep anxiety about his own hold on authority." In consonance with his name, Gershom will remain something of a stranger himself, as Machinist ("The Meaning of Moses," 14) observes: "Gershom has as well a curious genealogical niche. For while he has descendants, they are not arranged in a line of divine promise and

that Gershom's brother Eliezer is present in the background of Exod 4:24-6, since in v. 20 we read that Moses takes his wife and his sons (בניו) when he departed for Egypt, so there is no reason why Eliezer cannot be included in this company. Later in the story Eliezer's naming-speech by Moses is provided as a retrospect: "The God of my father has been my help and rescued me from the sword of Pharaoh" (Exod 18:4). If Eliezer (אליעזר) is also born in Midian, his name glances back to Moses' previous escape from Pharaoh and (unintentionally) reaches forward to the exodus event. In Exod 4:24-6 Eliezer's name likewise takes on another level of significance, as the mother's swift action with a sword of flint ensures the survival of her offspring, and just as Moses once rescued Zipporah, now he and his sons are rescued by her. Along with the midwives, Zipporah also saves the lives of Hebrew males and surely demonstrates the fear of God. Even if the reader never discovers the reason why she becomes the wife of Moses in Exod 2:21 rather than one of her sisters, it must be concluded that Zipporah is altogether a prudent match.

SHIFT IN PERSPECTIVE

The marriage of Moses and the birth of Gershom take the reader back to the outset of Exodus 2. As Carol Meyers notes, the chapter begins with the marriage of two Levites and the birth and naming of their son, and now the long section concludes with Moses' own marriage and naming-speech for his firstborn son: "These life cycle events form an inclusio. Between them is contained the emergence of the hero in narrative segments that account for his Egyptian identity, his Hebrew origins, and his Midianite connection — all important elements in the story about to unfold."[47] When Moses bequeaths a name for his son Gershom, and Eliezer as well at some undetermined point, it brings to mind the naming-speeches of Joseph in Gen 41:50-2. Prior to the arrival of the famine, Asenath daughter of Potiphera, priest of On,

---

authority such as is found with Abraham and his family (e.g., Genesis 26:2–5). Indeed, in Judges 18:30-1 (following here the textual tradition that reads the ancestor's name as Moses, not Manasseh), we learn that Gershom's descendants were priests to an idolatrous cult in the Israelite tribe of Dan."

[47] Meyers, *Exodus*, 46.

bore him Manasseh ("Because God has made me forget all my trouble and all my father's house") and Ephraim ("Because God has made me fruitful in the land of my affliction"). For Joseph and Moses, the naming of the son(s) takes place near the end of a lengthy period of exile from their families, and each character is shortly to reconcile with "their brothers" who previously rejected their leadership with rhetorical questions such as "will you govern over us?" or "who set you as a judge over us?" (Gen 37:8; Exod 2:14). The same brothers who angrily ask these questions are soon to be dependent on Joseph and Moses for deliverance from the ravages of famine and the slavery of Pharaoh, respectively. Naming the sons, therefore, is an ironic point of departure: "Both Joseph and Moses name their sons according to the past, but it occurs right before a change in their futures."[48] After the naming-speeches of Joseph in Genesis 41, the event of the famine is poised to begin, and this contingency sets the brothers on a journey of reunion. Similarly, right after the birth of Moses' firstborn, there is a death recorded in Exod 2:23 that will soon set Moses on a journey of reunion:

> During the course of those many days the king of Egypt died, and the Israelites groaned because of their slavery. They cried out for help, and their desperate plea because of their slavery went up to God.

Attention has been riveted on the travails of Moses since his flight to Midian, but meanwhile the drudgery of slave labor has continued for the Israelites. Pharaoh's obituary becomes the moment where these two narrative strands reconnect. The death notice of such an imposing figure in the text is terse considering how many Israelite lives he has taken—or attempted to take, including Moses' own—and the new king dies shrouded in the same anonymity with which he lived. An abrupt contrast emerges in these two verses: Gershom has an elaborate and multivalenced naming-speech that symbolically captures several elements of the forthcoming plot, whereas the dead king retains the namelessness that has marked his entire career.[49] Mention of this death returns us to the king's manic but ultimately unsuccessful effort to invalidate the divine promise to Abraham, that his name will be great and through his offspring every family on earth will be blessed. The naming of Gershom right before the obituary of the old

---

[48] Nohrnberg, *Like Unto Moses*, 153.   [49] Cf. Hamilton, *Exodus*, 41.

The Stranger in Midian 169

king suggests that any successor will also fail to eradicate the promise. For Nahum Sarna, the naming of Gershom echoes the divine word to Abraham in Gen 15:13-14, where the ancestor is told that his descendants will be strangers (גר) and slaves in a foreign land but afterwards will be brought out with great judgments and possessions, and therefore the "fulfillment of the predicted slavery evokes the associated promise of liberation, so that the birth of the child may be seen as symbolic of the coming regeneration of downtrodden Israel."[50] The death of the old king—who did not know Joseph—is reported right after yet another allusion to Joseph, further implying that Moses, like Joseph before him, preserves the family of Israel: Joseph rescued them by bringing them into Egypt, while Moses participates in their rescue by bringing them out of Egypt.

Within the immediate frame of the story, however, what is most jarring about the king's death is how inconsequential it is for the Israelites under the burden of slavery: "The death of the old king (2:23) who was instrumental to the oppression of the Israelites (as told in Exodus 1) could have presumably introduced a new set of affairs that could have led to the alleviation of the suffering of the Israelites. Just as a change of policy was effected when 'a new king arose over Egypt who did not acknowledge Joseph' (1:8), hope for a reversal of policy was ripe with the death of this king."[51] It is reasonable to think that a surge of hope for the slaves may have accompanied the death of such a notorious king, but the result is seemingly antithetical, as there is, if anything, an increase in their burden.[52] On two occasions, therefore, the new king marks a transition

---

[50] Sarna, *Exodus*, 12-13. In terms of Exodus 2 as a whole, see Greenberg's (*Understanding Exodus*, 46) summary remark: "Moses' advent in the story serves as a response to Pharaoh's last and most drastic measure; it is therefore fitting that the narrative of his early life in 2:1-22 begin and end with a birth notice—an echo of the proliferation formula of verse 7. Thus the pattern: repressive measure—frustrating response is carried to its conclusion. Noteworthy too is the balanced ending of the main passages: verse 10 and verse 22 each concludes with a name-giving."

[51] Gorospe, *Narrative and Identity: An Ethical Reading of Exodus 4*, 152.

[52] Greifenhagen, *Egypt on the Pentateuch's Ideological Map*, 68; Meyers, *Exodus*, 46. On the structural function of the king's death, see Ackerman, "The Literary Context of the Moses Birth Story," 107: "The opening passage, in describing the fruitful proliferation of the descendants of Israel, mentions the death of Joseph, God's agent through whom the life of the people had been preserved (cf. Gen. 50:20). The closing passage gives us another death—the death of Pharaoh, the death-bringer. Paradoxically, the people of Israel experience the deathlike quality of bondage even more strongly as a result."

in the story. When he arises to power the oppression of Israel begins, and when he dies there is arguably more oppression. The lack of any sign of a decrease in their burdens may trigger an increase in groaning, and while a string of verbs are detonated to express the Israelite frustration, scholars observe the *absence* of any direct object for their cries. Walter Brueggemann notes that the terms of lament are general and "constitute a characteristic vocabulary of those who cry out in rage, protest, insistence, and expectation concerning an intolerable situation. The two terms groan and groaning serve as an unfocused expression of distress. The other terms serve to summon help. None of the terms, however, is addressed to anyone in particular."[53] Similarly, Thomas Dozeman comments: "There is no object to the cry of the Israelites. Instead, their groan finds its own way to God."[54] The oppressed Israelites may not direct their plea for help directly to God, but God hears nonetheless because their cry "ascends" (עלה).[55] At this point in the story—quite possibly at the nadir of Israel's experience in Egypt—God enters the fray with an activation of covenant-memory, and in Exod 2:24-5 there is a responsiveness that is deeply personal:

> God heard their groaning, and God remembered his covenant with Abraham, Isaac, and Jacob. God saw the Israelites, and God knew.

Divine involvement to this point in the book of Exodus has been understated, and while it may be assumed that the growth of Israel is a fulfillment of the promise to the ancestors, the only indication of direct activity is God giving houses to the midwives. But even that case, as Gordon Davies explains, is quite different from God's response in the final lines of this chapter: "With the midwives in

---

[53] Brueggemann, "The Book of Exodus," 706. [54] Dozeman, *Exodus*, 91.
[55] Jacob, *The Second Book of the Bible: Exodus*, 45: "Their outcries were directed to God, as the rest of this verse and Deut 26:7 indicate." For a different view, see Ackerman, "The Literary Context of the Moses Birth Story," 107-8: "the first four descriptions of Israel in verse 23 show her at her lowest ebb. Though Pharaoh is dead, there is no one to hope in. Moses is far removed from the scene, and the God who had been with the forefathers has apparently faded from the people's memory. It is quite remarkable that there is no direct object for the outcry of Israel. They scream into the void, underlining their utter despair. But God heard... remembered... saw... knew. Their cry goes into the void, but God is there also. We know that the story is ready for a dramatic new turn."

1:20, God intervened silently; we learned nothing of his thoughts: 'God dealt well with the midwives; the people increased and became very strong.' Now we see briefly within his mind, and his salvation is all the more to be hoped for."[56] Some familiar language creates a parallel in this chapter: Moses sees (ראה) the Israelite abuse but ineffectively mediates in v. 11, yet now God sees (ראה) and the act of remembering will lead to a successful intervention. Indeed, the verb remember (זכר) is first used in Gen 8:1 when God remembers Noah, and this act of memory generates a wind that causes the floodwaters to recede. When God remembers, it is a preface to action based on a prior commitment. In Exod 2:24 the act of remembrance joins two narrative strands: the preparation of Moses, and God's covenant with the ancestors, thus positioning the story to move to another level. The final statement of the chapter—"and God knew" (וידע אלהים)—glances back to Chapter 1 and the rise of the new king who does not "know" Joseph: "And so וידע forms a contrasting inclusio with 1.8: the new king did not know of Joseph and brutalized the relations between the Egyptians and the Israelites."[57] The new king of Egypt did not acknowledge Joseph and changed national policy, but God knows the descendants of Joseph and is about to implement a radical shift in that same Egyptian policy. A measure of suspense is created by the final statement because there is no object, only the declaration that God "knows." While it may not qualify as a cliffhanger ending, Robert Alter notes that the concluding statement

> marks the end of the narrative segment with a certain mystifying note—sufficiently mystifying that the ancient Greek translators sought to "correct" it—because it has no object. "God knew," but what did He know? Presumably the suffering of the Israelites, the cruel oppression of history in which they are now implicated, the obligations of the covenant with the patriarchs, and the plan He must undertake to liberate the

---

[56] Davies, *Israel in Egypt*, 167. Cf. Meyers, *Exodus*, 46: "Although the divine presence may have been hovering in the background of the fortuitous saving of the infant Moses, the narrator does not tell us anything about God's response to the suffering of the people until this passage."

[57] Davies, *Israel in Egypt*, 172; a similar point is made by Durham (*Exodus*, 26): "Just as these two chapters are begun with the names of the descendants of the fathers, in and through which the first part of the covenant-promise has been fulfilled, so they are closed with the names of the fathers themselves, a reminder that God remembers the whole of his promise. Thus is the fulfillment of the second part of the promise anticipated by a reference to the fathers to whom it was made."

enslaved people. And so the objectless verb prepares us for the divine address from the burning bush and the beginning of Moses' mission.[58]

The death of the old king paves the way for a change in regime, and for the arrival of a new Pharaoh who will be the principal antagonist from now until his drowning in Exod 14:28 that is subsequently commemorated in the Song of the Sea.[59] But in addition to Moses, the new Pharaoh will find himself locked against an even more formidable opponent, and so it is fitting that his first direct speech stands in the firm tradition of his predecessor: "Who is the LORD that I should listen to his voice and release Israel? I do not know the LORD, and moreover, I won't release Israel!" (Exod 5:2). It could be that the frequent use of "God" in Exod 2:23-5 prepares the way for the revelation of the divine name in Exodus 3, as Moses "knows" the LORD whom Pharaoh refuses to acknowledge.[60] Overall, there is an *envelope structure* at work in Exodus 1-2, as the narrative unit begins (1:1-5) with an evocation of God's promise to the ancestors, and draws to a close (2:23-5) with a reference to the same promise, as well as the rise of the new king (1:8) and his eventual death (2:23).[61]

---

[58] Alter, *The Five Books of Moses*, 317. For Greenberg (*Understanding Exodus*, 45), "The increasing vagueness of the objects in verse 25—with the last verb entirely lacking an express object—similarly heightens the reader's anticipation."

[59] Cf. Greifenhagen, *Egypt on the Pentateuch's Ideological Map*, 68.

[60] Singled out as he is in the first two chapters of Exodus, it might be argued that Moses is prefigured as "the hero of close encounter, while the people are confined to a lower level of reality," (Martin Ravndal Hauge, *The Descent from the Mountain: Narrative Patterns in Exodus 19–40* [JSOTSup 323; Sheffield: Sheffield Academic Press, 2001] 31). On the frequency of God's name, note also Utzschneider and Oswald, *Exodus 1–15*, 105: "From the final sentence of v. 23 on, the divine denomination אלהים appears in every sentence, five times in all, even though in vv. 24-5 grammatically it is no longer required. Beyond this, the depiction implies a theologically significant characteristic of God: on the one hand, he nobly transcends earthly-human events: the complaint ascends to him—yet presumably to heaven. On the other hand, he is simultaneously immanent to the people of his future nation (whether their cries intend this or not). His distance is not tantamount to dwelling apathetically in an inaccessible sphere; the gulf is bridged by his ability and willingness to take notice."

[61] A comparable envelope structure can be found in 2 Samuel 11-12, as the Ammonite war frames the story of David and Bathsheba; see Shemaryahu Talmon, "1 and 2 Chronicles," pp. 365-72 in *The Literary Guide to the Bible*, edited by Robert Alter and Frank Kermode (Cambridge, MA: Belknap Press of Harvard University Press, 1987) 366; note also Shimon Bar-Efrat, *Narrative Art in the Bible* (JSOTSup 70; Sheffield: Almond Press, 1989) 98-9.

Contained within these bookends is a tightly organized story with a number of allusions to important moments in the book of Genesis, and such references collectively contribute to the theological map of forthcoming deliverance for the family of slaves that leads ultimately to their encounter with God in the wilderness.

7

Exodus 1–2 and the Sojourn of Israel

> *Of all the books in the Hebrew Bible, Exodus perhaps has had the greatest impact beyond the ancient community in which it took shape. The account of escape from oppression has become a great narrative of hope for peoples all over the world. The tale of courageous prophetic activity often has served as a model for struggling community leaders. The values embodied in the legal traditions are reflected in the law codes of many countries. The attention to the physical setting as well as the moral issues involved in the service of God reverberates in houses of worship everywhere. The establishment of a final form of Exodus as part of Hebrew scripture was both the end product of a long process of tradition formation and, at the same time, part of the beginning of the book's profound and enduring role in Christianity and Islam as well as Judaism.*
>
> Carol Meyers[1]

The opening sequence of the book of Exodus unfolds an exceptional narrative that foreshadows a significant amount of the forthcoming storyline in the rest of the Pentateuch and establishes a lasting paradigm of redemption for Israel. Major points of continuity with Genesis are immediately apparent: the people of Israel remain in Egypt after traveling to be reunited with Joseph and survive the ravages of famine, and their prolific growth in Egypt accords with God's promise to Abraham about his multitude of descendants. But there is also an immediate sense of *discontinuity* as the Exodus narrative begins, reflected in the stylistic shift and more accelerated

---

[1] Meyers, *Exodus*, xv.

Exodus 1–2 and the Sojourn of Israel 175

pace to the story.[2] Several reasons could be posited for the change of pace and style, but from a narrative-critical perspective it could be argued that different kinds of emplotment and characterization are at work in Exodus 1–2 because of the nature of the theological drama that is presented. Here the reader might usefully compare the opening segment of 1 Samuel as somewhat distinct from the preceding book of Judges. Walter Brueggemann notes, "The framers of the canonical books of I and II Samuel have a lively, daring 'sense of a beginning.' Their subject is the new narrative of Israel's new social possibility of monarchy." As one recalls, in the final form of the Deuteronomistic History the reader moves from the action-packed and horrific civil conflict at the end of Judges to a much more pedestrian commencement of the book of 1 Samuel, with its genealogical prologue and patient explanation of annual worship at Shiloh. Brueggemann maintains that the biblical writers "wish to assert that the monarchy did not appear in Israel either because of the initiative of dazzling personalities, nor because of large concentrations of socioeconomic, military power, but because of the inscrutable, inexplicable initiative of Yahweh."[3] Just as 1 Samuel transitions to the story of the inauguration of Israel's monarchy from the comparative anarchy and decentralization of Judges, so Exodus moves from the ancestral peregrinations and internal family dynamics in Genesis to the national story of oppression and enslavement in the early sectors of Exodus, and this topical change is met with a shift in narrative discourse.

Although the techniques of literary characterization in Exodus 1–2 differ from Genesis—with the latter having on the whole more developed

---

[2] See Brian Richardson, "Origins, Paratexts, and Prototypes" in *Narrative Beginnings: Theories and Practices*, edited by Brian Richardson (Lincoln and London: University of Nebraska Press, 2008) 13: "In his seminal book on beginnings, Edward Said draws attention to a number of paradoxes with which the concept is entwined. Beginnings seem always predetermined, yet they also appear to mark a distinct break from that which precedes them" (referring to Said, *Beginnings: Intention and Method*). Note also Alter, *The Five Books of Moses*, 299: "As the long historical narrative of the Five Books of Moses moves from the patriarchs to the Hebrew nation in Egypt, it switches gears. The narrative conventions deployed, from type-scenes and thematic keywords to the treatment of dialogue, remain the same, but the angle from which events are seen and the handling of characters are notably different." For a source-critical alternative, see Konrad Schmid, "Genesis and Exodus as Two Formerly Independent Traditions of Origins for Ancient Israel," *Biblica* 93 (2012) 187–208.
[3] Walter Brueggemann, "I Samuel 1: A Sense of a Beginning," *ZAW* 102 (1990) 33, referring to Frank Kermode, *The Sense of an Ending: Studies in the Theory of Fiction* (Oxford: Oxford University Press, 1967).

major characters, often infused with humor or embedded within more decorative measure-for-measure retributive frameworks—the early cast of Exodus is impressive in its own right and undeniably creates its own literary effect. An early example is the collective representation of the teeming Israelites, a particularly striking picture because this is presumably how the group would have appeared in the eyes of the new king of Egypt.[4] The swarming growth of Israel resonates with the divine promise of Genesis, but also provides grounds for the king's insinuation that they pose a quantifiable threat to Egyptian security. As for the new king himself, the most memorable aspect of his characterization, albeit one that has proven endlessly frustrating for historians, is the absence (or erasure) of a proper name, and Ronald Hendel argues it is entirely possible that by "leaving the name of Pharaoh a blank, the memory of Egyptian oppression could extend to all who had felt the oppression of Pharaoh at any time in the remembered past."[5] Within the portrait of the new king, therefore, is the image of a tyrant with a range of applications, and combined with the highly generic portrayal of Egypt in the book of Exodus, the reader assumes that this particular literary style allows for the story to transcend the period of Egyptian tyranny and have relevance for multiple situations of captivity, and by extension, the hope for deliverance in such circumstances. Of course, the namelessness of the new king is a stunning contrast to the midwives, Shifrah and Puah, who not only are explicitly identified—in what must be a satire of the Egyptian potentate—but also given (dynastic) houses as a reward for their courageous resistance of the despotic command to destroy the male offspring of Israel. The midwives are the first in a

---

[4] Note the succinct theoretical discussion of collective characterization in Pardes, *The Biography of Ancient Israel*, 10–11. On collective characterization in the Songs of Songs, see Yair Mazor, *Who Wrought the Bible? Unveiling the Bible's Aesthetic Secrets* (Madison: University of Wisconsin Press, 2009) 73–94; for an example from renaissance theatre, see Edward W. Rosenheim, *What Happens in Literature: A Guide to Poetry, Drama and Fiction* (Chicago: University of Chicago Press, 2000) 116–17.

[5] Hendel, "The Exodus in Biblical Memory," 604–5. He further notes (621): "The historically true and the symbolically true are interwoven in such a way that the past authorizes and encompasses the present. The exodus, in this sense, is not a punctual past but ongoing, a past continuous.... The story as a whole defines the collective identity and ethnic boundaries of the people, providing a common foundation for social and religious life. The social function of history is evident in the processes of ethnic self-definition in the story and in the annual festival (Passover) that reenacts this collective memory."

Exodus 1–2 and the Sojourn of Israel 177

parade of strong female characters, 12 by most counts, a cast of characters who are catalysts for the survival of the 12 tribes of Israel. Along with the Levite mother, the sister, Pharaoh's daughter, and the seven daughters of Reuel, these characters are the heroes of the initial installment of Exodus and a foil to Pharaoh and his taskmasters.[6] As the midwives resist Pharaoh, so Pharaoh's daughter resists conventional grammar, insisting on the active participle for her adopted son, who will indeed liberate the Hebrews and enable them to go up from the land *just as her father inadvertently predicts in his first speech*. The daughter of the king rescues Moses from the water of the Nile, but in a kind of reimbursement Moses then rescues the daughters of the priest by the well of water in Midian, in turn anticipating the national deliverance of Israel from the oppression of slavery.

Perhaps the easiest character to overlook is Reuel the priest of Midian, but he too provides another example of a non-Israelite figure who comes to the aid of Moses at a crucial moment in the narrative. While his timely gesture of hospitality to the newcomer may not be on quite the same dramatic plane as the rescue of the infant Moses by Pharaoh's daughter or his own daughter Zipporah's surgical intervention later in Exod 4:25, the name(s) of this Midianite priest nonetheless live on. This foreign priest of Midian becomes an ironic foil himself to the recalcitrant Israelites, represented by the brawler whom Moses encounters in Exod 2:13–14. One of the prime reasons Moses has to flee from Egypt is because he is sarcastically asked "who made you a judge (שפט)," only to take refuge with the priest of Midian who later offers great help when Moses is judging (שפט) the Israelites in Exod 18:13–26. The father-in-law suggests the appointment of other judges to whom Moses can delegate the easier cases, and in so doing the priest of Midian arrives at a sensible solution to an obvious problem. Not only does this help ease the legal burden of Moses, but it also casts a retrospective glance back to the insult in Exodus 2. Overall, the later episode coheres with the portrait of Moses in the early chapters of the book, since an early insult or point of adversity is revisited, overturned, and often transformed as his career progresses. Yet Moses' own life story is not without some ironic constriction of its

---

[6] Greenberg, *Understanding Exodus*, 50: "Here we may observe that the point of these narratives is precisely the contrast between the success of the feeble champions of Israel and the thwarting of their all-powerful opponents. Nothing could express so clearly the providential nature of the events."

own, as seen in the larger envelope structure to his narrative presentation in the Pentateuch: the grown Moses formally enters the story by striking and attempting to secretly bury the abusive Egyptian, and finally departs the story in Deut 34:6 when God buries him in secret outside the land of promise for his unauthorized striking of the rock in the wilderness (Num 20:10–12).[7]

A signature example of the literary sophistication of the story is the ark on the Nile in Exod 2:3, activating a compelling allusion to the ark of Noah in Genesis 6–8. At first glance there is a parallel dynamic in both stories. In the days of Noah "the earth was filled (ותמלא הארץ) with violence" (Gen 6:11), culminating in divine judgment through the chaotic floodwaters. The ark of Noah is constructed to preserve the mandate of creation, as Noah enters into a covenant with God (6:18) and hears a reaffirmation of the divine invitation to be fruitful and multiply when the floodwaters recede (9:1). In the contours of the Exodus narrative, the land of Egypt is filled (ותמלא הארץ) with the descendants of Israel, but the promise to Abraham appears imperiled when the violence of slavery is augmented by the king's command to throw the male offspring into the chaotic waters of the Nile. Again a covenant promise is protected by an ark, and when the ark of Moses is placed by the reeds of the Nile it is endowed with global significance. The schematics of the ark in Genesis 6 suggest that it is configured as a floating sanctuary, and with its side door and three levels it is a prototype of the Solomonic temple in Jerusalem. Because the Jerusalem temple on Mount Zion is a natural extension of the wilderness sanctuary, there is a powerful intertextual fusion when the ark of Exodus 2 protects the infant who will grow up to be the mediator of God's instructions for building the tabernacle. In a number of respects Moses is a forerunner of Israel's national experience, and when he is rescued from the waters of the Nile there is a foreshadowing of Israel's rescue at the edge of another body of water. The people of Israel are forced to build supply-cities for the king of Egypt as slaves, but are liberated from such coercion and instead directed to build the portable sanctuary in the wilderness as servants of the God who established a covenant with their ancestors.

---

[7] Cf. Sabo, "Drawing Out Moses," 435: "Water threatened Moses' life as an infant, it was what he drew out for his future wife, what he parted in order to save a nation, what he had miraculously provided in the desert, and it was, at least indirectly, the cause of his untimely death and denied entrance to the land of Canaan."

Exodus 1-2 and the Sojourn of Israel 179

Due to the importance of the story and its extraordinary literary concentration, it is not surprising that Exodus 1-2 has an enduring legacy and influence that can be felt in other sectors of the Hebrew Bible and even into the New Testament.[8] By way of conclusion to this present study, it is suggested that the book of Esther holds promise for further research. Modern readers might demur that the book of Esther is an unlikely candidate for a cluster of allusions to some of the grand images in the book of Exodus—about God's miraculous rescue of Israel and the submerging of the Egyptian army—because there are no overt references to God or explicit mention of any of the customary institutions of Israel's faith in the book. Something of a statistical outlier in this regard, it may seem odd to argue that echoes of Exodus can be heard in the post-exilic book of Esther, but that is exactly the kind of case that recent scholarship has been building. In general terms the commentary of Gillis Gerleman several decades ago "has made the most extensive comparison between Moses/Passover and Esther/Purim, a comparison that is, at points, compelling. Both share the setting in the court, the threat of annihilation, the desire for revenge and the institution of a festival."[9]

---

[8] As one example that was mentioned briefly in the introduction to this book, it can be posited that Matthew 1-2 has a host of allusions to the book of Exodus: "The existence of a Moses typology in Matt. 1-2 has been affirmed by many modern commentators, and rightly so," notes Dale C. Allison, Jr., in a comprehensive study of the issue (*The New Moses: A Matthean Typology* [Minneapolis: Fortress, 1993]). Cf. the summary of Brown, *The Birth of the Messiah*, 112-13: "The NT king who seeks to kill the infant Jesus takes on the physiognomy of the second Pharaoh; and the basic story line is established on the parallel between OT Joseph/wicked Pharaoh/infant Moses and NT Joseph/wicked King Herod/infant Jesus.... Just as there is an infancy narrative of Moses in the Book of Exodus showing God's hand in his career even before he began his ministry of redeeming Israel from Egypt and of mediating a covenant between God and His people, so Matthew has given us an infancy narrative of Jesus before he begins his ministry of redemption and of the new covenant." On the congruence between the larger plot lines of Matthew 1-5 and Exodus (e.g., the massacre of infants, exile and return of the hero, passage through a body of water, temptation in the desert, and the mountain of law-giving), see B. J. Oropeza, *Paul and Apostasy: Eschatology, Perseverance, and Falling Away in the Corinthian Congregation* (WUNT II/115; Tübingen: Mohr Siebeck) 83-4. Other studies that address this topic include Brian M. Nolan, *The Royal Son of God: The Christology of Matthew 1-2 in the Setting of the Gospel* (OBO 23; Göttingen: Vandenhoeck & Ruprecht, 1979), and David D. Kupp, *Matthew's Emmanuel: Divine Presence and God's People in the First Gospel* (SNTSMS 90; Cambridge: Cambridge University Press, 1996).

[9] Timothy S. Laniak, "Esther's *Volkcentrism* and the Reframing of Post-Exilic Judaism," pp. 77-90 in *The Book of Esther in Modern Research*, edited by Sidnie White Crawford and Leonard J. Greenspoon (JSOTSup 380; London: T & T Clark,

Consider, for instance, the series of correspondences between the central protagonists of each narrative, not least being the motif of adoption and concealed identity after an improbable entrance into the royal family. Pharaoh's daughter retrieves the ark and protects its Hebrew occupant seemingly in defiance of her father's directive. The boy becomes her son—after being nursed by his own mother at royal expense—and there is reason to suspect that Pharaoh is oblivious to the entire affair, at least until he tries to kill Moses over the matter of the murdered Egyptian. Despite the substantial gulf in time and space—the book of Esther takes place centuries later in the foreign court of Susa—certain aspects of Esther's career are not dissimilar to Moses. The first chapter of the book of Esther begins with a description of Ahasuerus' empire that stretches from India to Cush, then launches into a lavish description of the 180-day banquet where each guest drinks without restriction in an opulent garden setting. If Exodus 1 is more generic in its stylization, then Esther 1 is the opposite and quite literally a more colorful setting with a lush and exotic flavor, maybe to subtly draw attention to the seductive threat of assimilation that faces the post-exilic community as well as the gruesome threat of annihilation by royal fiat that comes later. Esther herself is not introduced until the next chapter, after the scandalous events of Vashti's refusal and the king's advisors formulate a strategy to find her replacement.

> There was a Jewish man in the citadel of Susa whose name was Mordecai—the son of Jair, the son of Shimei, the son of Kish, a Benjaminite—who had been taken into exile from Jerusalem with those exiled alongside Jeconiah king of Judah, whom Nebuchadnezzar king of Babylon had exiled. He was the guardian of Hadassah—that is, Esther—his uncle's daughter, because she did not have a father or mother. The young woman was beautiful of form and handsome in

2003) 85, citing Gilles Gerleman, *Esther* (BKAT 21; Neukirchen-Vluyn: Neukirchener Verlag, 1973). Note also the summary of Gerleman's work by Carey A. Moore ("Book of Esther," in *The Anchor Bible Dictionary*, 6 volumes, edited by David Noel Freedman [New York: Doubleday, 1992] 2:633-43): "According to Gerleman, because Moses was adopted (Exod 2:9) and had kept his racial identity a secret while in Pharaoh's house (Exod 2:6-10), had at first been unwilling to act on behalf of his people (Exod 3:11; 4:1, 10), and had to appear before Pharaoh several times (Exod 7:14-12:28) before the Egyptian enemies perished in great numbers (Exod 12:29-30; 14:27-28), only to find himself still later opposed by the Amalekites (Exod 17:8-16), so comparable things had to happen in the book of Esther." For his further reflections see, Carey A. Moore, "Esther Revisited Again: A Further Examination of Certain Esther Studies of the Past Ten Years," *HAR* 7 (1983) 173-6.

appearance, and when her father and mother died Mordecai took her as his own daughter. (Esther 2:5-7)

Moses has two parents who play a crucial but limited role in the story, while Esther loses her parents and this loss somehow necessitates or results in her adoption by Mordecai. There is no specific indication in the text that the Babylonian invasion by Nebuchadnezzar is responsible for the death of her parents, but her orphan status in the wake of a superpower's domination is surely not lost on the reader. So, a fortuitous adoption *around a time of national crisis* is a point of similarity between Moses and Esther, as is the respective entry of each protagonist into the foreign palace.[10] Esther's winning the favor of Ahasuerus and having the royal diadem placed on her head is on par with Moses' removal from the Nile by the princess of Egypt, especially since any of a vast number of other women could have been chosen in the empire-wide search for Vashti's successor. But while Pharaoh's daughter is well aware of her adopted son's ethnicity from the outset, Ahasuerus—like the king of Egypt—remains in the dark because Mordecai forbids his adopted niece to disclose any genealogical details ("Now Esther had not revealed her people or her lineage, because Mordecai commanded her not to reveal," 2:10). In retrospect, this reticence proves strategically useful later on when Esther confounds the plot of Haman, and her acquaintance with the court protocols also are utilized, even as Moses appears familiar with the customs of the Egyptian court during his confrontation with Pharaoh. Intelligent women triumphing over powerful men is a key feature of each narrative, as Haman and Pharaoh are both outflanked in their respective schemes. Furthermore, the speeches of both antagonists are similar, since the new king of Egypt (Exod 1:9-10) and Haman (Esther 3:8-9) use careful rhetoric in order to persuade their

---

[10] Note the summary of David J. A. Clines, *The Esther Scroll: The Story of the Story* (JSOTSup 30; Sheffield: JSOT Press, 1984) 154-5: "The narrative of the Esther scroll (whether in its proto-Masoretic or Masoretic form) recounts the gravest threat to the survival of the Jewish people since the pharaoh gave orders for the slaughter of the Israelites' male children. No Jewish author could have told the Esther story without a consciousness that the exodus story lay in the background as a prototype. The exodus story too had Israelites in a foreign land, threatened by a royal decree, represented at court by one from their own nation, and ultimately safely delivered. In the Exodus story the causality of the deliverance is entirely explicit: the Israelites are 'brought out' (Exod. 12.51) by the 'strong hand' (13.9) of Yahweh the 'man of war' (15.3); in the Esther story the causality is implicit, but none the less patent."

respective audiences about the threat that is allegedly posed by a certain people group: the new king is explicit about the Israelites while Haman uses indirection. The genocidal plots contain a high degree of cunning, but the various female characters are able to subvert and contribute to the vanquishing of lethal decrees. It may not be a coincidence that the demise of Haman and the end of Pharaoh have some common characteristics. Earlier in our study a large-scale irony was pointed out: the new king of Egypt attempts to destroy Israel through the waters of drowning, but later in the story the army of Egypt is destroyed by the waters of drowning as they attempt to destroy Israel one last time in what has to be interpreted as an ironic retribution. Haman's fate has a remarkably similar trajectory, as he—followed by his ten sons in due course—is impaled on the gibbet he had erected for Mordecai. So, in Exodus 14 and Esther 7–9 the genocidal opponents of Israel are suffocated by their own mechanisms of death.

Both Moses and Esther have symbolic names that connect with some deeper themes in each story. As discussed previously, the name of Moses forms a hybrid wordplay in the story: not only does it involve the Egyptian word for son/born (perhaps one of the ways Moses the Israelite is "hidden" from Pharaoh), but the same consonants in Hebrew mean *to draw out*. When the princess names the boy she finds in the ark, she uses the active participle, and in the process it is a poignant anticipation of exactly what Moses will do in the story: he becomes the instrument through whom God draws Israel out of Egypt, and thus the personal experience of Moses foreshadows the rescue of the nation. In Esther's case, there is no reason given in the text as to why two names are provided in the text. The proper name Hadassah (הדסה) just occurs here, and based on Isa 55:13 and Neh 8:15 means "myrtle tree" (הדס). Hadassah is only used in 2:7, but Esther is the name that is used in the rest of the book, and so the name Hadassah—a clue to her Hebrew identity—is "hidden" for the remainder of the story. In my view it is possible to argue that Esther and Moses have a similar hybrid nameplay, since scholars often note that Esther is a Babylonian name ostensibly derived from the goddess Ishtar.[11] The foreign court name of Moses protects his Israelite

---

[11] Adele Berlin, *Esther* (The JPS Bible Commentary; Philadelphia: The Jewish Publication Society, 2001) 26: "Esther is either a Babylonian name, derived from the name of the goddess Ishtar, or a Persian name from the word *stâra*, meaning 'star.'

Exodus 1–2 and the Sojourn of Israel

identity even as his Hebrew name anticipates the plot, and Esther's foreign name likewise has an important thematic function within the overall narrative plotline. Timothy Beal notes a particular aspect of Esther's (אסתר) name within the larger thematic framework of the book: "Rabbinic tradition suggests reading Esther as a book of divine hiding. Thus, for example, the Talmud passage quoted above finds in Esther's name an allusion to Deuteronomy 31:18, where God declares, 'I will surely hide [הסתר אסתיר] my face/presence from them.'"[12] The apparent divine absence is a major issue in the book of Esther, and the same matter has been raised by readers of Exodus 1–2:

> The reason for the hiddenness of God in Exodus 1–2 is that God has descended with his people into the pit of Egypt. He is not being portrayed as a transcendent God, far removed from his suffering people. If anything, he is even more immanent than in the "mighty acts" which follow. He remains quiet and hidden because he is totally identified with his people in their powerlessness and suffering. The prospering of the oppressed emphasizes the mystery that, despite their descent, God and his people will not succumb to the powers of death and evil.[13]

A comparable theology arguably is articulated in the book of Esther, and if so, it deserves consideration since many interpreters have been discomfited by the lack of any concrete reference to God or explicit divine activity in the narrative. However, if the reader appreciates a wealth of subtle allusions to Exodus 1–2 along the lines presented here, the reasons for the seeming lack of divine involvement may need to be recalibrated. As Aaron Koller notes, it can be understood that "the claim made in Esther is that God's covert operation in Persia was the equivalent of his overt operation in Egypt. Thus, the Esther story takes itself very seriously—as seriously as the Exodus is taken. The changed details in the narrative are just details, but the themes and dominant ideas are the same: this, too, tells a salvation history, and God's differing modes of operation reflect nothing more than a

---

Jews in the Diaspora often bore both a Jewish and a vernacular name, as, for example, did Daniel and his friends and Judah Maccabee and his brothers. It is possible that Mordecai had a Jewish name also, but that it is not recorded. (The name Hadassah is not included in the Greek versions.)"

[12] Timothy K. Beal, *The Book of Hiding: Gender, Ethnicity, Annihilation, and Esther* (Biblical Limits; London and New York: Routledge, 1997) 117, citing Talmud Hullin 139b, "Where is Esther indicated in the Torah? 'And I will surely hide [*'astîr*] my face.'"

[13] Ackerman, "The Literary Context of the Moses Birth Story," 119.

multi-talented deity."[14] There are other facets that could be further explored—for example, reluctant leaders are used as agents of deliverance, and the ethnicity of Haman the Amalekite as the architect of genocide (cf. Exod 17:8-16)—but among the most compelling intertextual features is the matter of *timing*.[15] As Jon Levenson explains, there are grounds for suggesting that the Esther narrative weaves a number of references to Passover into the story: "If Esther's intercession occurs immediately at the conclusion of the three-day fast (4:16), and if the fast immediately followed the issuance of the genocidal decree on the thirteenth of the first month (3:12), then she approached Ahasuerus during Passover (Lev. 23:5-6)—a most auspicious date for the Jews."[16] When combined with other factors such as the institution

---

[14] Aaron Koller, *Esther in Ancient Jewish Thought* (Cambridge: Cambridge University Press, 2014) 92-3.

[15] On the configuration of Haman, see Ori Z. Soltes, "Images and the Book of Esther: From Manuscript Illumination to Midrash," pp. 137-75 in *The Book of Esther in Modern Research*, edited by Sidnie White Crawford and Leonard J. Greenspoon (JSOTSup 380; London: T & T Clark, 2003) 138: "The death of Haman's ten sons—visually emphasized almost invariably in the Megillah by offering their names in an enlarged font and often by illustrating the scene within the body of text—and the ten plagues of the Exodus share a numerological focus on the suffering of others as the price of Israelite-Judean redemption."

[16] Jon D. Levenson, *Esther*, 89. See also Laniak, "Esther's *Volkcentrism* and the Reframing of Post-Exilic Judaism," 86: "The most subtle intertextuality may be the most significant: the month of 'fate' in Esther 3 (Nisan) was the very month God had originally chosen for Jewish triumph in the first chapter of their history (cf. Levenson 1997: 73). The specific date that the edict of annihilation was issued was the day Jewish readers would recognize as the eve of Passover (3.12). On this very day Esther called for a radical fast for both Jews and her personal attendants (Est. 4.16)." Cf. Gregory R. Goswell, "Keeping God out of the Book of Esther," *EQ* 82 (2010) 104: "The evil edict was written 'on the thirteenth day of the first month [Nisan]' (3:12), which is the eve of the Passover, with the planned slaughter of the Jews to take place 11 months later, on 'the thirteenth day of the twelfth month, which is the month of Adar' (3:13). The coincidence in time implies that an exodus-style deliverance may be anticipated." A slightly different angle is taken by Carolyn J. Sharp, *Irony and Meaning in the Hebrew Bible*, 76: "The finger of God had inscribed the ritual practices of Israelite religion on Sinai. What can it mean that the author of Esther says that the Jews had 'laid down for themselves' regulations concerning their fasts and lamentations? Beal notes that a number of scholars 'have argued that the story of deliverance and the festival established to commemorate that deliverance in the book of Esther are presented in ways that closely parallel the Exodus story, the initial institution of Passover, and the giving of the law at Sinai' (citing Beal, *Esther* [Berit Olam. Collegeville, MN: Liturgical Press, 1999] 117). Indeed; but we may say more about the silences that envelop these apparent congruences. Surely there is a staggering difference between the events of Sinai and the events of Susa. I read these parallels as most certainly intended—and as ironic. The Purim decree seems to be scripture, but it is

of the Purim festival to commemorate deliverance and the paired leadership of Moses and Aaron as a parallel to Esther and Mordecai, an intriguing case emerges for the story of Exodus being used as a prototype for Esther and an example of the enduring legacy of a narrative whose literary nuances were creatively appropriated in emerging Judaism. The beginning of the book of Exodus, therefore, is the introduction to an expansive story and makes a lasting contribution to the far-reaching narrative of Israel's sojourn.

not. It is a flawed imitation with none of the authority given the real Scripture by its divine source."

Bibliography

Ackerman, James S. "The Literary Context of the Moses Birth Story," pp. 74–119 in *Literary Interpretation of Biblical Narrative*, Volume 1, edited by Kenneth R. R. Gros Louis, James S. Ackerman, and Thayer S. Warshaw. Nashville: Abingdon, 1974.

Alexander, T. Desmond. *From Paradise to the Promised Land: An Introduction to the Pentateuch*, Third Edition. Grand Rapids: Baker Academic, 2012.

Allen, Joel S. *The Despoliation of Egypt in Pre-Rabbinic, Rabbinic and Patristic Traditions*. Supplements to Vigiliae Christianae 92; Leiden: Brill, 2008.

Allison, Dale C., Jr. *The New Moses: A Matthean Typology*. Minneapolis: Fortress, 1993.

Alter, Robert. *Genesis: Translation and Commentary*. New York: W. W. Norton, 1996.

Alter, Robert. *The David Story: A Translation with Commentary of 1 & 2 Samuel*. New York: Norton, 1999.

Alter, Robert. *The Five Books of Moses: A Translation with Commentary*. New York: W. W. Norton, 2008.

Alter, Robert. *Ancient Israel: The Former Prophets: Joshua, Judges, Samuel, and Kings: A Translation with Commentary*. New York: W. W. Norton, 2013.

Anderson, Gary A. "Exodus 12:1–14," pp. 85–8 in *The Lectionary Commentary: Theological Exegesis for Sunday's Texts. Volume 1, The First Readings: The Old Testament and Acts*, edited by Roger E. Van Harn. Grand Rapids, MI: Eerdmans, 2001.

Auerbach, Erich. *Mimesis: The Representation of Reality in Western Literature*. Princeton: Princeton University Press, 1953.

Baden, Joel S. "The Violent Origins of the Levites: Text and Tradition," pp. 103–16 in *Levites and Priests in Biblical History and Tradition*, edited by Mark Leuchter and Jeremy M. Hutton. Ancient Israel and Its Literature 9; Atlanta: Society of Biblical Literature, 2011.

Baden, Joel S. *The Composition of the Pentateuch: Renewing the Documentary Hypothesis*. New Haven: Yale University Press, 2012.

Baden, Joel S. "From Joseph to Moses: The Narratives of Exodus 1–2." *VT* 62 (2012) 133–58.

Bar-Efrat, Shimon, *Narrative Art in the Bible*. JSOTSup 70; Sheffield: Almond Press, 1989.

Barr, James. "'Why?' in Biblical Hebrew." *JTS* 36 (1985) 1–33.
Beal, Timothy K. *The Book of Hiding: Gender, Ethnicity, Annihilation, and Esther*. Biblical Limits; London and New York: Routledge, 1997.
Beal, Timothy K. *Esther*. Berit Olam; Collegeville, MN: Liturgical Press, 1999.
Bellis, Alice Ogden. *Helpmates, Harlots, and Heroes: Women's Stories in the Hebrew Bible*. Louisville, KY: Westminster/John Knox Press, 1984.
Bergsma, John Sietze, and Scott Walker Hahn, "Noah's Nakedness and the Curse on Canaan (Genesis 9:20–27)." *JBL* 124 (2005) 25–40.
Berlin, Adele. *Esther*. The JPS Bible Commentary; Philadelphia: The Jewish Publication Society, 2001.
Berlin, Adele. "Giving Birth to a Nation," pp. 305–23 in *The Torah: A Women's Commentary*, edited by Tamara Cohn Eskenazi and Andrea L. Weiss. New York: URJ Press and Women of Reform Judaism, 2008.
Berlin, Adele. "Literary Approaches to Biblical Literature: General Observations and a Case Study of Genesis 34," pp. 45–75 in *The Hebrew Bible: New Insights and Scholarship*, edited by Frederick E. Greenspahn. New York and London: New York University Press, 2008.
Biddle, Mark E. *Deuteronomy*. Macon, GA: Smyth & Helwys, 2003.
Billings, Rachel M. *"Israel Served the Lord": The Book of Joshua as Paradoxical Portrait of Faithful Israel*. Notre Dame, Indiana: University of Notre Dame Press, 2013.
Bird, Phyllis A. "The Harlot as Heroine: Narrative Art and Social Presupposition in Three Old Testament Texts." *Semeia* 46 (1989) 119–39.
Bloom, Harold. *The Book of J: Translated from the Hebrew by David Rosenberg, Interpreted by Harold Bloom*. New York: Grove Weidenfeld, 1990.
Bodner, Keith. *1 Samuel: A Narrative Commentary*. Hebrew Bible Monographs 19; Sheffield: Sheffield Phoenix Press, 2008.
Bodner, Keith, "Go Figure: Narrative Strategies for a New Generation," pp. 9–24 in *Go Figure! Figuration in Biblical Interpretation*, edited by Stanley D. Walters. Princeton Theological Monograph Series 81; Eugene, OR: Pickwick, 2008.
Bodner, Keith. *Jeroboam's Royal Drama*. Oxford: Oxford University Press, 2012.
Bodner, Keith. *The Artistic Dimension: Literary Explorations of the Hebrew Bible*. LHBOTS 590; London: T & T Clark, 2013.
Bodner, Keith. *Elisha's Profile in the Book of Kings: The Double Agent*. Oxford: Oxford University Press, 2013.
Bodner, Keith. *After the Invasion: A Reading of Jeremiah 40–44*. Oxford: Oxford University Press, 2015.
Brenner, Athalya. "Female Social Behavior: Two Descriptive Patterns within the 'Birth of the Hero' Paradigm." *VT* 36 (1986) 257–73.
Brichto, Herbert Chanan. *The Names of God: Poetic Readings in Biblical Beginnings*. New York: Oxford University Press, 1998.

Britt, Brian. "Prophetic Concealment in a Biblical Type Scene." *CBQ* 64 (2002) 37–58.
Britt, Brian. *Rewriting Moses: The Narrative Eclipse of the Text*. JSOTSup 402; London: T & T Clark, 2004.
Brown, Raymond E., S. S. *The Birth of the Messiah: A Commentary on the Infancy Narratives in the Gospels of Matthew and Luke*, New Updated Edition. The Anchor Bible Reference Library; New York: Doubleday, 1993.
Brueggemann, Walter. *Genesis*. Interpretation; Atlanta: John Knox Press, 1982.
Brueggemann, Walter. "I Samuel 1: A Sense of a Beginning." *ZAW* 102 (1990) 33–48.
Brueggemann, Walter. "The Book of Exodus: Introduction, Commentary and Reflections," pp. 675–981 in *The New Interpreter's Bible*, Volume 6, edited by L. E. Keck. Nashville: Abingdon, 1994.
Brueggemann, Walter and Tod Linafelt, *An Introduction to the Old Testament: The Canon and Christian Imagination*, Second Edition. Louisville: WJKP, 2012.
Buber, Martin. *Moses: The Revelation and the Covenant*. New York: Harper Torchbacks, 1958.
Carr, David M. *Reading the Fractures of Genesis: Historical and Literary Approaches*. Louisville: Westminster John Knox, 1996.
Carr, David M. "The Moses Story: Literary–Historical Reflections." *Hebrew Bible and Ancient Israel* 1 (2012) 7–36.
Cassuto, Umberto. *A Commentary on the Book of Exodus*. Jerusalem: Magnes Press, 1967.
Chan, Michael J. "Joseph and Jehoiachin: On the Edge of Exodus." *ZAW* 125 (2013) 566–77.
Childs, Brevard S. "Birth of Moses." *JBL* 84 (1965) 109–22.
Childs, Brevard S. *Biblical Theology in Crisis*. Philadelphia: Westminster, 1970.
Childs, Brevard S. *The Book of Exodus: A Critical, Theological Commentary*. Old Testament Library. Louisville: Westminster, 1974.
Christensen, Duane L. "The Identity of King So of Egypt (2 Kings xvii 4)." *VT* 39 (1989) 140–53.
Clines, David J. A. *The Esther Scroll: The Story of the Story*. JSOTSup 30; Sheffield: JSOT Press, 1984.
Clines, David J. A. *The Theme of the Pentateuch*, Second Edition. JSOTSup 10; Sheffield: Sheffield Academic Press, 1997 (originally published 1978).
Coats, George W. "A Structural Transition in Exodus." *VT* 22 (1972) 129–42.
Coats, George W. *Moses: Heroic Man, Man of God* (JSOTSup 57; Sheffield: Sheffield Academic Press, 1988.
Collins, John J. *The Bible after Babel: Historical Criticism in a Postmodern Age*. Grand Rapids: Eerdmans, 2005.

Coogan, Michael D. "In the Beginning: The Earliest History," pp. 3–24 in *The Oxford History of the Biblical World*, edited by Michael D. Coogan. New York: Oxford University Press, 1998.

Cotter, David W. *Genesis*. Berit Olam; Collegeville: Liturgical Press, 2003.

Crawford, Cory D. "Between Shadow and Substance: The Historical Relationship of Tabernacle and Temple in Light of Architecture and Iconography," pp. 117–33 in *Levites and Priests in Biblical History and Tradition*, edited by Mark Leuchter and Jeremy M. Hutton. Ancient Israel and Its Literature 9; Atlanta: Society of Biblical Literature, 2011.

Crawford, Cory D. "Noah's Architecture: The Role of Sacred Space in Ancient Near Eastern Flood Myths," pp. 1–22 in *Constructions of Space IV: Further Developments in Examining Ancient Israel's Social Space*, edited by Mark K. George. LHBOTS 569; London: Bloomsbury, 2013.

Crawford, Sidnie White. "The Book of Esther: Introduction, Commentary, and Reflections," pp. 855–941 in *The New Interpreter's Bible*, Volume 3. Nashville: Abingdon, 1999.

Curtis, Adrian. *Oxford Bible Atlas*, Fourth Edition. Oxford: Oxford University Press, 2007.

Davies, G. I. "Introduction to the Pentateuch," in *The Oxford Bible Commentary*, edited by John Barton and John Muddiman. Oxford: Oxford University Press, 2001.

Davies, Gordon F. *Israel in Egypt: Reading Exodus 1–2*. JSOTSup 135; Sheffield: Sheffield Academic Press, 1992.

Davies, John A. *A Royal Priesthood: Literary and Intertextual Perspectives on an Image of Israel in Exodus 19.6*. JSOTSup 395; London: T & T Clark, 2004.

Day, John. *Yahweh and the Gods and Goddesses of Canaan*. JSOTSup 265; Sheffield: Sheffield Academic Press, 2000.

Dennis, Trevor. *Sarah Laughed: Women's Voices in the Old Testament*. Nashville: Abingdon, 1994.

Dozeman, Thomas B. "The Wilderness and Salvation History in the Hagar Story." *JBL* 117 (1998) 23–43.

Dozeman, Thomas B. *Exodus*. ECC; Grand Rapids: Eerdmans, 2009.

Dozeman, Thomas B., editor. *Methods for Exodus*. Methods in Biblical Interpretation; New York: Cambridge University Press, 2010.

Durham, John I. *Exodus*. WBC; Waco: Word, 1987.

Edelman, Diana, Philip R. Davies, Christophe Nihan, and Thomas Römer. *Opening the Books of Moses: Volume One of the Books of Moses*. Sheffield: Equinox, 2011.

Edelman, Diana. "The Nile in Biblical Memory," pp. 77–102 in *Thinking of Water in the Early Second Temple Period*, edited by Ehud Ben Zvi and Christoph Levin. BZAW 461; Berlin: Walter de Gruyter, 2014.

Enns, Peter. *Exodus*. NIVAC; Grand Rapids, Zondervan, 2000.

Bibliography 191

Exum, J. Cheryl. "'You Shall Let Every Daughter Live': A Study of Exodus 1:8–2:10." *Semeia* 28 (1983) 63–82, reprinted in pp. 37–61 in *A Feminist Companion to Exodus to Deuteronomy*, edited by Athalya Brenner. FCB 6; Sheffield: Sheffield Academic Press, 1994.

Exum, J. Cheryl. "Second Thoughts About Secondary Characters: Women in Exodus 1.8–2.10," pp. 75–87 in *A Feminist Companion to Exodus to Deuteronomy*, edited by Athalya Brenner. FCB 6; Sheffield: Sheffield Academic Press, 1994.

Feldman, Louis H. "Josephus' Portrait of Moses." *JQR* 82 (1992) 285–328.

Fewell, Danna Nolan. *Circle of Sovereignty, A Story of Stories in Daniel 1–6*. JSOTSup 72; Sheffield: JSOT Press, 1988.

Fewell, Donna Nolan, and David M. Gunn. *Gender, Power, and Promise: The Subject of the Bible's First Story*. Nashville: Abingdon, 1993.

Fishbane, Michael. *Text and Texture: Close Readings of Selected Biblical Texts*. New York: Schocken Books, 1979 (republished as *Biblical Text and Texture: A Literary Reading of Selected Texts* [Oxford: Oneworld, 1998]).

Fishbane, Michael. *Biblical Interpretation in Ancient Israel*. Oxford: Clarendon Press, 1985.

Fokkelman, J. P. "Exodus," pp. 56–65 in *The Literary Guide to the Bible*, edited by Robert Alter and Frank Kermode. Cambridge, MA: Belknap Press, 1987.

Freedman, David Noel, editor. *The Anchor Bible Dictionary*, 6 volumes. New York: Doubleday, 1992.

Fretheim, Terence E. *Exodus. Interpretation: A Bible Commentary for Teaching and Preaching*. Louisville: John Knox, 1991.

Fretheim, Terence E. "The Book of Genesis: Introduction, Commentary, and Reflections," pp. 321–674 in *The New Interpreter's Bible*, Volume 6, edited by L. E. Keck; Nashville: Abingdon, 1994.

Fretheim, Terence E. "Numbers," in *The Oxford Bible Commentary*, edited by John Barton and John Muddiman. Oxford: Oxford University Press, 2001.

Fretheim, Terence E. *Abraham: Trials of Family and Faith*. Columbia, SC: University of South Carolina Press, 2007.

Friedman, Richard Elliot. *Commentary on the Torah, with a New English Translation*. San Francisco: HarperCollins, 2001.

Frymer-Kensky, Tikva. *Reading the Women of the Bible*. New York: Schocken Books, 2002.

Fuchs, Esther. "A Jewish–Feminist Reading of Exodus 1–2," pp. 307–26 in *Jews, Christians, and the Theology of the Hebrew Scriptures*, edited by Joel S. Kaminsky and Alice Ogden Bellis. SBL Symposium Series 8; Atlanta: Society of Biblical Literature, 2000.

Galvin, Garrett. *Egypt as a Place of Refuge*. FAT II/51; Tübingen: Mohr Siebeck, 2011.

Geller, Stephen A. "The Sack of Shechem: The Use of Typology in Biblical Covenant Religion." *Prooftexts* 10 (1990) 1–15.
Gerleman, Gillis. *Esther*. BKAT 21; Neukirchen-Vluyn: Neukirchener Verlag, 1973.
Gertz, Jan Christian. "The Transition between the Books of Genesis and Exodus," pp. 73–87 in *A Farewell to the Yahwist? The Composition of the Pentateuch in Recent European Interpretation*, edited by Thomas B. Dozeman and Konrad Schmid. SBLSymS 34; Atlanta: Society of Biblical Literature, 2006.
Gillmayr-Bucher, Susanne. "'She Came to Test Him with Hard Questions': Foreign Women and Their View on Israel." *BibInt* 15 (2007) 135–50.
Gilmour, Rachelle. *Juxtaposition and the Elisha Cycle*. LHBOTS 594; New York and London: T & T Clark, 2014.
Goldingay, John. "Jeremiah and the Superpower," pp. 59–77 in *Uprooting and Planting: Essays on Jeremiah for Leslie Allen*, edited by John Goldingay. LHBOTS 459; New York: T & T Clark, 2007.
Gorospe, Athena E. *Narrative and Identity: An Ethical Reading of Exodus 4*. BIS 86; Leiden: Brill, 2007.
Goswell, Gregory R. "Keeping God out of the Book of Esther." *EQ* 82 (2010) 99–110.
Graetz, Naomi. "Did Miriam Talk Too Much?" pp. 231–42 in *A Feminist Companion to Exodus to Deuteronomy*, edited by Athalya Brenner. FCB 6; Sheffield: Sheffield Academic Press, 1994.
Green, Barbara, O. P. "The Determination of Pharaoh: His Characterization in the Joseph Story (Genesis 37–50)," pp. 150–71 in *The World of Genesis: Persons, Places, Perspectives*, edited by Philip R. Davies and David J. A. Clines. JSOTSup 257; Sheffield: Sheffield Academic Press, 1998.
Greenberg, Moshe. *Understanding Exodus: A Holistic Commentary on Exodus 1–11*, Second Edition, edited with a foreword by Jeffrey H. Tigay. Eugene, OR: Wipf & Stock, 2013.
Greifenhagen, F. V. *Egypt on the Pentateuch's Ideological Map: Constructing Biblical Israel's Identity*. JSOTSup 361; London: Sheffield Academic Press, 2002.
Gurtner, Daniel M. *Exodus: A Commentary on the Greek Text of Codex Vaticanus*. Septuagint Commentary Series; Leiden: Brill, 2013.
Hall, Sarah Lebhar. *Conquering Character: The Characterization of Joshua in Joshua 1–11*. LHBOTS 512; London: T & T Clark, 2010.
Halpern, Baruch, *David's Secret Demons: Messiah, Murderer, Traitor, King*. Grand Rapids: Eerdmans, 2001.
Hamilton, Victor P. *The Book of Genesis: Chapters 1–17*. NICOT. Grand Rapids: Eerdmans, 1990.
Hamilton, Victor P. *The Book of Genesis: Chapters 18–50*. NICOT. Grand Rapids: Eerdmans, 1995.

Hamilton, Victor P. *Exodus: An Exegetical Commentary*. Grand Rapids: Baker, 2011.
Harvey, John E. "Jehoiachin and Joseph: Hope at the Close of the Deuteronomistic History," pp. 51-61 in *The Bible as a Human Witness to Divine Revelation: Hearing the Word of God through Historically Dissimilar Traditions*, edited by Randall Heskett and Brian Irwin. LHBOTS 469; London: T & T Clark, 2010.
Hauge, Martin Ravndal. *The Descent from the Mountain: Narrative Patterns in Exodus 19-40*. JSOTSup 323; Sheffield: Sheffield Academic Press, 2001.
Hawk, L. Daniel. *Joshua*. Berit Olam; Collegeville, MN: Liturgical Press, 2000.
Hendel, Ronald. "The Exodus in Biblical Memory." *JBL* 120 (2001) 601-22.
Hendel, Ronald S. *Remembering Abraham: Culture, Memory, and History in the Hebrew Bible*. New York: Oxford University Press, 2005.
Hendel, Ronald. *The Book of Genesis: A Biography*. Princeton: Princeton University Press, 2013.
Herzberg, Bruce. "Deborah and Moses." *JSOT* 38.1 (2013) 15-33.
Holloway, Steven W. "What Ship Goes There? The Flood Narratives in the Gilgamesh Epic and Genesis Considered in Light of Ancient Near Eastern Temple Ideology." *ZAW* 103 (1991) 328-55.
Houston, Walter. "Exodus," in *The Oxford Bible Commentary*, edited by John Barton and John Muddiman. Oxford: Oxford University Press, 2001.
Houtman, Cornelis. *Exodus I*. HCOT; Leuven: Peeters, 1993.
Hughes, Paul E. "Moses' Birth Story: A Biblical Matrix for Prophetic Messianism," pp. 10-22 in *Eschatology, Messianism, and the Dead Sea Scrolls*, edited by Craig A. Evans and Peter W. Flint. Studies in the Dead Sea Scrolls and Related Literature; Grand Rapids: Eerdmans, 1997.
Hyatt, J. P. *Exodus*. NCB; London: Marshall, Morgan & Scott, 1971.
Isbell, Charles. "Exodus 1-2 in the Context of Exodus 1-14: Story Lines and Key Words," pp. 37-61 in *Art and Meaning: Rhetoric in Biblical Literature*, edited by David J. A. Clines, David M. Gunn, and Alan J. Hauser. JSOTSup 19; Sheffield: JSOT Press, 1982.
Jackson, Melissa. *Comedy and Feminist Interpretation of the Hebrew Bible: A Subversive Collaboration*. Oxford Theological Monographs; Oxford: Oxford University Press, 2012.
Jacob, Benno. *The Second Book of the Bible: Exodus*. Hoboken, NJ: Ktav, 1992.
Janzen, J. Gerald. *Abraham and All the Families of the Earth: A Commentary on the Book of Genesis 12-50*. ITC; Grand Rapids: Eerdmans, 1993.
Janzen, J. Gerald. *Exodus*. Westminster Bible Companion; Louisville: Westminster John Knox Press, 1997.
Johnson, Benjamin J. M. "What Type of Son is Samson? Reading Judges 13 as a Biblical Type-Scene." *JETS* 53 (2010) 269-86.
Josipovici, Gabriel. *The Book of God: A Response to the Bible*. New Haven: Yale University Press, 1988.

Kawashima, Robert S. "Sources and Redaction," pp. 47–70 in *Reading Genesis: Ten Methods*, edited by Ronald Hendel. New York: Cambridge University Press, 2010.

Kee, Min Suc. "The Heavenly Council and Its Type-scene." *JSOT* 31 (2007) 259–73.

Keiter, Sheila Tuller. "Outsmarting God: Egyptian Slavery and the Tower of Babel." *JBQ* 41 (2013) 200–4.

Kermode, Frank. *The Sense of an Ending: Studies in the Theory of Fiction*. Oxford: Oxford University Press, 1967.

Kermode, Frank. *The Uses of Error and Other Essays*. Cambridge, MA: Harvard University Press, 1991.

Kim, Koowon. *Incubation as a Type-Scene in the 'Aqhatu, Kirta, and Hannah Stories: A Form-Critical and Narratological Study of KTU 1.14 I–1.15 III, 1.17 I–II, and 1 Samuel 1:1–2:11*. VTSup 145; Leiden: Brill, 2011.

Klein, Lillian R. *The Triumph of Irony in the Book of Judges*. JSOTSup 68; Bible and Literature Series 14; Sheffield: Almond Press, 1989.

Knauf, Ernst Axel. "Hagar," in *The Anchor Bible Dictionary*, 6 volumes, edited by David Noel Freedman. New York: Doubleday, 1992, 3:18–19.

Koller, Aaron. *Esther in Ancient Jewish Thought*. Cambridge: Cambridge University Press, 2014.

Kruschwitz, Jonathan. "The Type-Scene Connection between Genesis 38 and the Joseph Story," *JSOT* 36 (2012) 383–410.

Kupp, David D. *Matthew's Emmanuel: Divine Presence and God's People in the First Gospel*. SNTSMS 90; Cambridge: Cambridge University Press, 1996.

LaCocque, André. "Whatever Happened in the Valley of Shinar? A Response to Theodore Hiebert." *JBL* 128 (2009) 29–41.

Langston, Scott M. *Exodus through the Centuries*. Blackwell Bible Commentaries; Oxford: Blackwell, 2006.

Laniak, Timothy S. "Esther's *Volkcentrism* and the Reframing of Post-Exilic Judaism," pp. 77–90 in *The Book of Esther in Modern Research*, edited by Sidnie White Crawford and Leonard J. Greenspoon. JSOTSup 380; London: T & T Clark, 2003.

Letellier, Robert I. *Day in Mamre, Night in Sodom: Abraham and Lot in Genesis 18 and 19*. BIS 10; Leiden: Brill, 1995.

Leuchter, Mark. "The Fightin' Mushites." *VT* 62 (2012) 479–500.

Leveen, Adriane. *Memory and Tradition in the Book of Numbers*. Cambridge: Cambridge University Press, 2008.

Levenson, Jon D. *The Death and Resurrection of the Beloved Son: The Transformation of Child Sacrifice in Judaism and Christianity*. New Haven: Yale University Press, 1993.

Levenson, Jon D. *Creation and the Persistence of Evil: The Jewish Drama of Divine Omnipotence*, Second Edition. Princeton, NJ: Princeton University Press, 1994.

Levenson, Jon D. *Esther: A Commentary*. OTL; Louisville: Westminster John Knox Press, 1997.

Levenson, Jon D. "The Conversion of Abraham to Judaism, Christianity, and Islam," pp. 3–40 in *The Idea of Biblical Interpretation: Essays in Honor of James L. Kugel*, edited by Hindy Najman and Judith H. Newman. JSJSup 83; Leiden: Brill, 2004.

Levenson, Jon D. *Resurrection and the Restoration of Israel: The Ultimate Victory of the God of Life*. New Haven and London: Yale University Press, 2006.

Levenson, Jon D. *Inheriting Abraham: The Legacy of the Patriarch in Judaism, Christianity and Islam*. Princeton: Princeton University Press, 2012.

Levine, Baruch. "Leviticus," in *The Anchor Bible Dictionary*, edited by David Noel Freedman, 6 vols. New York: Doubleday, 1992.

Lohr, Joel N. "Chosen and Unchosen: Conceptions of Election in the Pentateuch and Jewish–Christian Interpretation." PhD diss., Durham University, 2007.

Lyke, Larry L. *King David with the Wise Woman of Tekoa: The Resonance of Tradition in Parabolic Narrative*. JSOTSup 255; Sheffield: Sheffield Academic Press, 1997.

Machinist, Peter. "Assyria and Its Image in the First Isaiah." *JAOS* 103 (1983) 719–37.

Machinist, Peter. "The Meaning of Moses." *Harvard Divinity Bulletin* 27 (1998) 14–15.

Marks, Herbert. "Biblical Naming and Poetic Etymology." *JBL* 114 (1995) 21–42.

Martin, Michael W. "Betrothal Journey Narratives." *CBQ* 70 (2008) 505–23.

Matties, Gordon H. *Joshua*. BCBC; Harrisonburg, VA: Herald Press, 2012.

Mazor, Yair. *Who Wrought the Bible? Unveiling the Bible's Aesthetic Secrets*. Madison: University of Wisconsin Press, 2009.

McCarter, P. Kyle. *I Samuel: A New Translation with Introduction and Commentary*. AB 8; Garden City, NY: Doubleday, 1980.

McConville, J. Gordon. *God and Earthly Power. An Old Testament Political Theology: Genesis–Kings*. LHBOTS 454; London: T & T Clark, 2006.

Mendenhall, George E. "Midian," *ABD* IV 815–18.

Meyers, Carol. *Exodus*. New Cambridge Bible Commentary; New York: Cambridge University Press, 2005.

Middlemas, Jill. "Ships and Other Seafaring Vessels in the Old Testament," pp. 407–21 in *Let Us Go Up to Zion: Essays in Honour of H. G. M. Williamson on the Occasion of his Sixty-Fifth Birthday*, edited by Iain Provan and Mark J. Boda. VTSup 153; Leiden: Brill, 2012.

Miller, J. Hillis, *Reading Narrative*. Oklahoma Project for Discourse and Theory 18; Norman: University of Oklahoma Press, 1998.

Mitchell, Christine. "The Ironic Death of Josiah in 2 Chronicles." *CBQ* 68 (2006) 421-35.
Moberly, R. W. L. *The Theology of the Book of Genesis*. OTT; Cambridge: Cambridge University Press, 2009.
Moore, Carey A. "Esther Revisited Again: A Further Examination of Certain Esther Studies of the Past Ten Years." *HAR* 7 (1983) 169-86.
Moore, Carey A. "Book of Esther," pp. 633-43 in Volume 2 of *The Anchor Bible Dictionary*, edited by David Noel Freedman, 6 vols. New York: Doubleday, 1992.
Montgomery, J. A., and H. S. Gehman, *A Critical and Exegetical Commentary on the Books of Kings*. ICC; Edinburgh: T & T Clark, 1951.
Morschauser, Scott. "Potters' Wheels and Pregnancies: A Note on Exodus 1:16." *JBL* 122 (2003) 731-3.
Morson, Gary Saul. *Narrative and Freedom: The Shadows of Time*. New Haven: Yale University Press, 1994.
Nikaido, S. "Hagar and Ishmael as Literary Figures: An Intertextual Study." *VT* 51 (2001) 219-42.
Nohrnberg, James. "Moses," pp. 35-57 in *Images of Man and God: Old Testament Short Stories in Literary Focus*, edited by Burke O. Long. Bible and Literature 1; Sheffield: Almond Press, 1981.
Nohrnberg, James. *Like Unto Moses: The Constituting of an Interruption*. Indiana Studies in Biblical Literature; Bloomington and Indianapolis: Indiana University Press, 1995.
Nolan, Brian M. *The Royal Son of God: The Christology of Matthew 1-2 in the Setting of the Gospel*. OBO 23; Göttingen: Vandenhoeck & Ruprecht, 1979.
Noth, Martin. *Exodus: A Commentary*. OTL; Philadelphia: Westminster, 1962.
Nuttall, Anthony David. *Openings: Narrative Beginnings from the Epic to the Novel*. Oxford: Clarendon Press, 1992.
O'Connell, Robert H. "Proverbs vii 16-17: A Case of Fatal Deception in a 'Woman and the Window' Type-Scene." *VT* 41 (1991) 235-41.
Olson, Dennis T. *The Death of the Old and the Birth of the New: The Framework of the Book of Numbers and the Pentateuch*. Brown Judaic Studies 71. Chico, CA: Scholars Press, 1985.
Olson, Dennis T. "Exodus," pp. 27-40 in *Theological Bible Commentary*, edited by Gail R. O'Day and David L. Petersen. Louisville: Westminster John Knox Press, 2009.
Olson, Dennis T. "Genesis," pp. 1-32 in *The New Interpreter's Bible One-Volume Commentary*, edited by Beverly Roberts Gaventa and David L. Petersen. Nashville: Abingdon, 2010.
Olson, Dennis T. "Literary and Rhetorical Criticism," pp. 13-54 in *Methods For Exodus*, edited by Thomas B. Dozeman. Methods in Biblical Interpretation; Cambridge: Cambridge University Press, 2010.

Olson, Dennis T. "From Horeb to Nebo: Exile, The Pentateuch, and the Promise of Home in Exodus 2:1–3:6 and Deuteronomy 34:1–12," pp. 82–92 in *By the Irrigation Canals of Babylon: Approaches to the Study of the Exile*, edited by John J. Ahn and Jill Middlemas. LHBOTS 526; London: Bloomsbury, T & T Clark, 2012.

Oropeza, B. J. *Paul and Apostasy: Eschatology, Perseverance, and Falling Away in the Corinthian Congregation*. WUNT II/115; Tübingen: Mohr Siebeck, 2000.

Osherow, Jacqueline. "Brides of Blood: Women at the Outset of Exodus," pp. 46–51 in *From the Margins 1: Women of the Hebrew Bible and their Afterlives*, edited by Peter S. Hawkins and Lesleigh Cushing Stahlberg. The Bible in the Modern World 18; Sheffield: Sheffield Phoenix Press, 2009.

Pardes, Ilana. *The Biography of Ancient Israel: National Narratives in the Bible*. Berkeley: University of California Press, 2002.

Pixley, Jorge. "Liberation Criticism," pp. 131–62 in *Methods for Exodus*, edited by Thomas B. Dozeman. Methods in Biblical Interpretation; Cambridge: Cambridge University Press, 2010.

Propp, William H. C. *Exodus 1–18: A New Translation with Introduction and Commentary*. Anchor Bible 2. New York: Doubleday, 1999.

Rad, Gerhard von. *Genesis: A Commentary*. OTL; Philadelphia: Westminster, 1972.

Ray, J. D. "Egyptian Wisdom Literature," pp. 17–29 in *Wisdom in Ancient Israel: Essays in Honour of J. A. Emerton*, edited by John Day, Robert P. Gordon, and H. G. M. Williamson. Cambridge: Cambridge University Press, 1995.

Reed, Walter L. *Dialogues of the Word: The Bible as Literature According to Bakhtin*. New York: Oxford University Press, 1993.

Reno, R. R. *Genesis*. Brazos Theological Commentary on the Bible; Grand Rapids: Brazos Press, 2010.

Richardson, Brian, editor. *Narrative Beginnings: Theories and Practices*. Lincoln and London: University of Nebraska Press, 2008.

Rickett, Daniel. "Rethinking the Place and Purpose of Genesis 13." *JSOT* 36.1 (2011) 31–53.

Rofé, Alexander. "Moses' Mother and her Slave-Girl According to 4QExod[b]." *Dead Sea Discoveries* 9 (2002) 38–43.

Römer, Thomas. "The Exodus in the Book of Genesis." *Svensk Exegetisk Årsbok* 75 (2010) 1–20.

Römer, Thomas C. *The So-Called Deuteronomistic History: A Sociological, Historical, and Literary Introduction*. London: T & T Clark International, 2005.

Rosenberg, Joel. *King and Kin: Political Allegory in the Hebrew Bible*. Bloomington: Indiana University Press, 1986.

Rosenberg, Marvin. *The Masks of Othello: The Search for the Identity of Othello, Iago, and Desdemona by Three Centuries of Actors and Critics*. Berkeley: University of California Press, 1961.

Rosenheim, Edward W. *What Happens in Literature: A Guide to Poetry, Drama and Fiction*. Chicago: University of Chicago Press, 2000.

Russell, Stephen C. *Images of Egypt in Early Biblical Literature: Cisjordan-Israelite, Transjordan-Israelite, and Judahite Portrayals*. BZAW 403; Berlin: Walter de Gruyter, 2009.

Sabo, Peter. "Drawing Out Moses: Water as a Personal Motif of the Biblical Character," pp. 409–36 in *Thinking of Water in the Early Second Temple Period*, edited by Ehud Ben Zvi and Christoph Levin. BZAW 461; Berlin: Walter de Gruyter, 2014.

Sacks, Jonathan. "Righteousness Knows No Racial or Religious Boundaries." *The Times* (24 May 2003).

Said, Edward. *Beginnings: Intention and Method*. New York: Basic Books, 1975.

Sarna, Nahum M. *Exploring Exodus: The Origins of Biblical Israel*. New York: Schocken Books, 1986.

Sarna, Nahum. *Exodus*. JPS Torah Commentary; Philadelphia: Jewish Publication Society, 1991.

Savran, George. "Theophany as Type Scene." *Prooftexts* 23 (2003) 119–49.

Schmid, Konrad. "Genesis and Exodus as Two Formerly Independent Traditions of Origins for Ancient Israel." *Biblica* 93 (2012) 187–208.

Schmid, Konrad. "Exodus in the Pentateuch," pp. 27–60 in *The Book of Exodus: Composition, Reception, and Interpretation*, edited by Thomas B. Dozeman, Craig A. Evans, and Joel N. Lohr. VTSup 164; Leiden: Brill, 2014.

Schor, Esther. "Saviors and Liars: The Midwives of Exodus 1," pp. 31–45 in *From the Margins 1: Women of the Hebrew Bible and their Afterlives*, edited by Peter S. Hawkins and Lesleigh Cushing Stahlberg. The Bible in the Modern World 18; Sheffield: Sheffield Phoenix Press, 2009.

Scott, James C. *Weapons of the Weak: Everyday Forms of Peasant Resistance*. New Haven, CT: Yale University Press, 1985.

Scott, James C. *Domination and the Arts of Resistance: Hidden Transcripts*. New Haven, CT: Yale University Press, 1990.

Seow, Choon Leong. "1 & 2 Kings," in *The New Interpreter's Bible*, Volume 3. Nashville: Abingdon, 1999.

Seow, Choon Leong. "Adoniram," p. 54 in *The New Interpreter's Dictionary of the Bible*, edited by Katharine Doob Sakenfeld. Nashville: Abingdon, 2009.

Setel, Drorah O'Donnell. "Exodus," pp. 26–35 in *The Women's Bible Commentary*, edited by Carol A. Newsom and Sharon H. Ringe. Louisville: Westminster/John Knox, 1992.

Sharp, Carolyn J. *Irony and Meaning in the Hebrew Bible*. Bloomington: Indiana University Press, 2009.

Bibliography 199

Siebert-Hommes, Jopie. "Twelve Women in Exodus 1 and 2: The Role of Daughters and Sons in the Stories Concerning Moses." *ACEBT* 9 (1988) 47–58.

Siebert-Hommes, Jopie. "But if She Be a Daughter... She May Live! 'Daughters' and 'Sons' in Exodus 1-2," pp. 62–74 in *A Feminist Companion to Exodus to Deuteronomy*, edited by Athalya Brenner. FCB 6; Sheffield: Sheffield Academic Press, 1994.

Siebert-Hommes, Jopie. *Let the Daughters Live! The Literary Architecture of Exodus 1-2 as a Key for Interpretation*. BIS 37; Leiden: Brill, 1998.

Ska, Jean-Louis. *Le passage de la Mer: Etude de la construction, du style et de la symbolique d' Ex 14,1–31*. AnBib 109; Rome: Pontificium Institutum Biblicum, 1986.

Smith, Mark S., with contributions by Elizabeth M. Bloch-Smith. *The Pilgrimage Pattern in Exodus*. JSOTSup 239; Sheffield: Sheffield Academic Press, 1997.

Smith, Mark S. *Exodus*. New Collegeville Bible Commentary; Collegeville: Liturgical Press, 2011.

Soltes, Ori Z. "Images and the Book of Esther: From Manuscript Illumination to Midrash," pp. 137–75 in *The Book of Esther in Modern Research*, edited by Sidnie White Crawford and Leonard J. Greenspoon. JSOTSup 380; London: T & T Clark, 2003.

Sparks, Kenton L. "Genre Criticism," pp. 55–94 in *Methods For Exodus*, edited by Thomas B. Dozeman. Methods in Biblical Interpretation; Cambridge: Cambridge University Press, 2010.

Speiser, E. A. *Genesis*. Anchor Bible 1A. Garden City: Doubleday, 1964.

Spencer, John R. "Levi," in *The Anchor Bible Dictionary*, edited by David Noel Freedman, 6 vols. New York: Doubleday, 1992.

Stackert, Jeffrey. *A Prophet Like Moses: Prophecy, Law, and Israelite Religion*. New York: Oxford University Press, 2014.

Stambovsky, Phillip. *The Depictive Image: Metaphor and Literary Experience*. Amherst: The University of Massachusetts Press, 1988.

Sternberg, Meir. *The Poetics of Biblical Narrative: Ideological Literature and the Drama of Reading*. Indiana Studies in Biblical Literature; Bloomington: Indiana University Press, 1985.

Sternberg, Meir. *Hebrews Between Cultures: Group Portraits and National Literature*. Indiana Studies in Biblical Literature; Bloomington: Indiana University Press, 1998.

Strawn, Brent A. "Pharaoh," pp. 631–6 in *Dictionary of the Old Testament: Pentateuch*, edited by T. Desmond Alexander and David W. Baker. Downers Grove: InterVarsity Press, 2003.

Strawn, Brent A. "Exodus," in *The New Interpreter's Bible One-Volume Commentary*. Nashville: Abingdon, 2010.

Strine, Casey A. *Sworn Enemies: The Divine Oath, the Book of Ezekiel, and the Polemics of Exile.* BZAW 436: Berlin: Walter de Gruyter, 2013.
Sweeney, Marvin A. *I & II Kings.* OTL. Louisville, KY: Westminster John Knox Press, 2007.
Sweeney, Marvin A. "The Portrayal of Assyria in the Book of Kings," pp. 274–84 in *The Bible as a Human Witness to Divine Revelation: Hearing the Word of God through Historically Dissimilar Traditions,* edited by Randall Heskett and Brian Irwin. LHBOTS 469; London: T & T Clark, 2010.
Talmon, Shemaryahu. "1 and 2 Chronicles," pp. 365–72 in *The Literary Guide to the Bible,* edited by Robert Alter and Frank Kermode. Cambridge, MA: Belknap Press of Harvard University Press, 1987.
Thimmes, Pamela Lee. *Studies in the Biblical Sea-Storm Type-scene: Convention and Invention.* San Francisco: Mellen Research University Press, 1992.
Toorn, Karel van der. *Scribal Culture and the Making of the Hebrew Bible.* Cambridge, MA: Harvard University Press, 2007.
Trible, Phyllis. "Depatriarchalizing in Biblical Interpretation." *JAAR* 41 (1973) 30–48.
Trible, Phyllis. "The Pilgrim Bible on a Feminist Journey." *Princeton Seminary Bulletin* 11 (1990) 232–9.
Trible, Phyllis. "Difference Among the Distaff: A Reading of Exodus 1.1–2.10," pp. 292–306 in *Making a Difference: Essays on the Bible and Judaism in Honor of Tamara Cohn Eskenazi,* edited by David J. A. Clines, Kent Harold Richards, and Jacob L. Wright. HBM 49; Sheffield: Sheffield Phoenix Press, 2012.
Turner, Laurence A. *Genesis.* Readings; Sheffield: Sheffield Academic Press, 2000.
Utzschneider, Helmet, and Wolfgang Oswald. *Exodus 1–15.* Translated by Philip Sumpter; International Exegetical Commentary on the Old Testament; Stuttgart: Kohlhammer, 2015.
Van Seters, John. *The Life of Moses: The Yahwist as Historian in Exodus–Numbers.* Louisville: Westminster John Knox Press, 1994.
Van Seters, John. "The Geography of the Exodus," pp. 255–76 in *The Land that I Will Show You: Essays on the History and Archaeology of the Ancient Near East in Honour of J. Maxwell Miller,* edited by J. Andrew Dearman and M. Patrick Graham. JSOTS 343; Sheffield: Sheffield Academic Press, 2001.
Van Wijk-Bos, Johanna W. H. *Ezra, Nehemiah, and Esther.* Westminster Bible Companion; Louisville, KY: Westminster John Knox, 1998.
Walsh, Jerome T. *1 Kings.* Berit Olam; Collegeville: Liturgical Press, 1996.
Warning, Wilfried. *Literary Artistry in Leviticus.* BIS 35; Leiden: Brill, 1998.
Watson, Wilfred G. E. *Classical Hebrew Poetry.* JSOTSup 26; Sheffield: JSOT Press, 1986.
Watts, James W. *Ritual and Rhetoric in Leviticus: From Sacrifice to Scripture.* New York: Cambridge University Press, 2007.

Weems, Renita J. "The Hebrew Women are Not Like the Egyptian Women: The Ideology of Race, Gender, and Sexual Reproduction in Exodus 1." *Semeia* 59 (1992) 25–34.

Weinfeld, Moshe. *Deuteronomy and the Deuteronomic School.* Oxford: Clarendon Press, 1972.

Weitzman, Steven. *Solomon: The Lure of Wisdom.* New Haven: Yale University Press, 2011.

Wenham, Gordon J. *Genesis 1–15.* WBC; Waco: Word, 1987.

Wenham, Gordon J. *Genesis 16–50.* WBC; Dallas: Word, 1994.

Whybray, R. N. "Genesis," pp. 38–66 in *The Oxford Bible Commentary,* edited by John Barton and John Muddiman. Oxford: Oxford University Press, 2001.

Wicke, D. W. "The Literary Structure of Exodus 1.2–2.10." *JSOT* 24 (1982) 99–107.

Williamson, H. G. M. *A Critical and Exegetical Commentary on Isaiah 1–27,* Volume 1: *Commentary on Isaiah 1–5.* ICC; London: T & T Clark, 2006.

Willis, John T. *Yahweh and Moses in Conflict: The Role of Exodus 4:24–26 in the Book of Exodus.* Bern: Peter Lang, 2010.

Ziolkowski, Theodore. *Disenchanted Images: A Literary Iconology.* Princeton: Princeton University Press, 1977.

Index

Aaron brother of Moses 31, 71, 75, 92, 103, 126–27, 131–32, 135–36, 154, 183–85
Abel 48, 131
Abida son of Midian 141
Abigail 85
Abimelech the Philistine 76
Abram/Abraham 12–13, 18–30, 32, 35, 37, 39–40, 42, 46, 49–52, 59–61, 67, 73–74, 76, 84–85, 87, 91, 96, 115, 136, 141, 143–44, 148–150, 155, 164, 166–70, 174, 178
Absalom 130
Achan son of Carmi 125
Ackerman, James S. 7–8, 45–46, 52, 55, 62–63, 69–70, 95, 103–4, 110, 122–23, 157, 169–70, 183
Adam 26, 98
Adonijah son of David 84, 110
Adoniram 58
Ahasuerus of Persia 56–57, 180–81, 184
Ahaziah king of Judah 107–8
Ahijah of Shiloh 139
Ahmose of Egypt 115
Alexander, T. Desmond 33
Allen, Joel S. 159
Allen, Leslie 18
Allison, Dale C., Jr. 179
Alter, Robert 3, 22, 34–35, 38, 68, 81–82, 95, 105, 113, 124, 132–33, 138, 142, 144, 148, 150, 166, 171–72, 175
Amnon son of David 59
Amram father of Moses 91
Aristotle 10, 146
Asenath 151, 167
Asher son of Jacob 42
Asshurim son of Dedan 141
Athaliah the queen 107–8

Baden, Joel S. 13, 128, 141
Baker, David W. 33
Baker of Pharaoh 51, 78
Balaam the soothsayer 53, 61, 161
Balak king of Moab 53, 61, 161
Barak of Naphtali 80–81

Bar-Efrat, Shimon 140, 172
Barr, James 77
Barton, John 39, 135, 146
Bathsheba 84, 113, 172
Beal, Timothy K. 183–84
Bellis, Alice Ogden 9–10
Ben Zvi, Ehud 17, 109
Benaiah 111
Benjamin son of Jacob 35, 41–42, 67
Bergsma, John Sietze 95
Berlin, Adele 10, 55, 98, 155, 182
Billings, Rachel M. 82
Bird, Phyllis A. 84
Bithya daughter of Pharaoh 69
Bloch-Smith, Elizabeth M. 115
Bloom, Harold 166
Boda, Mark J. 94
Bodner, Keith 11, 68, 108, 143–44
Brenner, Athalya 8, 26, 164
Britt, Brian 120, 142
Brown, Raymond E. 84, 179
Brueggemann, Walter 10–11, 18, 21–22, 68, 79, 96, 103, 114, 118–19, 140–41, 149, 154, 156–57, 170, 175
Buber, Martin 8

Cain 48, 131, 137
Cassuto, Umberto 44, 47, 65, 71, 73, 86, 107, 121, 156–57
Chan, Michael J. 50
Childs, Brevard S. 7, 10, 49, 51, 55, 61, 69, 78, 95, 112, 126, 129, 152, 162
Christensen, Duane L. 49
Clines, David J. A. 8–9, 19, 32, 181
Coats, George W. 4, 95
Coogan, Michael D. 17
Cotter, David W. 29
Crawford, Cory D. 97
Crawford, Sidnie White 109, 179, 184
Cupbearer of Pharaoh 51, 69, 78
Cyrus of Persia 90

Dan son of Jacob 42
Daniel 50, 183

Index

David 58, 68, 77, 84–85, 108, 110, 113, 130–31, 148, 172
Davies, Gordon F. 4–5, 7, 14, 54–55, 65, 68–69, 75–76, 86, 95, 122, 125, 130–31, 138, 140, 150, 153–54, 162–63, 170–71
Davies, Philip R. 32, 95
Day, John 48
Deborah the prophetess 80–81
Dedan son of Jokshan 141
Dennis, Trevor 101, 106
Dinah daughter of Jacob 59, 91, 128
Dozeman, Thomas B. 10–11, 26–27, 41, 45, 52, 66, 84–85, 95, 99, 101, 127, 134, 140, 160
Durham, John I. 10, 46–47, 61, 72, 92, 156, 171

Edelman, Diana 17, 95
Eldaah son of Midian 141
Eli the priest 68
Eliakim 116
Eliezer son of Moses 91, 163, 167
Elisha the prophet 87
Elizabeth wife of Zechariah 143
Enns, Peter 87, 92, 137, 139, 141
Ephah son of Midian 141
Epher son of Midian 141
Ephraim son of Joseph 168
Esau 60, 65, 144
Eskenazi, Tamara Cohn 9–10
Esther 16, 55, 179–85
Evans, Craig A. 41, 116
Eve 112–3
Exum, J. Cheryl 8, 10, 13, 57, 70, 88, 94, 99, 107
Ezekiel 48

Feldman, Louis H. 126
Fewell, Danna Nolan 43, 80, 104
Fishbane, Michael 4, 98, 121
Flint, Peter W. 116
Fokkelman, Jan P. 166
Freedman, David Noel 17
Fretheim, Terence E. 3, 12–13, 19, 22, 25, 36, 38, 52, 59, 62, 67, 76, 90–91, 93, 96, 112, 135, 150, 161–62, 164
Friedman, Richard Elliot 43–44
Frye, Northrop 6
Fuchs, Esther 9

Gabriel the angel 143
Gad son of Jacob 42
Gaventa, Beverly Roberts 20
Gehman, H. S. 95
Geller, Stephen A. 98
George, Mark K. 97
Gerleman, Gillis 179–80
Gershom son of Moses 33, 135, 162–63, 166–69
Gillmayr-Bucher, Susanne 82
Gilmour, Rachelle 87
Goldingay, John 18
Goswell, Gregory R. 184
Gordon, Robert P. 48
Gorospe, Athena E. 140, 166, 169
Graetz, Naomi 164
Green, Barbara 32
Greenberg, Moshe 10, 59, 69, 91, 104, 124, 155, 169, 172, 177
Greenspahn, Frederick E. 98
Greenspoon, Leonard J. 179, 184
Greifenhagen, F. V. 22–23, 26, 29, 31, 38, 69, 79, 88, 124, 139, 141, 164–65, 169, 172
Gros Louis, Kenneth R. R. 7
Gunn, David M. 8, 80, 104
Gurtner, Daniel M. 75, 109, 136

Hadassah (Esther) 180, 182–83
Hagar mother of Ishmael 12, 19, 23, 25–27, 30, 69, 87, 101
Hahn, Scott Walker 95
Hall, Sarah Lebhar 82
Halpern, Baruch 77
Haman the Agagite 55–57, 181–84
Hamilton, Victor P. 36, 57–58, 61, 71, 76, 80, 85, 87, 101, 106, 116, 128, 136, 146, 154, 158, 168
Hannah 47, 112–3, 143
Hanoch son of Midian 141
Harvey, John E. 50
Hauge, Martin Ravndal 172
Hauser, Alan J. 8
Hawk, L. Daniel 82
Hawkins, Peter S. 85
Heber the Kenite 80–81
Hendel, Ronald 24, 120, 164, 176
Herod the king 179
Herodotus 17
Heskett, Randall 18, 50
Hiebert, Theodore 53
Hobab of Midian 149

Index

Holloway, Steven W. 97
Hophra of Egypt 49
Houston, Walter 146
Houtman, Cornelis 10, 45, 47, 77, 86–87, 92, 104, 111, 114, 129–30, 153
Hughes, Paul E. 116
Hutton, Jeremy M. 128
Hyatt, J. P. 71

Iphigenia 146
Isaac son of Abraham 12, 16, 27, 39, 61, 65, 80, 84, 91, 111, 141, 143–47, 152, 170
Isbell, Charles 7, 53, 92, 97, 159
Ishbak son of Keturah 141
Ishmael son of Hagar 29, 30, 87, 101–2
Ishtar the goddess 182
Issachar son of Jacob 42
Irwin, Brian 18, 50

Jabin of Canaan 80
Jackson, Melissa 123
Jacob 2, 12–13, 16, 27, 37–42, 44–47, 60–61, 65–67, 80, 91, 125, 127–29, 144, 147, 152, 155, 160–63, 170
Jacob, Benno 53, 71, 80, 94, 101, 114, 116, 131, 134, 170
Jael wife of Heber 9, 80–81
Janzen, J. Gerald 20, 122, 144, 147
Jehoahaz of Judah 116
Jehoiachin/Jeconiah 50, 180
Jehoiada the priest 108
Jehoiakim king of Judah 43, 116
Jehoshaphat king of Judah 159
Jehosheba 108
Jehu son of Nimshi 107
Jeremiah 48–49
Jeroboam 18, 48, 139
Jesus of Nazareth 73, 179
Jethro of Midian 76, 142, 149–50, 156, 162
Jezebel 107
Joab 130
Joash 108
Jochebed mother of Moses 85, 91
Johnson, Benjamin J. M. 143
Jokshan son of Keturah 141
Joram 108
Joseph 2, 12, 19, 27–39, 41–42, 45–48, 50–55, 57–58, 60–61, 69–70, 75–76, 78, 87, 95, 116, 126, 136–37, 141, 144, 146, 151, 158, 164, 167–69, 171, 174, 179
Joseph (NT) 179
Josephus 126
Joshua son of Nun 81–84, 98–99
Josiah 49
Josipovici, Gabriel 118
Judah brother of Joseph 28, 41–43, 47, 50, 53–54, 68, 144
Judah Maccabee 183

Kaminsky, Joel S. 9
Kawashima, Robert S. 24
Keck, L. E. 11, 22
Kee, Min Suc 142
Keiter, Sheila Tuller 67
Kermode, Frank 120, 166, 172, 175
Keturah wife of Abraham 29, 141
Kim, Koowon 142
Klein, Lillian R. 81
Knauf, Ernst Axel 25
Koller, Aaron 183–84
Kruschwitz, Jonathan 144
Kugel, James L. 32
Kupp, David D. 179

Laban the Aramean 60, 65, 80, 144, 160–63
LaCocque, André 53
Langston, Scott M. 85, 120, 126
Laniak, Timothy S. 179, 184
Leah wife of Jacob 127
Letellier, Robert I. 23
Letushim son of Dedan 141
Leuchter, Mark 128
Leummim son of Dedan 141
Leveen, Adriane 127
Levenson, Jon D. 20, 28, 32, 55, 92–93, 110, 140, 184
Levi son of Jacob 42, 91, 127–29
Levin, Christoph 17, 109
Linafelt, Tod 18, 96
Lohr, Joel N. 41, 92, 104–5, 112, 114
Long, Burke O. 80
Lot nephew of Abraham 12, 17, 19, 23–27, 136, 149
Lyke, Larry L. 131

Machinist, Peter 18, 136, 166
Manasseh 167
Manasseh son of Joseph 33, 168
Mann, Thomas 120

Marks, Herbert 135
Martin, Michael W. 144, 148
Matties, Gordon H. 83
Mazor, Yair 176
McCarter, P. Kyle 113
McConville, J. Gordon 67
McLuhan, Marshall 6
Medan son of Keturah 141
Melchizedek 149–50
Mendenhall, George E. 141
Merneptah of Egypt 70
Meyers, Carol 10, 42–44, 49, 62, 68, 138, 159, 167, 169, 171, 174
Middlemas, Jill 94
Midian son of Keturah 141
Miller, J. Hillis 10, 40
Miriam sister of Moses 9, 85, 92, 105, 135–36
Mitchell, Christine 49
Moberly, R. W. L. 20, 32
Montgomery, J. A. 95
Moore, Carey A. 180
Mordecai 55–56, 180–85
Morschauser, Scott 73
Morson, Gary Saul 89–90
Moses
  accusation by the Hebrew fighter 133–38
  allusions to Sargon 94–95
  befriended by Reuel 155–60
  comparisons with Hagar 26–27
  concealed in an ark 93–100
  encounter at the well 142–55
  flight to Midian 138–41
  hiding like Rahab 82–83
  intervention in a fight 127–33
  Joshua's succession 98–99
  Levite parentage 91–93
  marriage to Zipporah 160–67
  murder of the Egyptian 120–27
  named by Pharaoh's daughter 107–116
  observed by Miriam 100–107
  parallels to Esther 179–85
  violence of Levi 128–9
Muddiman, John 39, 135, 146

Najman, Hindy 32
Naphtali son of Jacob 42
Nebuchadnezzar king of Babylon 43, 116, 180
Neco of Egypt 49, 116

Newman, Judith H. 32
Newsom, Carol A. 10
Nihan, Christophe 95
Nikaido, S. 29–30
Noah 1, 14, 44–45, 95–98, 100, 117, 118, 178
Nohrnberg, James 5–7, 57, 79–80, 107, 116–17, 129, 137–38, 141, 146, 158, 168
Nolan, Brian M. 179
Noth, Martin 74

O'Connell, Robert H. 142
O'Day, Gail R. 42
Oedipus 89, 146
Olson, Dennis T. 11, 20, 42, 88, 90, 137
Oropeza, B. J. 179
Osherow, Jacqueline 71
Oswald, Wolfgang 11, 41, 46, 85, 94, 109, 122, 144, 160, 166, 172
Othello 117

Pardes, Ilana 114, 176
Perez son of Judah 60, 67
Petersen, David L. 20, 42
Pixley, Jorge 84
Potiphar of Egypt 30, 32, 141
Potiphar's wife 30, 66, 69
Potiphera priest of On 151, 167
Propp, William H. C. 5, 44, 47, 52, 57, 60–62, 69, 73, 79, 92, 101, 112, 123, 130, 142, 149–51, 155
Provan, Iain 94
Ptahmose of Egypt 115
Puah the midwife 67–72, 76, 82, 84–85, 107, 176

Qimchi, David 28

Rachel 67, 80, 87, 92, 144, 150, 155, 160, 163
Rad, Gerhard von 19, 36
Rahab 9, 64, 81–84, 93–94, 125
Ramose 115
Ramses II 115
Rashi 123
Ray, J. D. 48
Rebekah 65, 80, 92, 101, 143–44, 147, 150, 155, 163
Reed, Walter L. 99
Rehoboam 47–48
Reno, R. R. 22

Index

Reuben firstborn of Jacob 34, 42
Reuel of Midian 77, 149–50, 156–65, 177
Richards, Kent Harold 9
Richardson, Brian 10, 175
Rickett, Daniel 23
Ringe, Sharon H. 10
Rofé, Alexander 94
Römer, Thomas C. 33, 95
Rosenberg, David 166
Rosenberg, Joel 29
Rosenberg, Marvin 117
Rosenheim, Edward W. 176
Ruth 84, 148
Russell, Stephen C. 18

Sabo, Peter 109, 144, 160, 178
Sacks, Jonathan 104
Said, Edward 10, 44, 175
Sakenfeld, Katharine Doob 58
Salmon husband of Rahab 84
Samuel the prophet 55, 112–3
Sarai/Sarah wife of Abraham 12–13, 20–23, 25–27, 30, 32, 51, 73, 77, 82, 92, 101, 106, 143
Sargon 94–95
Sargon II 95
Sarna, Nahum M. 10, 47, 69, 76, 86, 90, 97, 115, 129, 137, 141, 156–57, 169
Saul son of Kish 55, 77, 104, 112–13, 132–33, 147–50
Savran, George 142
Schmid, Konrad 41, 175
Schor, Esther 85
Scott, James C. 93
Seow, Choon Leong 58, 95
Setel, Drorah O'Donnell 10, 80
Sharp, Carolyn J. 81, 184
Sheba son of Jokshan 141
Shechem the Canaanite 58–59, 91, 128
Shifrah the midwife 66–72, 76, 82, 84–85, 107, 176
Shishak of Egypt 18, 48
Shuah son of Jokshan 141
Shunammite woman 61, 143
Siebert-Hommes, Jopie 5–8, 44, 58, 74, 94, 99, 106
Simeon son of Jacob 34–36, 42, 128–29
Sisera of Canaan 80–81
Ska, Jean-Louis 75
Smith, Mark S. 49, 115, 133, 149
So of Egypt 49

Solomon 17–18, 47–48, 58–59, 84, 97, 110–11, 113, 139, 178
Soltes, Ori Z. 184
Sophocles 89
Sparks, Kenton L. 94–95
Speiser, E. A. 29
Spencer, John R. 128
Stackert, Jeffrey 143
Stahlberg, Lesleigh Cushing 85
Stambovsky, Phillip 64
Stephen (NT) 126
Sternberg, Meir 4, 34–35, 66, 70–71, 76, 86, 122, 137, 146
Steward of Joseph's house 35–37, 70, 76
Strawn, Brent A. 33
Strine, Casey A. 93
Sumpter, Philip 11
Sweeney, Marvin A. 18, 48–49

Talmon, Shemaryahu 172
Tamar daughter of David 59
Tamar daughter-in-law of Judah 60, 67, 84, 144
Tekoa, wise woman of 130–31
Thimmes, Pamela Lee 142
Thotmose 115
Tigay, Jeffrey H. 59
Trible, Phyllis 9, 57, 60, 86, 88, 106–7, 114
Turner, Laurence A. 23, 36

Uriah the Hittite 84, 113
Utzschneider, Helmet 11, 41, 46, 85, 94, 109, 122, 144, 160, 166, 172

Van Seters, John 55
Van Wijk-Bos, Johanna W. H. 56
Vashti 180–81

Walsh, Jerome T. 48
Walters, Stanley D. 144
Warshaw, Thayer S. 7
Watson, Wilfred G. E. 115
Weems, Renita J. 74
Weiss, Andrea L. 10
Weitzman, Steven 113
Wenham, Gordon J. 21, 24, 26, 35, 58
Wette, W. M. L. de 5
Whybray, R. N. 39
Wicke, D. W. 4
Williams, Bruce B. 17
Williamson, H. G. M. 48, 94, 158

Willis, John T. 165
Wright, Jacob L. 9

Zaphenath-paneah (Joseph) 116, 151
Zebulun son of Jacob 42
Zechariah the priest (NT) 143
Zedekiah king of Judah 116
Zerah brother of Perez 67
Zimran son of Keturah 141
Ziolkowski, Theodore 64
Zipporah wife of Moses 16, 71, 135–36, 162–67, 177